Get the eBook FREE!
(PDF, ePub, Kindle, and liveBook all included)

We believe that once you buy a book from us, you should be able to read it in any format we have available. To get electronic versions of this book at no additional cost to you, purchase and then register this book at the Manning website.

Go to https://www.manning.com/freebook and follow the instructions to complete your pBook registration.

That's it!
Thanks from Manning!

Seriously Good Software

Code that Works, Survives, and Wins

MARCO FAELLA

Foreword by Cay Horstmann

MANNING
SHELTER ISLAND

For online information and ordering of this and other Manning books, please visit www.manning.com. The publisher offers discounts on this book when ordered in quantity.
For more information, please contact

    Special Sales Department
    Manning Publications Co.
    20 Baldwin Road
    PO Box 761
    Shelter Island, NY 11964
    Email: orders@manning.com

Manning Publications Co.
20 Baldwin Road
PO Box 761
Shelter Island, NY 11964

Development editor:	Toni Arritola
Technical development editor:	Kostas Passadis
Production editor:	Janet Vail
Copy editor:	Carl Quesnel
Proofreader:	Keri Hales
Technical proofreader:	Serge Simon
Typesetter:	Paolo Brasolin
Cover designer:	Marija Tudor

ISBN 9781617296291
Printed in the United States of America

brief contents

contents

foreword

I have written quite a few programming books in the last 30 years, so it is perhaps not surprising that every so often someone contacts me seeking advice about writing a book. I always ask for a sample chapter. In most cases, I hear nothing further, and I don't feel bad about that. Obviously, if someone can't produce a chapter, no book will materialize, and there is nothing to discuss.

In January 2018, I got an email from Marco Faella, a professor from the University of Naples, whom I had previously met when he worked at the University of California in Santa Cruz. He asked for advice about a book project. And he had already finished several chapters! I liked what I saw and replied with encouragement and a few suggestions. I didn't hear anything further. I wasn't surprised. One of my editors once told me that he knew a great number of people who started a book . . . but only a few who finished one.

In April 2019, I got another email. The book was going to be published by Manning. And it looked really good. In August, Marco asked me to write the foreword, which I am delighted to do.

When I write a book about a programming language (such as the classic *Core Java* book), I focus on the constructs and APIs that are specific to that language. I assume that the reader has a good grasp of data structures, algorithms, and software engineering principles such as testing, refactoring, and design patterns. Of course, having been a professor, I am aware that university curricula do not always do a good job of teaching those topics in a practical and accessible manner.

That is where this book fills a real need. You, the reader, are expected to be familiar with the fundamentals of Java programming, and Marco will show you the way to higher quality programs. You probably have experience with algorithm design, API design, testing, and concurrency, but Marco puts a new spin on these classic themes. He takes one example and derives an astounding number of insights from it by implementing it over and over in different ways. Normally, I dislike the "running example" technique because it forces me to read a book sequentially. I can't just dive in at a spot that interests me because I need to know the evolutionary state of the running example. But Marco's example (whose nature I don't want to reveal in the foreword) is very cleverly designed. You need to master a couple of surprising—and interesting—core concepts when you first see it. Afterwards, each chapter evolves the code in an independent direction. It is quite a tour de force.

In each of the principal chapters, you will find a section titled "And now for something completely different." At this point, you are invited to apply the chapter's techniques to a different situation. I encourage you to work through these challenges, as well as the pop quizzes and end-of-chapter exercises.

Building high-quality software is never simple, and it is always a good idea to re-examine the principles of good design and craftsmanship. In this book, you will find a fresh perspective that I hope you will enjoy as much as I did

—Cay Horstmann
Author of *Core Java, Java/Scala/JavaScript for the Impatient,* and many other books for beginning and professional programmers

preface

My personal title for this book is "Java: Exercises in Style." After the wise people at Manning taught me about catchiness, this preface is all that's left of that title and its literary overtone. Indeed, in the modern classic *Exercises in Style*, French writer Raymond Queneau writes the same story in 99 different ways. The point of the book is not the story, which is intentionally unremarkable, but rather the whimsical exploration of the virtually endless expressive capabilities of natural languages.

Programming is certainly not literature, despite efforts by renowed personalities such as Donald Knuth to bring the two closer together. In fact, beginner programmers may be forgiven if they think there's one best way to solve each programming assignment, just like simple math problems have a single solution. In reality, modern day programming can be much more similar to literature than to math. Programming languages have evolved to include ever more abstract constructions, multiplying the ways to achieve the same goal. Even after their introduction, languages evolve, often by acquiring new ways of doing the same things. The most used languages, such as Java, have been evolving at an accelerated pace to keep up with the younger languages trying to take their positions.

In this book, I try to give a taste of the wide range of concerns and solutions that you should consider, or at least be aware of, when undertaking any programming task. The task I propose is quite mundane: a class representing water containers that you can connect with pipes and fill with liquid. Clients interact continuously with the containers, adding or removing water and placing new pipes at any time. I present and discuss 18 different implementations for this task, each striving to maximize a different objective, be it performance, code clarity, or some other software quality. This book is not a dry sequence of code snippets. Whenever the context calls for it, I take the opportunity to discuss a number of specialized topics pertaining to computer science (various data structures, complexity theory, and amortized complexity); Java programming (thread synchronization and the Java memory model); and software engineering (the design-by-contract methodology and testing techniques). My objective is to show you that even a relatively simple case study, when analyzed in depth, is linked to a vast network of topics, all of which contribute to writing better code.

FURTHER READING

One of the objectives of this book is to stimulate your curiosity about the various disciplines related to software development. That's why each chapter ends with a *Further reading* section, where I briefly introduce the best resources I could find on the chapter's topic. I think the preface should be no exception, so here it goes:

- Raymond Queneau. *Exercises in Style.* New Directions, 2013.
  The original "exercises in style" book. (Actually, the original was written in French in 1947.)
- Cristina Videira Lopes. *Exercises in Programming Style.* CRC, 2014.
  The author solves a simple programming task in 33 different styles using Python. Rather than optimizing different code qualities, every style results from obeying certain constraints. Among other things, it teaches you a lot about the history of programming languages.
- Matt Madden. *99 Ways to Tell a Story: Exercises in Style.* Jonathan Cape, 2006.
  When you need a break from coding, check out this comic book featuring a simple story drawn in 99 different styles.

acknowledgments

I expected to work hard on this book. I didn't expect that so many other people would work on it equally hard. I'm talking about the people at Manning, who in various capacities pushed the quality of this book close to my personal limit. A number of external reviewers took time to write detailed reports that helped refine the content. I hope they're happy with the result.

I've learned Java from Cay's books, and I've been recommending them to my students for many years. I'm honored that he kindly agreed to write the foreword for this book.

To all the reviewers: Aditya Kaushik, Alexandros Koufoudakis, Bonnie Bailey, Elio Salvatore, Flavio Diez, Foster Haines, Gregory Reshetniak, Hessam Shafiei Moqaddam, Irfan Ullah, Jacob Romero, John Guthrie, Juan J. Durillo, Kimberly Winston-Jackson, Michał Ambroziewicz, Serge Simon, Steven Parr, Thorsten Weber, and Travis Nelso, your suggestions helped make this a better book.

The origin of my passion for programming can be traced back to my father teaching a curious eight-year-old me how to draw a circle with a `for` loop and two enchantments called *cos* and *sin*. *Grazie!*

about this book

The core idea of this book is to convey the mindset of an experienced developer by comparing and contrasting different code qualities (aka nonfunctional requirements).

The figure inside the front cover relates the content of this book to the wider landscape of the knowledge required of professional developers. First, you start by learning the basics of a programming language. In Java, that entails knowing about classes, methods, fields, and so on. This book won't teach you those basics. Then, you should ideally follow three paths:

- *The programming language path*—Learn about the more advanced language features, such as generics and multithreading.
- *The algorithmic path*—Learn about solid theoretical principles, standard algorithms and data structures, and ways to measure their performance.
- *The software engineering path*—Learn about design principles, methodologies, and best practices that help manage complexity, especially in large projects.

This book covers all of these areas, with a twist. Rather than teaching these different aspects separately, I'll mix and match them according to the needs of each chapter.

Each chapter focuses on a specific software quality, like time efficiency or readability. I've selected the chosen qualities not only because of their importance and universality, but also as those that you can meaningfully apply to a small code unit (a single class). Moreover, I try to focus on general principles and coding techniques, rather than specific tools. When appropriate, I'll point to tools and libraries that can help you assess and optimize a given software quality.

WHO SHOULD READ THIS BOOK

This book is the ideal starting point for a junior developer with limited formal training to widen their perspective on software development. Specifically, the book targets two objectives and audiences:

- For working developers with little formal training, or training in a different area than CS/CE, it provides a tour of computer science and engineering techniques, elucidating the trade-offs inherent in any nontrivial programming task.
- For computer science and engineering students, it provides a unifying case study for a variety of topics that are traditionally taught in different courses. As such, it may supplement your textbooks for programming and software engineering classes.

In both cases, to make the most out of this book you should be familiar with the following:

- Basic programming notions, such as iteration and recursion
- Basic object-oriented programming notions, such as encapsulation and inheritance
- Intermediate Java language skills, including generics, standard collections, and basic multithreading (thread creation and the `synchronized` keyword)

BOOK STRUCTURE

Here's a breakdown of the chapters and their corresponding code qualities. Don't overlook the hands-on exercises at the end of all chapters. They come with detailed solutions and complete the core chapter content by applying those techniques in different contexts.

Chapter 1 The first chapter describes the programming task to be solved (a water container class), followed by a naive implementation showcasing common misconceptions that affect inexperienced programmers.

Chapter 2 I detail the reference implementation (which I subsequently refer to as *Reference*), which strikes a balance between different qualities.

Chapter 3 Focusing on time efficiency, you'll improve the running time of *Reference* by up to two orders of magnitude (500x), and discover that different use cases lead to different performance trade-offs.

Chapter 4 This chapters experiments with space (memory) efficiency. Compared to *Reference*, you'll shrink the memory footprint of containers by more than 50% when using objects and by 90% when forgoing an object for each water container.

Chapter 5 To achieve reliability via monitoring, I introduce the *design by contract* methodology and show you how to harden the *Reference* class with runtime checks and assertions based on method contracts and class invariants.

Chapter 6 To achieve reliability via unit testing, I discuss techniques for designing and executing a test suite for a class, including code coverage measures and tools.

Chapter 7 In this chapter on readability, you'll refactor *Reference* to follow the best practices for clean self-documenting code.

Chapter 8 As we examine concurrency and thread safety, you'll recall the basic notions of thread synchronization and discover that our running example needs non-trivial techniques to avoid deadlocks and race conditions.

Chapter 9 With a focus on reusability, using generics, you'll generalize our reference class to embrace other applications with a similar general structure.

Appendix A In discussing succinctness, I present a compact implementation of the recurring example whose source code is only 15% as long as *Reference*. As expected, the result is an unreadable, geekily satisfying tangle of code that would immediately get you kicked out of any code review session.

Appendix B Finally, I put together the most important software qualities to give you the ultimate water container class.

THE ONLINE REPOSITORY

All the code I've presented in the book is available in a public online `git` repository (https://bitbucket.org/mfaella/exercisesinstyle) organized by chapter. The bulk of the code consists of many different versions of the same `Container` class. Each version has a nickname, corresponding to the name of its package. For example, the first version is presented in section 1.8 with the nickname *Novice*. In the repository, the corresponding class is `eis.chapter1.novice.Container`. The table inside the back cover lists the main classes and their characteristics.

The code for the examples in this book is also available for download from the Manning website at https://www.manning.com/books/seriously-good-software.

WHY JAVA? WHICH JAVA?

As you know, Java is evolving at an accelerated pace, with a new version coming out every six months. As of this writing, the current version is Java 12.

This book, on the other hand, isn't about Java programming in and of itself. It's about acquiring the habit of evaluating and balancing different software qualities, whatever language you happen to be using. The examples are in Java because of my own expertise with it, and because it's one of the most used languages around.

The principles I teach in this book work equally well in other languages. The closer your language is to Java, the more content from this book you can export to it without modification. For example, C# is very close to Java, and indeed the book is sprinkled with C# notes highlighting the differences that are relevant to that chapter's content.

As for the Java code shown in the book and stored in the online repository, 99% of it is Java 8. In a few places, I'm using minor Java 9 utilities like the ability to construct a list with the static method `List.of`.

LIVEBOOK DISCUSSION FORUM

Purchase of Seriously Good Software includes free access to a private web forum run by Manning Publications where you can make comments about the book, ask technical questions, and receive help from the author and from other users. To access the forum, go to https://livebook.manning.com/#!/book/seriously-good-software/discussion. You can also learn more about Manning's forums and the rules of conduct at https://livebook.manning.com/#!/discussion.

Manning's commitment to our readers is to provide a venue where a meaningful dialogue between individual readers and between readers and the author can take place. It is not a commitment to any specific amount of participation on the part of the author, whose contribution to the forum remains voluntary (and unpaid). We suggest you try asking the author some challenging questions lest his interest stray! The forum and the archives of previous discussions will be accessible from the publisher's website as long as the book is in print.

about the author

MARCO FAELLA is an associate professor of computer science at the University of Naples Federico II, in Italy. Besides his research on theoretical computer science, he's a passionate teacher and programmer. He's been teaching an advanced programming class for the last 13 years. He published a Java certification manual and a video course on Java streams.

about the cover

The figure on the cover of *Seriously Good Software* is captioned "Homme Tscheremiss," or man of the Tscheremiss tribe, which was a clan of people from the area near present-day Finland. The illustration is taken from a collection of dress costumes from various countries by Jacques Grasset de Saint-Sauveur (1757–1810), titled *Costumes de Différents Pays*, published in France in 1797. Each illustration is finely drawn and colored by hand. The rich variety of Grasset de Saint-Sauveur's collection reminds us vividly of how culturally apart the world's towns and regions were just 200 years ago. Isolated from each other, people spoke different dialects and languages. In the streets or in the countryside, it was easy to identify where they lived and what their trade or station in life was just by their dress.

The way we dress has changed since then and the diversity by region, so rich at the time, has faded away. It is now hard to tell apart the inhabitants of different continents, let alone different towns, regions, or countries. Perhaps we have traded cultural diversity for a more varied personal life—certainly for a more varied and fast-paced technological life.

At a time when it is hard to tell one computer book from another, Manning celebrates the inventiveness and initiative of the computer business with book covers based on the rich diversity of regional life of two centuries ago, brought back to life by Grasset de Saint-Sauveur's pictures.

Part 1

Preliminaries

The idea of this book is to separately optimize different software qualities guided by a single running example. In this first part, I introduce software qualities in general and present the simple programming task that you'll repeatedly solve throughout the book.

Two preliminary implementations follow: a naive version that an inexperienced programmer might author, and a reference version that strikes reasonable compromises between different quality criteria.

Software qualities and a problem to solve

1

This chapter covers

- Evaluating software from different points of view and for different objectives
- Distinguishing internal from external software qualities
- Distinguishing functional from nonfunctional software qualities
- Assessing interactions and trade-offs between software qualities

The core idea of this book is to convey the mindset of an experienced developer by comparing and contrasting different code qualities (aka nonfunctional requirements). Most of these qualities—like performance or readability—are universal, in the sense that they're relevant to any piece of software. To emphasize this fact, you'll revisit the same recurring example in each chapter: a simple class representing a system of water containers.

In this chapter, I'll introduce the software qualities that this book addresses, and I'll present the specifications for the water container example, followed by a preliminary implementation.

1.1   Software qualities

In this book, you should interpret the word *quality* as a characteristic that a piece of software may or may not have, not as its overall value. That's why I talk about multiple qualit*ies.* You can't consider all characteristics qualities; for example, the programming language in which a piece of software is written is certainly a characteristic of that software but not a quality. Qualities are characteristics that you can grade on a scale, at least in principle.

As with all products, the software qualities that people are mostly interested in are those that measure the extent to which the system fulfills its requirements. Unfortunately, just describing—let alone fulfilling—the requirements of a piece of software is no easy task. Indeed, the entire field of Requirements Analysis is devoted to it. How is that possible? Isn't it enough for the system to reliably and consistently offer the services its users need?

First of all, often the users themselves don't exactly know what services they need—they need time and assistance to figure that out. Second, fulfilling those needs isn't the end of the story at all. Those services may be offered more or less quickly, with more or less accuracy, after a long user training or after just a quick glance at a well-designed UI, and so on. In addition, over time you need to modify, fix, or improve any system, which leads to more quality variables: How easy is it to understand the system's inner workings? How easy is it to modify and extend it without breaking other parts? The list goes on and on.

To put some order in this multitude of criteria, experts suggest organizing them according to two characteristics: internal versus external and functional versus nonfunctional.

1.1.1   Internal vs. external qualities

The end user can perceive external qualities while interacting with the system, whereas you can appraise internal ones only by looking at the source code. The boundary between these two categories isn't clear-cut. The end user can indirectly perceive some internal qualities. Vice versa, all external qualities ultimately depend on the source code.

Software quality standards

The ISO and IEC standardization bodies have defined software quality requirements since 1991 in standard 9126, which was superseded by standard 25010 in 2011.

For example, maintainability (how easy it is to modify, fix, or extend the software) is an internal attribute, but end users will become aware of it if a defect is found and programmers take a long time to fix it. Conversely, robustness to incorrect inputs is generally considered an external attribute, but it becomes internal when the piece of software under consideration—perhaps a library—isn't exposed to the end user and only interacts with other system modules.

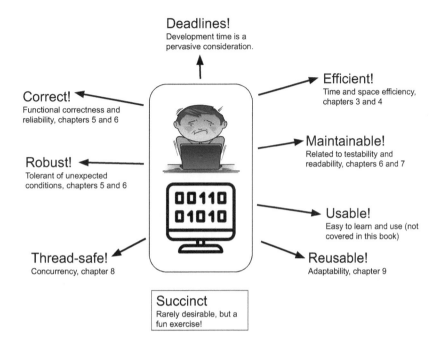

Figure 1.1 Functional and nonfunctional requirements pull software in different directions. It's your job to find a balance.

1.1.2 *Functional vs. nonfunctional qualities*

The second distinction is between qualities that apply to what the software *does* (functional qualities) and those that refer to how the software *is* (nonfunctional qualities) (figure 1.1). The internal-external dichotomy applies to this distinction as well: if the software does something, its effect is visible to the end user, one way or another. Therefore, all functional qualities are external. On the other hand, nonfunctional qualities can be either internal or external, depending on whether they're more related to the code itself or to its emerging traits. The following sections contain examples of both kinds. In the meantime, take a look at figure 1.2, which puts all the qualities addressed in this chapter in a 2D spectrum, representing the internal-external distinction on the horizontal axis and the functional versus nonfunctional distinction on the vertical one. The next section presents the main software qualities that the end user can directly appraise.

1.2 *Mostly external software qualities*

External software qualities pertain to the observable behavior of the program and as such are naturally the primary concern of the development process. Besides attributing these qualities to software, I'll discuss them in relation to a plain old toaster to try and

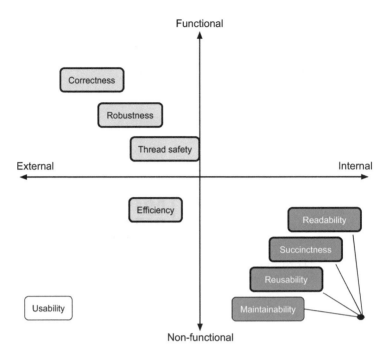

Figure 1.2 Software qualities classified according to two dichotomies: internal versus external (horizontal axis) and functional versus nonfunctional (vertical axis). The qualities that I specifically address in the book have a thick border.

frame them in the most general and intuitive sense. The following subsections provide a description of the most important external qualities.

1.2.1 Correctness

Adherence to stated objectives, aka requirements or specifications

For a toaster to be correct, it must cook sliced bread until it's brown and crispy. Software, on the other hand, must offer the functionalities that were agreed on with the customer. This is *the* functional quality, by definition.

There's no secret recipe for correctness, but people employ a variety of best practices and development processes to improve the likelihood of writing correct software in the first place, and catching defects after the fact. In this book, I'll focus on the small-scale techniques that a single programmer can employ on the job, regardless of the specific development process their company has adopted.

First of all, there can be no correctness if the developer doesn't have a clear idea of the specifications they're aiming at. Thinking of specifications in terms of *contracts* and implementing safeguards to enforce those contracts are useful ideas I explore in chapter 5. The primary way to catch the inevitable defects is to put the software through simulated interactions, that is, testing. Chapter 6 discusses systematic ways to design test cases and measure their effectiveness. Finally, adopting the best practices for readable code benefits correctness by helping both the original author and their peers spot problems, before and after they're exposed by failed tests. Chapter 7 presents a selection of such best practices.

1.2.2 Robustness

Resilience to incorrect inputs or adverse/unanticipated external conditions (such as the lack of some resource)

Correctness and robustness are sometimes lumped together as *reliability*. A robust toaster doesn't catch fire if a bagel, a fork, or nothing at all is pushed in instead of bread. It has safeguards in place against overheating, and so on.[1]

Robust software, among other things, checks that its inputs are valid values. If they're not, it signals the problem and reacts accordingly. If the error condition is fatal, a robust program aborts after salvaging as much as possible of the user data or the computation that has been performed so far. Chapter 5 addresses robustness by promoting rigorous specification and runtime monitoring of method contracts and class invariants.

1.2.3 Usability

A measure of the effort needed to learn how to use software and to achieve its goals; ease of use

Modern pop-up toasters are very easy to use, doing away with a lever to push the bread in and start toasting, and a knob to adjust the amount of toasting desired. Software usability is tied to the design of its user interface (UI) and is addressed by such disciplines as human-computer interaction and user experience (UX) design. This book doesn't address usability because it's focused on software systems with no direct exposure to the end user.

1.2.4 Efficiency

Adequate consumption of resources

Toaster efficiency may refer to how much time and electricity is needed to complete its toasting task. For software, time and space (memory) are the two resources that all programs consume. Chapters 3 and 4 deal with time and space efficiency, respectively. Many programs also require network bandwidth, database connections, and many other resources. Trade-offs commonly arise between different resources. A more powerful toaster may be faster but require more (peak) electricity. Analogously, some programs may be made faster by employing more memory (more on this later).

Although I'm listing efficiency among the external qualities, its true nature is ambiguous. For example, execution speed is definitely noticeable on the part of the end user, especially when it's limited. Consumption of other resources, like network bandwidth, is instead hidden from the user, and you can appraise it only with specialized tools or

---

[1] Toaster robustness is no joke: an estimated 700 people worldwide are killed every year in toaster-related accidents.

by analyzing the source code. That's why I put efficiency somewhat in the middle in figure 1.2.

Efficiency is a mostly nonfunctional quality, because in general the user doesn't care if some service is offered in one or two milliseconds, or whether one or two kilobytes of data is sent over the network. It becomes a functional issue in two contexts:

- *In performance-critical applications*—In these cases, performance guarantees are part of the specifications. Think of an embedded device that interacts with physical sensors and actuators. The response time of its software must obey precise timeouts. Failure to do so may result in functional inconsistencies in the best case, all the way to life-threatening incidents in industrial, medical, or automotive applications.
- *Whenever the efficiency is so bad that it affects normal operations*—Even for a consumer-oriented, noncritical program, there's a limit to the sluggishness and memory hunger that the user is willing to put up with. Beyond that, the lack of efficiency rises to the level of a functional defect.

1.3   *Mostly internal software qualities*

You can appraise internal qualities better by looking at the source code of a program than by running it. The following subsections provide a list of the most important internal qualities.

1.3.1   *Readability*

Clarity, understandability by fellow programmers

It may seem odd to speak of toaster readability, until we realize that, as for all internal qualities, we are talking about its structure and design. In fact, the relevant international standard for software qualities dubs this characteristic *analyzability*. So, a *readable* toaster, once opened for inspection, is easy to analyze, revealing a clear internal layout, with the heating elements well separated from the electronics, an easily identifiable power circuit and timer, and so on.

A readable program is just what it sounds like: easy to understand by another programmer, or by the author after the program's mental model has faded from their mind. Readability is an extremely important, and often undervalued, code quality. It's the topic of chapter 7 of this book.

1.3.2   *Reusability*

Ease of reusing the code to solve similar problems, and amount of changes needed to do so—aka adaptability

You may consider a toaster reusable in our sense if the company that makes it can adapt its design and its parts to build other appliances. For example, its power cord is likely to be standard and, as such, compatible with similar small appliances. Perhaps its timer could be used in a microwave, and so on.

Code reuse was one of the historical selling points of the object oriented (OO) paradigm. Experience has proven that the vision of building complex systems out of widely reusable software components was exaggerated. The modern trend, instead, favors libraries and frameworks that are intentionally designed for reusability, on top of which lies a not-so-thin layer of application-specific code that doesn't aim at reusability. I address reusability in chapter 9 of this book.

1.3.3 Testability

The ability to write tests, and how easy it is to do so, that can trigger all relevant program behaviors and observe their effects

Before discussing testable toasters, let's try to figure out what a toaster test might look like.[2] A reasonable test procedure would involve inserting suitable thermometers into the slots and starting a toasting run. You'd measure success by the temperature change in time being sufficiently close to a predetermined nominal one. A testable toaster makes this procedure easy to perform repeatedly and automatically, with as little human intervention as possible. For example, a toaster that you can start by pushing a button is more testable than a toaster requiring a lever to be pulled down, because it's easier for a machine to push or bypass a button than to pull or bypass a lever.

Testable code exposes an API that allows the caller to verify all expected behaviors. For example, a `void` method (aka a procedure) is less testable than a method returning a value. This book addresses testing techniques and testability in chapter 6.

1.3.4 Maintainability

Ease of finding and fixing bugs, as well as evolving the software

A maintainable toaster is easy to pull apart and service. Its schematics are widely available, and its components are replaceable. Similarly, maintainable software is readable and modular, with different parts having clearly defined responsibilities and interacting in clearly defined ways. Testability and readability, addressed in chapters 6 and 7, are among the main contributors to maintainability.

The FURPS model

Large companies with strong technical traditions develop their own quality model for their software development processes. For example, Hewlett-Packard developed the well-known FURPS model, which classifies software characteristics in five groups: Functionality, Usability, Reliability, Performance, and Supportability.

---

[2] According to some reports, "how to test a toaster" is a recurring question in software engineering job interviews.

**Table 1.1   Typical interactions between code qualities: ↓ stands for "hurts" and - for "no interaction."
Inspired by Figure 20-1 in *Code Complete* (see the *Further reading* section at the end of this chapter).**

	Readability	Robustness	Space efficiency	Time efficiency
Readability				
Robustness	-			
Space efficiency	↓	-		
Time efficiency	↓	↓	↓	

1.4   *Interactions between software qualities*

Some software qualities represent contrasting objectives, while others go hand-in-hand. The result is a balancing act common to all engineering specialties. Mathematicians have a name for this type of problem: *multi-criteria optimization*; that is, finding optimal solutions with respect to multiple competing quality measures. Contrary to an abstract mathematical problem, software qualities may be impossible to quantify (think readability). Luckily, you don't need to find a truly optimal solution, just one that's good enough for your purposes.

Table 1.1 summarizes the relationships between four of the qualities that we examine in this book. Both time and space efficiency may hinder readability. Seeking maximum performance leads to sacrificing abstraction and writing lower level code. In Java, this may entail using primitive types instead of objects, plain arrays instead of collections, or, in extreme cases, writing performance-critical parts in a lower level language like C and connecting them with the main program using the Java Native Interface.

Minimizing memory requirements also favors the use of primitive types, as well as special encodings, where a single value is used as a compact way to represent different things. (You'll see an example of this in section 4.4.) All these techniques tend to hurt readability, and hence maintainability. Conversely, readable code uses more temporary variables and support methods and shies away from those low-level performance hacks.

Time and space efficiency also conflict with each other. For example, a common strategy for improving performance involves storing extra information in memory, instead of computing it every time it's needed. A prominent example is the difference between singly and doubly linked lists. Even though the "previous" link of every node could in principle be computed by scanning the list, storing and maintaining those links allows for constant-time deletion of arbitrary nodes. The class in section 4.4 trades improved space efficiency for increased running time.

Maximizing robustness requires adding code that checks for abnormal circumstances and reacts in the proper way. Such checks incur a performance overhead, albeit usually quite limited. Space efficiency need not be impacted in any way. Similarly, in principle, there's no reason why robust code should be less readable.

Software metrics

Software qualities are related to software *metrics*, which are quantifiable properties of a piece of software. Hundreds of metrics have been proposed in the literature, two of the most common being the mere number of lines of code (aka LOC) and the cyclomatic complexity (a measure of the amount of nesting and branching). Metrics provide objective means of evaluating and monitoring a project that are intended to support decisions related to project development. For example, a method having high cyclomatic complexity may require more testing effort.

Modern IDEs automatically compute common software metrics either natively or via plugins. The relative merits of these metrics, their relationships with the general software qualities described in this chapter, and their effective use are highly debated topics in the software engineering community. In this book, we'll make use of code coverage metrics in chapter 6.

Opposite to these software qualities sits another force that contrasts them all: development time. Business reasons push for writing software quickly, but maximizing any quality attribute requires deliberate effort and time. Even when management is sensitive to the prospective benefits of carefully designed software, it may be tricky to estimate how much time is enough time for a high-quality result. Development processes, of which there are a rich variety, propose different solutions to this problem, some advocating the use of the software metrics mentioned in the sidebar.

This book doesn't enter into the process debate (sometimes it feels like "war" is a more appropriate term), instead focusing on those software qualities that remain meaningful when applied to a small software unit consisting of a single class with a fixed API. Time and space efficiency make the cut, together with reliability, readability, and generality. I exclude other qualities, such as usability or security, from this analysis.

1.5 Special qualities

In addition to the quality attributes I've described in the previous sections, I'll consider two properties of a class that are not formally software qualities: thread safety and succinctness.

1.5.1 Thread safety

The ability of a class to work seamlessly in a multithreaded environment

This isn't a general software quality because it applies only to the specific context of multithreaded programs. Still, such context has become so ubiquitous and thread synchronization issues are so tricky that knowing your way around basic concurrency primitives is a valuable skill to have in any programmer's toolbox.

It's tempting to put thread safety among the internal qualities, but that would be a mistake. What's truly hidden from the user is whether a program is sequential or multithreaded. In the realm of multithreaded programs, thread safety is a basic prerequisite to correctness, and as such a very visible quality. Incidentally, thread safety issues lead to some of the hardest bugs to detect because of their apparent randomness and poor reproducibility. That's why in figure 1.2 I put thread safety in the same area as correctness and robustness. Chapter 8 is devoted to ensuring thread safety while avoiding common concurrency pitfalls.

1.5.2 *Succinctness*

Writing the shortest possible program for a given task

Generally speaking, this isn't a code quality at all. On the contrary, it leads to horrible, obscure code. I've included it in this book (in appendix A) as a fun exercise that pushes the language to its limits and challenges your knowledge of Java or any programming language of your choice.

Still, you can find practical scenarios where succinctness is a desired objective. Low-end embedded systems like smart cards, found in phones and credit cards, may be equipped with so little memory that the program must not only occupy little memory while running, but also exhibit a small footprint when stored on persistent memory. Indeed, most smart cards these days feature 4 KB of RAM and 512 KB of persistent storage. In such cases, the sheer number of bytecode instructions becomes a relevant issue, and shorter source code may lead to fewer issues in that area.

1.6   *The recurring example: A system of water containers*

In this section, I'll describe the programming problem that you'll solve repeatedly in the rest of the book, each time aiming at a different software quality objective. You'll learn the desired API, followed by a simple use case and a preliminary implementation.

Suppose you need to implement the core infrastructure for a new social network. People can register and, of course, connect with each other. Connections are symmetric (if I'm connected to you, you're automatically connected to me, as with Facebook), and one special feature of this network is that users can send a message to all the users to whom they're connected, directly or indirectly. In this book, I'll take the essential features of this scenario and put them in a simpler setting, where we don't have to worry about the content of the messages or the attributes of the people.

Instead of people, you'll deal with a set of water containers, all identical and equipped with a virtually unlimited capacity. At any given time, a container holds a certain amount of liquid, and any two containers can be permanently connected by a pipe. Instead of sending messages, you can pour water in or remove it from a container. Whenever two or more containers are connected, they become communicating vessels, and from that time on they split equally the liquid contained in them.

1.6.1 *The API*

This section describes the desired API for the water containers. At the very least, you'll build a `Container` class, endowed with a public constructor that takes no arguments and creates an empty container, and the following three methods:

- `public double getAmount()`—Return the amount of water currently held in this container.
- `public void connectTo(Container other)`—Permanently connect this container with `other`.

- `public void addWater(double amount)` —Pour amount units of water into this container. This method automatically and equally distributes water among all containers that are connected, directly or indirectly, to this one.

    You can also use this method with a negative amount to remove water from this container. In that case, the group of connected containers should be holding enough water to satisfy the request—you wouldn't want to leave a negative amount of water in a container.

Most of the implementations I present in the following chapters conform exactly to this API, save for a couple of clearly marked exceptions, where tweaking the API helps optimizing a certain software quality.

A connection between two containers is symmetric: water can flow in both directions. A set of containers connected by symmetric links form what is known in computer science as an *undirected graph*. See the sidebar to learn the basic notions about such graphs.

Undirected graphs

In computer science, networks of pairwise connected items are called *graphs*. In this context, items are also known as *nodes* and their connections as *edges*. If connections are symmetric, the graph is called *undirected* because the connections don't have a specific direction. A set of items that are connected, directly or indirectly, is called a *connected component*. In this book, a maximal connected component is simply called a *group*.

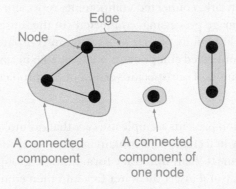

The elements of graphs according to computer science

A proper implementation of `addWater` in the container scenario requires that you know what components are connected because you have to spread (or remove) water evenly among all connected containers. In fact, the main algorithmic problem underlying the proposed scenario consists of maintaining knowledge of the connected components under node creation (`new Container`) and edge insertion (`connectTo` method), a type of *dynamic graph connectivity problem*.

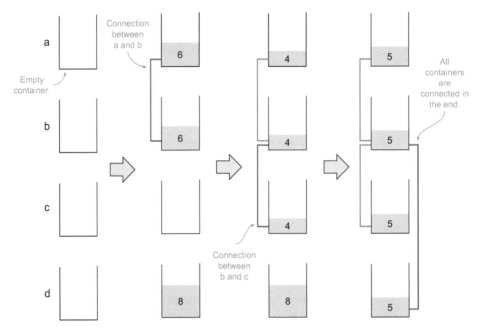

Figure 1.3   The four steps of the use case: from four empty isolated containers to a single group of connected containers

Such problems are central to many applications involving networks of items: in a social network, connected components represent groups of people linked by friendship; in image processing, connected (in the sense of adjacent) regions of same-color pixels help identify objects in a scene; in computer networks, discovering and maintaining connected components is a basic step in routing. Chapter 9 explores the reach and the limits of our specific version of the problem.

1.6.2   The use case

This section presents a simple use case that exemplifies the API outlined in the previous section. You'll create four containers, put some water in two of them, and then progressively connect them until they form a single group (figure 1.3). For this preliminary example, you'll insert the water first and then connect the containers. In general, you can freely interleave these two operations. What's more, you can create new containers at any time.

I've divided the use case (class UseCase in the online repository (https://bitbucket .org/mfaella/exercisesinstyle)) into four parts so that in the other chapters you can easily refer to specific points and examine how different implementations fulfill the same requests. The four steps are illustrated in figure 1.3. In the first part, which coincides with the following code snippet, you simply create four containers. Initially, they're empty and isolated (not connected).

```
Container a = new Container();
Container b = new Container();
Container c = new Container();
Container d = new Container();
```

Next, you add water to the first and last containers and connect the first two with a pipe. At the end, you print the water amount in each container to screen to check that everything worked according to the specifications.

```
a.addWater(12);
d.addWater(8);
a.connectTo(b);
System.out.println(a.getAmount()+" "+b.getAmount()+" "+
                   c.getAmount()+" "+d.getAmount());
```

At the end of the previous snippet, containers a and b are connected, so they share the water that you put into a, whereas containers c and d are isolated. The following is the desired output from the `println`:
6.0 6.0 0.0 8.0

Let's move on and connect c to b to check whether adding a new connection automatically redistributes the water among all connected containers.

```
b.connectTo(c);
System.out.println(a.getAmount()+" "+b.getAmount()+" "+
                   c.getAmount()+" "+d.getAmount());
```

At this point, c is connected to b and, indirectly, to a. Now a, b, and c are communicating vessels, and the total amount of water contained in all of them distributes equally among them. Container d is unaffected, leading to this output:
4.0 4.0 4.0 8.0

Pay special attention to the current point in the use case, as I will use it in the following chapters as a standard scenario to show how different implementations represent the same situation in memory.

Finally, connect d to b so that all containers form a single connected group:

```
b.connectTo(d);
System.out.println(a.getAmount()+" "+b.getAmount()+" "+
                   c.getAmount()+" "+d.getAmount());
```

As a consequence, in the final output, the water level is equal in all containers:
5.0 5.0 5.0 5.0

1.7 Data model and representations

Now that you know the requirements for your water container class, you can turn to designing an actual implementation. The specifications fix the public API, so the next step is to figure out which fields each `Container` object needs, and possibly the class itself (aka static fields) needs. The examples in later chapters show that you can come up with a surprisingly large number of different field choices, depending on which quality objective you're aiming for. This section presents some general observations that apply regardless of the specific quality objective.

First of all, the objects must include enough information to offer the services that the specifications require. Once this basic criterion is met, you still have two types of decisions to make:

1 Do you store any *extra* information, even if not strictly necessary?
2 How do you *encode* all the information you want to store? Which data types or structures are the most appropriate? And which object(s) will be responsible for it?

Regarding question 1, you may want to store unnecessary information for two possible reasons. First, you may do so for performance; this is the case of information that you could derive from other fields, but you prefer to have it ready because deriving it is more expensive than maintaining it. Think of a linked list storing its length in a field, even if that information could be computed on-the-fly by scanning the list and counting the number of nodes. Second, you sometimes store extra information to make room for future extensions. You'll encounter an example of this in section 1.7.2.

Once you establish what information is to be stored, it's time to answer question 2 by equipping classes and objects with fields of appropriate types. Even in a relatively simple scenario like our water containers, this step can be far from trivial. As the whole book tries to prove, several competing solutions may exist, all valid in different contexts and with different quality objectives in mind.

Focusing on our scenario, the information describing the current state of a container is composed of two aspects: the amount of water held in it and its connections with other containers. The next two sections deal with each aspect separately.

1.7.1 *Storing water amounts*

First of all, the presence of the `getAmount` method requires containers to "know" the amount of water in them. By "knowing," I don't mean that you should necessarily store this information in the container. It's too early to make that call. What I mean is simply that the container has some way to appraise that value and return it. Additionally, the API dictates that such an amount be represented by a `double`. The natural implementation choice is indeed to include an amount field of type `double` in each container. Under closer inspection, you might notice that each container in a group of connected containers holds the same amount of water. So, it might be preferable to store such amount information only once, in a separate object representing a group of containers. In this way, you'll only need to update a single object when `addWater` is called, even if the current container is connected to many others.

Finally, instead of a separate object, you also could store the group amount in a special container, chosen as the representative for its group. Summarizing, at least three approaches seem to make sense at this point:

1 Each container holds an up-to-date "amount" field.
2 A separate "group" object holds the "amount" field.

3 Only one container in each group—the *representative*—holds the up-to-date amount value, which applies to all containers in the group.

In the following chapters, various implementations side with each of these three alternative approaches (as well as a couple of extra approaches), and I'll discuss the pros and cons of each approach in detail.

1.7.2 *Storing connections*

When adding water to a container, the liquid must be distributed equally over all containers that are connected (directly or indirectly) to it. Each container therefore must be able to identify all the containers that are connected to it. An important decision is whether to distinguish direct from indirect connections. A direct connection between a and b can be established only via the call a.connectTo(b) or b.connectTo(a), whereas indirect connections arise as a consequence of direct ones.[3]

PICKING THE INFORMATION TO BE STORED

The operations that our specifications require don't distinguish direct from indirect connections, so you could just store the more general type: indirect connections. However, suppose that at some point in the future you want to add a "disconnectFrom" operation whose intent is to undo a previous "connectTo" operation. If you mix up direct and indirect connections, you can't hope to correctly implement "disconnectFrom."

Indeed, consider the two scenarios represented in figure 1.4, where direct connections are drawn as lines between containers. If you store only indirect connections in memory, the two scenarios are indistinguishable: in both cases, all containers are mutually connected. Hence, if the same sequence of operations is applied to both scenarios, they're bound to react in the exact same way. On the other hand, consider what *should* happen if the client issues the following operations:

```
a.disconnectFrom(b);
a.addWater(1);
```

If these two lines are executed on the first scenario (figure 1.4, left), the three containers are still mutually connected, so the extra water must be split equally among all of them. Conversely, in the second scenario (figure 1.4, right) disconnecting a from b makes container a isolated, so the extra water must be added to a only. This shows that only storing indirect connections is incompatible with a future "disconnectFrom" operation.

Summarizing, if you think that the future addition of a "disconnectFrom" operation is likely, you may have reason to store direct connections explicitly and separately from indirect ones. However, if you don't have specific information about the future evolution of your software, you should be wary of such temptations. Programmers are known to be prone to overgeneralization and tend to weigh the hypothetical benefits more than the certain costs that come with it. Consider that the costs associated with

---

[3] In mathematical terms, indirect connections correspond to the *transitive closure* of direct ones.

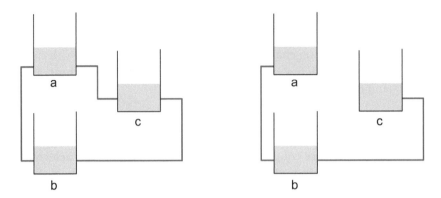

Figure 1.4   Two three-container scenarios. Lines between containers represent direct connections.

an extra feature aren't limited to development time, as each unnecessary class member needs to be tested, documented, and maintained just like the necessary ones.

Also, there's no limit to the amount of extra information you may want to include. What if you later want to remove all connections older than one hour? You should store the time when each connection was made! What if you want to know how many threads have created connections? You should store the set of all threads that have ever created a connection, and so on. In the following chapters, I'll generally stick to storing only the information that's necessary for present purposes,[4] with a few clearly marked exceptions.

PICKING A REPRESENTATION

Finally, assuming you're satisfied with storing indirect connections, the next step is to pick an actual representation for them. In this respect, the preliminary choice is between explicitly forging a new class, say `Pipe`, to represent the connection between two containers, or storing the corresponding information directly inside the container objects (an *implicit* representation).

The first choice is more inline with the OO orthodoxy. In the real world, containers are connected by pipes, and pipes are real objects, clearly distinguished from containers. Hence, the story goes, they deserve to be modeled separately. On the other hand, the specifications laid out in this chapter don't mention any `Pipe` objects, so they would remain hidden within containers, unknown to the clients. Moreover, and more importantly, those pipe objects would contain very little behavior. Each pipe would hold two references to the containers being connected, with no other attributes or nontrivial methods.

Balancing these reasons, it seems there would be a pretty meager benefit from having this extra class around, so you might as well follow the practical, implicit route and avoid it altogether. Containers will be able to reach their group companions without

---

[4] This principle has been formalized as the "You aren't gonna need it" (YAGNI) slogan by the Extreme Programming movement.

resorting to a dedicated "pipe" object. But how exactly will you arrange the references linking the connected containers? The core language and its API offer a variety of solutions: plain arrays, lists, sets, and more. We won't analyze them here because many of them occur naturally in the following chapters (especially chapters 4 and 5) when optimizing for different code qualities.

1.8 Hello containers! [Novice]

To break the ice, in this section we'll consider a `Container` implementation that could be authored by an inexperienced programmer who's just picked up Java after some exposure to a structured language like C. This class is the first in the long sequence of versions that you'll encounter throughout the book. I've assigned each version a nickname to help you navigate and compare them. The nickname for this version is *Novice*, and its fully qualified name in the repository is `eis.chapter1.novice.Container`.

1.8.1 Fields and constructor

Even seasoned professionals have been beginners at some point, navigating the syntax of a new language, unaware of the vast API hiding just around the corner. At first, arrays are the data structure of choice, and resolving syntax errors is too demanding to also worry about coding style issues. After some trial and error, the beginning programmer puts together a class that compiles and seems to fulfill the requirements. Perhaps it starts somewhat like listing 1.1.

Listing 1.1 Novice: Fields and constructor

```java
public class Container {

    Container[] g;        1 The group of connected containers
    int n;                2 The actual size of the group
    double x;             3 The water amount in this container

    public Container() {
        g = new Container[1000];    4 Look: a magic number!
        g[0] = this;                5 Puts this container in its group
        n = 1;
        x = 0;
    }
}
```

These few lines contain a wealth of small and not-so-small defects. Let's focus on the ones that are superficial and easy to fix, as the others will become apparent when we move to better versions in subsequent chapters.

The intent for the three instance fields is the following:

- g is the array of all containers connected to this one, including this one (as is clear from the constructor)
- n is the number of containers in g
- x is the amount of liquid in this container

The single quirk that immediately marks the code as amateurish is the choice of variable names: very short and completely uninformative. A pro wouldn't call the group g if a mobster gave them 60 seconds to hack into a super-secure system of water containers. Jokes aside, meaningful naming is the first rule of readable code, as you'll see in chapter 7.

Then we have the visibility issue. Fields should be `private` instead of *default*. Recall that default visibility is more open than private; it allows access from other classes residing in the same package. Information hiding (aka encapsulation) is a fundamental OO principle, enabling classes to ignore the internals of other classes and interact with them via a well-defined public interface (a form of separation of concerns). In turn, this allows classes to modify their internal representation without affecting existing clients.

The principle of separation of concerns also provides the very footing for this book. The many implementations I present in the following chapters comply with the same public API, and therefore, in principle, clients can use them interchangeably. The way each implementation realizes the API is appropriately hidden from the outside, thanks to the visibility specifiers. At a deeper level, the very notion of individually optimizing different software qualities is an extreme instance of separation of concerns. It's so extreme, in fact, to be merely a didactic tool and not an approach to pursue in practice.

Moving along, the array size, as shown in the sixth line of code in listing 1.1, is defined by a so-called *magic number*: a constant that's not given any name. Best practices dictate that you assign all constants to some `final` variable, so that (a) the variable name can document the meaning of the constant, and (b) you set the value of that constant at a single point, which is especially useful if you use the constant multiple times.

The choice of using a plain array is not very appropriate, as it puts an *a-priori* bound to the maximum number of connected containers: too small a bound, and the program is bound to fail; too large is just wasted space. Moreover, using an array forces us to manually keep track of the number of containers actually in the group (field n here). Better options exist in the Java API, and I discuss them in chapter 2. Nevertheless, plain arrays will come in handy in chapter 5, where the primary objective will be to save space.

1.8.2 Methods getAmount and addWater

Let's proceed and examine the source code for the first two methods, as shown in the following listing.

Listing 1.2 *Novice:* **Methods `getAmount` and `addWater`**

```java
public double getAmount() {  return x;  }

public void addWater(double x) {
    double y = x / n;
    for (int i=0; i<n; i++)
        g[i].x = g[i].x + y;
}
```

getAmount is a trivial getter, and addWater shows the usual naming problems with variables x and y, whereas i is acceptable as the traditional name for an array index. If the last line of the listing used the += operator, it wouldn't repeat g[i].x twice, and you wouldn't have to look back and forth to make sure the statement is actually incrementing the same variable.

Notice that addWater doesn't check whether its argument is negative and, in that case, whether the group holds enough water to satisfy the request. I'll deal with robustness issues like this one specifically in chapter 6.

1.8.3 Method connectTo

Finally, our novice programmer implements the connectTo method, whose task is to merge two groups of containers with a new connection. After this operation, all containers in the two groups must hold the same amount of water because they all become communicating vessels. First, the method will compute the total amount of water in both groups and the total size of the two groups. The water amount per container, after the merge, is simply the former divided by the latter.

You'll also need to update the arrays of all containers in the two groups. The naive way to do so involves appending all containers in the second group to all the arrays belonging to the first group, and vice versa. That's what the following listing does, using two nested loops. Finally, the method updates the size field n and the amount field x of all affected containers.

Listing 1.3 Novice: Method connectTo

```
public void connectTo(Container c) {
    double z = (x*n + c.x*c.n) / (n + c.n);   ❶ Amount per container
                                                  after merge
    for (int i=0; i<n; i++)                    ❷ For each container g[i] in lst group
        for (int j=0; j<c.n; j++) {            ❸ For each container c.g[j] in 2nd group
            g[i].g[n+j] = c.g[j];              ❹ Appends c.g[j] to group of g[i]
            c.g[j].g[c.n+i] = g[i];            ❺ Appends g[i] to group of c.g[j]
        }

    n += c.n;

    for (int i=0; i<n; i++) {                  ❻ Updates sizes and amounts
        g[i].n = n;
        g[i].x = z;
    }
}
```

As you can see, the connectTo method is where the naming issues hurt the most. All those single letter names make it really hard to understand what's going on. For a dramatic comparison, you may want to jump ahead and take a quick look at the readability-optimized version in chapter 7.

Readability would also be improved by replacing the three for-loops with enhanced-for (aka foreach statement in C#), but the representation based on fixed-size arrays makes that a little cumbersome. Indeed, imagine you replaced the last loop from listing 1.3 with the following:

```
for (Container c: g) {
    c.n = n;
    c.x = z;
}
```

This new loop is certainly more readable, but it's going to crash with a `NullPointer Exception` as soon as the `c` variable goes beyond the cells that actually contain a reference to a container. The remedy is quite simple—exiting the loop as soon as you detect a `null` reference:

```
for (Container c: g) {
    if (c==null) break;
    c.n = n;
    c.x = z;
}
```

Despite being utterly unreadable, the `connectTo` method in listing 1.3 is logically correct, with some restrictions. Indeed, consider what happens if `this` and `c` are *already* connected before you call the method. Let's make it concrete and assume the following use case, involving two brand new containers:

```
a.connectTo(b);
a.connectTo(b);
```

Can you see what's going to happen? Is the method tolerant to this slight misstep by the caller? Really think about it before reading ahead. I'll wait . . .

The answer is that connecting two already connected containers messes up their state. Container `a` ends up with two references to itself and two references to `b` in its group array, and a size field `n` equal to 4 instead of 2. Something similar happens to `b`. What's worse, the defect manifests itself even if `this` and `c` were only *indirectly* connected, which can't be considered ill usage on the part of the caller. I'm talking about a scenario like the following (once again, a, b, and c are three brand new containers):

```
a.connectTo(b);
b.connectTo(c);
c.connectTo(a);
```

Before the last line, containers a and c are already connected, albeit indirectly (as in figure 1.4, right). The last line adds a direct connection between them, which is legitimate according to the specifications and leads to the situation depicted in figure 1.4, left. But the `connectTo` implementation in listing 1.3, instead, adds a second copy of all three containers to all group arrays, while erroneously setting all group sizes to 6 instead of 3.

Another obvious limitation of this implementation is that if the merged group contains more than 1,000 members (the magic number), one of these two lines in listing 1.3:

```
g[i].g[n+j] = c.g[j];
c.g[j].g[c.n+i] = g[i];
```

will crash the program with an `ArrayIndexOutOfBoundsException`.

In the next chapter, I'll present a reference implementation that solves most of the superficial issues I've noted here, while striking a balance between different code qualities.

Summary

- You can distinguish between internal and external software qualities, as well as functional and nonfunctional software qualities.
- Some software qualities contrast with each other, and some go hand-in-hand.
- This book addresses software qualities using a system of water containers as a unifying example.

Further reading

This book tries to squeeze into 300 pages a varied range of topics that are seldom treated together. To pull this off, I can only scratch the surface of each topic. That's why I end each chapter with a short list of resources you can refer to for in-depth information on the chapter's content.

- Steve McConnell. *Code Complete.* Microsoft Press, 2nd edition, 2004.
  A valuable book on coding style and all-around good software. Among many other things, it discusses code qualities and their interactions.
- Diomidis Spinellis. *Code Quality: The Open Source Perspective.* Addison Wesley, 2006.
  The author takes you on a journey through quality attributes not unlike the one offered by this book, but with an almost opposite guiding principle: instead of a single running example, he employs a wealth of code fragments taken from various popular open source projects.
- Stephen H. Kan. *Metrics and Models in Software Quality Engineering.* Addison Wesley, 2003.
  Kan provides a systematic, in-depth treatment of software metrics, including statistically sound ways to measure them and use them to monitor and manage software development processes.
- Christopher W.H. Davis. *Agile Metrics in Action.* Manning Publications, 2015.
  Chapter 8 of this book discusses software qualities and the metrics you can use to estimate them.

Reference implementation

This chapter covers

- Using standard collections
- Creating diagrams to illustrate a software design
- Expressing performance in big-O notation
- Estimating the memory footprint of a class

In this chapter, you'll examine a version of the `Container` class that strikes a good balance between different qualities, such as clarity, efficiency, and memory usage.

As you recall from section 1.7, I made the assumption that storing and maintaining the set of indirect connections between containers would suffice. In practice, you do this by equipping each container with a reference to the collection of containers directly or indirectly connected to it, called its *group*. Being familiar with the Java Collections Framework (JCF) (see sidebar), let's go hunting for the best class to represent one of these groups.

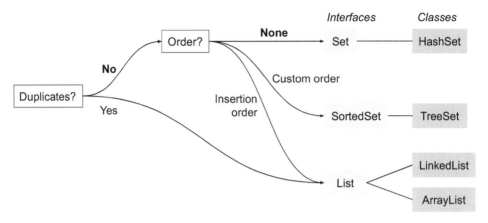

Figure 2.1   Choosing the right Java interface and class for a collection of items

Java Collections Framework

Most standard collections were introduced in Java 1.2 and were heavily redesigned for the 1.5 release (later renamed Java 5) to take advantage of the newly introduced generics. The resulting API is called the JCF and is one of the crown jewels of the Java ecosystem. It comprises approximately 25 classes and interfaces, providing common data structures such as linked lists, hash tables, and balanced trees, as well as concurrency-oriented facilities.

When choosing the right type to represent a collection of items, you should consider two questions: whether the collection will contain duplicates, and whether the ordering of the elements is relevant. In our case, the answer to both questions is "no." In other words, container groups function as mathematical sets, corresponding to the Set interface from the JCF, as shown in figure 2.1.

Next, you need to choose an actual implementation of Set, that is, a class that implements said interface. You have no reason to depart from the most common and generally most efficient choice: HashSet.

POP QUIZ 1 Which collection interface and class would you choose to represent your phone's contact list?

C# collections

C# collection hierarchy differs somewhat from Java's, but the range of concrete classes you ultimately instantiate is quite similar. For example, here are the C# closest matches to each of the classes I mentioned in figure 2.1:

Java	C#
HashSet	HashSet
TreeSet	SortedSet
ArrayList	List
LinkedList	LinkedList

2.1 *The code*   *[Reference]*

Let's design the reference version of the `Container` class, starting from its fields and constructor. The nickname for this version will be, well, *Reference*. According to the previous discussion on collections, you equip every new container with an initial group consisting of that container only and represented by a `HashSet`.

Following the *program to an interface* best practice, you should declare the group field as a `Set` and then instantiate it as a concrete `HashSet`. Think of this as hiding the concrete type from the rest of the class. A benefit of this approach is that if you later change your mind and switch the concrete type from `HashSet` to some other implementation of `Set`, the surrounding code stays unchanged because it refers only to the interface.

Programming to an interface...

...refers to the general idea of focusing your design efforts around APIs, rather than concrete implementations. It's akin to the design-by-contract methodology I discuss in chapter 5. Declaring a field with the most general interface type that gets the job done is a small-scale application of this principle.

Additionally, each container is aware of the amount of water in it, encoded by a `double` value that is implicitly initialized to zero. You should end up with code similar to the following listing.

Listing 2.1   *Reference*: Fields and constructor

```
import java.util.*;    ❶ The following listings will omit the import statements.

/* A water container.   ❷ This freestyle comment should be
 *                         in Javadoc instead (see chapter 7).
 * by Marco Faella
 */
public class Container {

    private Set<Container> group;   ❸ Containers connected to this one
    private double amount;          ❹ Amount of water in this container
```

```
/* Creates an empty container. */    ⑤ This should also be in Javadoc.
public Container() {
   group = new HashSet<Container>();
   group.add(this);                   ⑥ Group starts with this container.
}
```

For starters, compared with *Novice*, this version uses proper encapsulation and naming: fields are private and have reasonably descriptive names. Then, I have intentionally commented the code in a rather naive way to contrast this style with the more principled approach that I discuss in chapter 7, where readability becomes the central issue.

Before presenting the various methods, I'll introduce a couple of graphical devices that will be useful for visually comparing different versions of containers that I'll present in the following chapters.

2.1.1   *Memory layout diagrams*

For every version of `Container` that uses a different choice of fields to represent its data, I'll show a *memory layout* picture, which is an abstract illustration of how a given set of containers is realized in memory. The intent is to help you build a visual mental model of that representation, and to ease comparison between different versions. To that end, I'll always depict the same scenario, namely the standard use case I described in chapter 1, the way it looks when the first three parts have been executed. Recall that those parts create four containers (a to d) and execute the following lines:

```
a.addWater(12);
d.addWater(8);
a.connectTo(b);
b.connectTo(c);
```

At this point, three of the four containers are connected in a group, and the fourth one is isolated, as shown in figure 2.2. The memory layout diagram is a simplified scheme of how the objects are arranged in memory, similar to UML *object diagrams* (explained in the following subsection). Both display static snapshots of a set of objects, including the value of their fields and their relationships. In this book, I prefer to use my own style of object diagram because it's more intuitive and I can tailor it to the specific point I'm trying to make in each section. Figure 2.3 shows the memory layout of *Reference*, after the first three parts of *UseCase*. As you can see, I've omitted many low-level details, such as the type and width in bytes of each field. Additionally, I've completely hidden the internal composition of the `HashSet`, because right now I'd like you to focus on

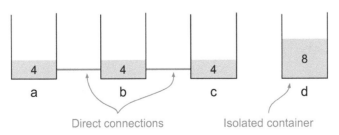

Figure 2.2   The situation after executing the first three parts of *UseCase*. You have connected together containers a through c and poured water into a and d.

Direct connections   Isolated container

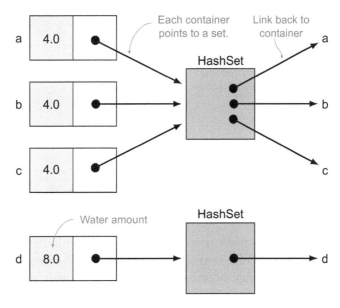

Figure 2.3   The memory layout of *Reference* after executing the first three parts of *UseCase*. To avoid clutter, I've pictured the references from the `HashSet`s back to the containers as reaching the name of the container.

which object contains each piece of information, and which object points to which other object. We'll return to the memory layout of a `HashSet` in section 2.2.1.

Naturally, in your job you're more likely to encounter standard UML diagrams, so here's a brief reminder of two common types of UML diagrams.

UML CLASS DIAGRAM
A class diagram is a description of the static properties of a set of classes, particularly regarding their mutual relationships, such as inheritance or containment. The just-mentioned object diagrams are closely

Unified Modeling Language

Unified Modeling Language (UML) is a standard providing a rich collection of diagrams for describing various aspects of a software system. Class diagrams and sequence diagrams are two of the most commonly used parts of the standard. You'll see an example of a sequence diagram in chapter 3.

related to class diagrams, except that they depict individual instances of those classes.

For example, a class diagram for *Reference* may look like figure 2.4. The `Container` box is quite self-explanatory, listing fields and methods, whose visibility is denoted by a plus (public) or minus (private) sign. The `HashSet` box doesn't specify any field or method, and that's perfectly fine for such diagrams; they can be as abstract or as detailed as you wish.

The line between the two boxes is called an *association* and represents a relation between two classes. At each end of the line, you can describe the role of each class in the association ("Member" and "Group" here) and the so-called cardinality of the

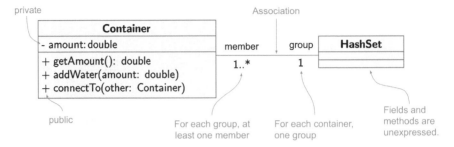

Figure 2.4   UML class diagram for *Reference* (detailed version)

association. The latter specifies how many instances of that class are in relation to each instance of the other class. In this case, each container belongs to a single group, and each group includes one or more members, denoted by "1..*" in UML.

Although formally correct, the class diagram in figure 2.4 is too detailed for most purposes. UML diagrams are intended to describe a *model* of the system, not the system itself. If a diagram becomes too detailed, you might as well replace it with the actual source code. Hence, you normally don't mention standard collections such as Hash Set explicitly. Rather, they're interpreted as just one possible implementation of an association between classes.

In this case, you can replace the HashSet with a more abstract association linking the Container class with itself. In this way, rather than describing the implementation, you're conveying the idea that each container may be connected to zero or more other containers. Figure 2.5 represents this graphically.

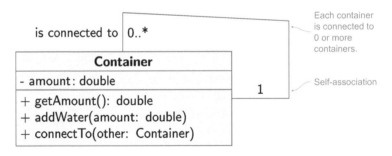

Figure 2.5   UML class diagram for *Reference* (abstract version)

POP QUIZ 2   Use a class diagram to represent the main attributes of Java classes and methods, and their mutual relationships.

UML OBJECT DIAGRAM

UML object diagrams appear very similar to class diagrams. You distinguish objects (that is, class instances) from classes by having their names and types underlined. For example, figure 2.6 shows the object diagram for *Reference*, after executing the first three parts of *UseCase*. That figure is consistent with the abstract class diagram in figure 2.5, where the `HashSets` are not explicitly modeled, but rather hidden within the association between containers.

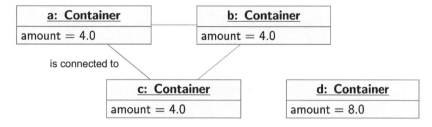

Figure 2.6   UML object diagram for *Reference* (abstract version)

In chapter 3, you'll learn about one more type of UML diagram: the sequence diagram, designed to visualize the dynamic interactions among a set of objects.

2.1.2   The methods

The `getAmount` method is a trivial getter—nothing to write home about.

Listing 2.2   *Reference*: The `getAmount` method

```
public double getAmount() { return amount; }
```

Next, you can develop the `connectTo` method (listing 2.3).[1] Start by observing that connecting two containers essentially entails merging their two groups. As a result, the method initially computes the total amount of water in the two groups and the amount of water in each container after the merge. Then, you modify the group of this container to absorb the second group, and you assign all containers of the second group to the new, larger group. Finally, you update the amount of water in each container with the precomputed new amount.

As before, listing 2.3 is heavily commented in an attempt to improve its readability. The modern trend, instead, would be to split it into smaller methods with suitably descriptive names. I'll discuss that in depth in chapter 7.

Listing 2.3   *Reference*: The `connectTo` method

```
public void connectTo(Container other) {

    // If they are already connected, do nothing
    if (group==other.group) return;

    int size1 = group.size(),          ❶ Computes the new amount
        size2 = other.group.size();       of water in each container
    double tot1 = amount * size1,
```

---

[1]   Here and in the following chapters, I'm taking some liberties with code formatting, like putting a loop and its body on the same line. I'm doing so to shorten the listing and make it fit in a single page.

```
        tot2 = other.amount * size2,
        newAmount = (tot1 + tot2) / (size1 + size2);

    // Merge the two groups
    group.addAll(other.group);
    // Update group of containers connected with other
    for (Container c: other.group) { c.group = group; }
    // Update amount of all newly connected containers
    for (Container c: group) { c.amount = newAmount; }
}
```

❷ You can replace comments like this with a properly named support method.

The `addWater` method simply distributes an equal amount of water to each container in the group.

> **Listing 2.4   *Reference*: The `addWater` method**

```
public void addWater(double amount) {
    double amountPerContainer = amount / group.size();
    for (Container c: group) c.amount += amountPerContainer;
}
```

As in *Novice*, this method accepts negative arguments—denoting water removal—and doesn't check whether the containers hold enough water to satisfy the request. It thus runs the risk of leaving a negative amount of water in one or more containers. (I address robustness issues like this in chapter 5.) In the next two sections, we'll analyze the memory and time consumption of the implementation I've presented in this section, so later you'll be able to compare its performance with that of the following versions.

2.2   *Memory requirements*

Despite the fact that primitive types have a fixed size, estimating the memory size of a Java object is not trivial. Three factors render the exact size of an object dependent on the architecture and even on the JDK vendor:

- Reference size
- Object headers
- Padding

How these factors influence the size of an object depends on the specific JVM you use to run your program. Recall that the Java framework is based on two official specifications: one for the Java language and one for the virtual machine (VM). Different vendors are free to implement their own compiler or VM, and, indeed, as of writing these lines, Wikipedia lists 18 actively developed JVMs.[2] In the following VM-dependent arguments, I'll refer to Oracle's standard JVM, which is called *HotSpot*.

Let's consider each of the three memory factors in more detail. First, the size of a reference is not fixed by the language. Whereas the size is 32 bits on 32-bit hardware,

---

[2] See http://mng.bz/zlm6.

on modern 64-bit processors it can be either 32 or 64 bits because of a technology called *compressed ordinary object pointers (OOPs).* Compressed OOPs allow the program to store references as 32-bit values, even when the hardware supports 64-bit addresses, at the cost of addressing "only" 32 GB of the total available heap space. In the following memory-occupancy estimates, assume a fixed reference size of 32 bits.

Compressed OOPs

Compressed OOPs work by implicitly adding three zeros at the end of each 32-bit address, so a stored address of, say, `0x1` is interpreted as the machine address `0x1000`. In this way, machine addresses effectively span 35 bits, and the program can access up to 32 GB of memory. The JVM must also take steps to align all variables to 8-byte boundaries, because the program can only refer to addresses that are multiples of eight.

Summarizing, this technology saves space for each reference but increases padding space and incurs a time overhead when mapping stored addresses to machine addresses (a quick left-shift operation). Compressed OOPs are turned on by default but are automatically disabled if you tell the VM that you intend to use more than 32 GB of memory (with command-line options `-Xms` and `-Xmx`).

Second, the memory layout of all objects starts with a header containing some standard information that the JVM needs. As a consequence, even an object with no fields (aka a *stateless* object) takes up some memory. The detailed composition of the object header goes beyond the scope of this book,[3] but three features of the Java language are ultimately responsible for it: reflection, multithreading, and garbage collection.

1   Reflection requires objects to know their type. Hence, each object must store a reference to its class, or a numeric identifier referring to a table of loaded classes. This mechanism allows the `instanceof` operator to check the dynamic type of an object and the `getClass` method of the `Object` class to return a reference to the (dynamic) class of the object.

On a related note, arrays also need to store the type of their cells because every write operation into an array is type-checked at runtime (and raises `Array StoreException` if incorrect). However, this information does *not* enlarge the overhead of a single array, because it's part of the type information and can be shared among all arrays of the same type. For example, all arrays of strings point to the same `Class` object, representing the type "array of strings."

2   Multithreading support assigns a *monitor* to each object (accessible via the `syn chronized` keyword). Hence, the header must accommodate a reference to a monitor object. Modern virtual machines create such a monitor on demand only when multiple threads actually compete for exclusive access to that object.

---

[3]   If you're curious for details, you can browse the source code for HotSpot, currently available https://hg.openjdk.java.net/jdk10/jdk10/hotspot. The object headers' content is described in the file src/share/vm/oops/markOop.hpp.

3 Garbage collection needs to store some information on each object, such as a *reference count*. In fact, modern garbage collection algorithms assign objects to different *generations*, based on the time since they were created. In that case, the header also contains an *age* field.

In this book, assume a fixed 12-byte per-object overhead, which is typical of modern 64-bit JVMs. Besides this standard object header, arrays also need to store their length, leading to a 16-byte total overhead (that is, even an empty array takes 16 bytes).

Finally, hardware architectures require or prefer data to be aligned to certain boundaries; that is, they work more efficiently if memory accesses employ addresses that are multiples of some power of two (usually four or eight). This circumstance leads compilers and virtual machines to employ *padding*: inflating the memory layout of an object with empty space so that each field is properly aligned and the whole object fits exactly into an integer number of words. For simplicity, we'll ignore such architecture-dependent padding issues in this book.

C# object size

The situation in C# is pretty similar to the one I've described here for Java, and the causes for memory overhead are exactly the same, leading to 12-byte headers for 32-bit architectures and 16 bytes for 64 bit.

2.2.1   *Memory requirements of Reference*

Now turn your attention to the actual memory occupancy of the *Reference* implementation. For starters, each `Container` object requires the following:

- 12 bytes for overhead
- 8 bytes for the `amount` field (type `double`)
- 4 bytes for the reference to the set, plus the size of the set itself

To estimate the memory footprint of a `HashSet`, you need to peek under the hood at its implementation. You typically implement a `HashSet` using an array of linked lists (called *buckets*), plus a couple of extra fields for bookkeeping. Ideally, each element goes into a different bucket, and there are exactly as many buckets as elements. Without going into too much detail,[4] in this ideal scenario a barebone `HashSet` takes up approximately 52 bytes. Each element in the set requires one reference (to its list) and a list with one element: approximately 32 more bytes. I'm using the word *barebone* instead of *empty* because an empty `HashSet` starts with a non-zero initial capacity (16 buckets in the current OpenJDK), but it's simpler and more orderly to ascribe that space to the first elements that will be inserted. Figure 2.7 shows in some detail the internals of the involved objects, with a breakdown of the memory requirements.

---

[4] The actual implementation of `HashSet` goes through `HashMap`, complicating the analysis.

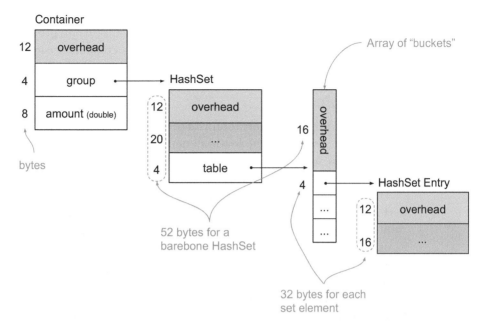

Figure 2.7 **The detailed memory footprint of a container in version *Reference*. The estimates for `HashSet` assume a perfectly sized table of buckets and a perfect hashing function, resulting in exactly one element in each bucket.**

Measuring object size

The JDK includes a tool called JOL (for Java Object Layout) that inspects the internal memory layout of a given class, including the object header. It's available at http://openjdk.java.net/projects/code-tools/jol/.

POP QUIZ 3 The class `android.graphics.Rect` contains four public fields of type `int`. How many bytes does a `Rect` object take?

To get actual numbers and ease comparisons with other implementations, I'll estimate the memory occupancy for two hypothetical scenarios: first, 1000 isolated containers; second, 1000 containers connected in 100 groups of 10 containers each. In those two scenarios, our reference implementation performs as reported in table 2.1. Are those numbers good or bad? Are 100 bytes too many for an isolated container?

Table 2.1 **Memory requirements of *Reference* in two conventional scenarios**

Scenario	Size (calculations)	Size (bytes)
1000 isolated	$1000 * (12 + 8 + 4 + 52 + 32)$	108000
100 groups of 10	$1000 * (12 + 8 + 4) + 100 * (52 + 10 * 32)$	61200

Can we do any better? It's hard to judge those numbers as they stand. In the next two chapters, you'll develop a number of alternative implementations, and then you'll be able to compare their memory occupancy and answer the previous questions with solid arguments. (Spoiler alert: I present the most compact version in chapter 4, and it requires just 4 KB for both scenarios, but it doesn't comply with the established API.)

2.3   Time complexity

When measuring the memory footprint of a program, you can use bytes as the standard basic unit. If you ignore the low-level details I discussed in the previous section, as a rule of thumb, a given Java program will take the same amount of memory when run on all computers.

The situation for time measurements is more complicated. The same program will perform in vastly different ways on different computers. Rather than measuring actual running time, you can count the number of *basic steps* that the program performs. Roughly speaking, you can define as a basic step any operation that requires a constant amount of time. For example, you can consider any arithmetic or comparison operation a basic step.[5]

Another issue is the fact that the same function can execute a different number of basic steps when given different inputs. For example, consider the `connectTo` method from listing 2.3. It takes two containers as inputs:

- Its only *explicit* input is the parameter `other` of type `Container`.
- Being an instance method, it also takes `this` as an *implicit* parameter, so the current container is also an effective input.

That method contains two `for` loops, whose lengths (that is, number of iterations) depend on the size of the two container groups being merged, which is a function of the inputs.

In such cases, you summarize with one or more numeric parameters what it is in the input that influences the running time of your algorithm. Usually, the summary involves measuring the *size* of the input in some way. If the number of basic steps of our algorithm varies even for same-sized inputs, we just consider the worst case—that is, the maximum number of steps performed on any input of a given size.

Going back to the `connectTo` method, as a first attempt you can consider two parameters: `size1` and `size2`, the sizes of the two groups of containers you're merging. Using these parameters, you can analyze the `connectTo` method as shown in the following listing.

---

[5]   The formal definition of basic step must be based on a formal model of computation, such as Turing machines. You may then define a basic step as any operation that requires a constant number of steps of a Turing machine.

Listing 2.5 *Reference*: The `connectTo` method (comments stripped)

```
public void connectTo(Container other) {

    if (group==other.group) return;         ❶ I step

    int size1 = group.size(),
        size2 = other.group.size();
    double tot1 = amount * size1,                    ❷ 5 steps
           tot2 = other.amount * size2,
           newAmount = (tot1 + tot2) / (size1 + size2);

    group.addAll(other.group);                               ❸ size2 steps
    for (Container c: other.group) { c.group = group; }      ❹ size2 steps
    for (Container c: group) { c.amount = newAmount; }       ❺ size1 + size2
}                                                                steps
```

I'm counting as one step anything that doesn't involve a loop, because its running time will be essentially constant, and in particular independent of the parameters `size1` and `size2`. I'm also sweeping a lot of detail under the rug when labeling the `group.addAll` line with "`size2` steps." In short, that estimate is the expected number of steps assuming the `hashCode` method spreads objects uniformly over the whole set of representable integers.

> **NOTE** For a deeper understanding of hash tables and their performance, refer to a book on data structures, such as the one I mention in the *Further reading* section at the end of this chapter.

According to this reasoning, the number of basic steps that `connectTo` performs is

$$6 + 2 * \texttt{size2} + (\texttt{size1} + \texttt{size2}) = 6 + \texttt{size1} + 3 * \texttt{size2} \qquad (*)$$

However, you should recognize that the number 6 in this expression is somewhat arbitrary. If you counted assembly lines instead of Java lines, you might get 6 thousand instead of 6, and 6 million steps if you counted the steps of a Turing machine. For the same reason, the 3 multiplier in front of `size2` is essentially arbitrary. In other words, the constants 3 and 6 depend on the *granularity* you choose for the basic steps.

A more interesting way to count steps that elegantly sidesteps the granularity issue is to focus on only how quickly the number of steps grows when the size parameters grow. This is called the *order of growth*, and it's the basic tenet of complexity theory, a branch of computer science. The order of growth frees you from the burden of establishing a specific granularity for the basic steps, thus providing performance estimates that are more abstract but easier to compare with one another. At the same time, the order of growth preserves the *asymptotic* behavior of our function, that is, the trend for large values of its parameter(s).

In practice, the most common way to indicate the order of growth is the so-called *big-O notation*. For example, the basic steps expression (*) in big-O notation becomes $O(\texttt{size1} + \texttt{size2})$, effectively hiding all arbitrary additive and multiplicative constants. In so doing, it highlights the fact that the number of steps is linearly proportional to `size1` and `size2`. More precisely, the big-O notation establishes an *upper bound* to the growth of a function. So, $O(\texttt{size1} + \texttt{size2})$ asserts that our running time grows *at most* linearly with respect to `size1` and `size2`.

The `connectTo` method is simple, always performing the same number of steps for the same values of `size1` and `size2`. Other algorithms are less regular in that their performance depends on some feature of the input that the size parameter(s) don't express. For example, searching for a specific value in an unordered array may find that value immediately (constant time) or may involve scanning the whole array before realizing the value isn't actually there (linear time). In that case, complexity analysis suggests that you consider the input that requires the most steps to complete, aka the *worst case*. That's why the standard performance estimate for algorithms is called *worst-case asymptotic complexity*. Summarizing, the (worst-case asymptotic) complexity of searching in an unordered array is $O(n)$. Table 2.2 presents some common big-O bounds, their names, and examples of array algorithms matching that bound. For algorithms running on arrays, the parameter n refers to the size of the array.

Table 2.2 Common complexity bounds in big-O notation

Notation	Name	Example
$O(1)$	Constant time	Checking whether the first element in an array is zero
$O(\log n)$	Logarithmic time	Binary search: the smart way to look for a specific value in a sorted array
$O(n)$	Linear time	Finding the maximum value in an unsorted array
$O(n \log n)$	Quasilinear time	Sorting an array using merge sort
$O(n^2)$	Quadratic time	Sorting an array using bubble sort

POP QUIZ 4   Given an unordered array of integers, what is the complexity of checking whether the array is a palindrome?

Before we delve a little deeper into the asymptotic notation, let's further simplify the analysis of `connectTo` by switching from two size parameters to a single one. If you call n the total number of containers ever created, then `size1` + `size2` is at most equal to n (distinct groups are disjoint by definition). Because the upper bound $O(\texttt{size1}+\texttt{size2})$ holds for our function, so does $O(n)$, which is greater than the first upper bound. In other words, the time that a `connectTo` operation requires grows at most linearly with the total number of containers around. This may seem like a brutal approximation, and it is. After all, `size1` and `size2` are likely to be much smaller than n. However, rough as it is, this type of upper bound will be accurate enough to distinguish the efficiency of the various implementations presented in the following chapters.

The formal definition of big-O notation

When someone says that an algorithm has complexity $O(f(n))$ for some function f, they mean that $f(n)$ is an upper bound to the number of basic steps that the algorithm performs on any input of size n. This makes sense if we agree on how to measure the size of the input with a single parameter n.

More formally, you can apply the big-O notation to any function $f(n)$, representing the number of steps an algorithm requires when run on an input of size n. Consider an algorithm and let $g(n)$ be the actual number of "steps"—however they may be defined—performed by the algorithm on an input of size n. Then, writing that the algorithm has time complexity $O(f(n))$ means that two numbers m and c exist such that, for all $n \geq m$

$$g(n) \leq c \cdot f(n)$$

In other words, for sufficiently large inputs, the actual number of steps is at most equal to a constant times the value of the f function.

Complexity theory includes several other notations, denoting lower bounds, simultaneous lower and upper bounds, and so on.

2.3.1 Time complexity of Reference

You can now precisely state the time complexity of all the methods from *Reference*. The `getAmount` method is a simple getter and takes constant time. Methods `connectTo` and `addWater` need to cycle over all containers in a group. Because a group can be as large as the whole set of all containers, their complexity in the worst case is linear with the total number n of containers. Table 2.3 summarizes these observations. In chapter 3, you'll learn how to improve these time complexities.

Table 2.3 Time complexities for *Reference*, with n standing for the total number of containers

Method	Time complexity
`getAmount`	$O(1)$
`connectTo`	$O(n)$
`addWater`	$O(n)$

2.4 Applying what you learned

This section, and the similar sections in the following chapters, applies the notions developed in the chapter to different contexts. Because the whole book is based on the idea of using a single example to tie together a variety of topics, it's particularly important to read and work through these applications. For this reason, I've framed them as exercises. Naturally, you should try to solve them on your own. If you don't have the time or the inclination to do that, *at least read the exercises and their solutions.* I believe you'll find that the solutions are carefully explained and sometimes add useful insight to the core chapter contents. Besides, several exercises throughout the chapters guide you in a behind-the-scenes exploration of various classes from the JDK and other libraries.

EXERCISE 1

1. What is the complexity of the following method?

```
public static int[][] identityMatrix(int n) {
   int[][] result = new int[n][n];
   for (int i=0; i<n; i++) {
      for (int j=0; j<n; j++) {
         if (i==j) {
            result[i][j] = 1;
         }
      }
   }
   return result;
}
```

2. Can you make it more efficient without changing its output?
3. If you were able to come up with a more efficient version, does that version have a lower complexity?

EXERCISE 2

The class `java.util.LinkedList<T>` realizes a doubly linked list of references to objects of type `T`. Check out its source code[6] and estimate the size in bytes of a `LinkedList` with *n* elements (excluding the space occupied by the *n* objects).

EXERCISE 3 (MINI-PROJECT)

Implement the class `User`, representing a person in a social network, with the following functionalities:

- Each user has a name. Provide a public constructor accepting that name.
- Users can befriend each other using the following method:

      public void befriend(User other)

  Friendships are symmetric: `a.befriend(b)` is equivalent to `b.befriend(a)`.
- Clients can check whether two users are direct friends or indirect friends (friends of friends) using the following two methods:

      public boolean isDirectFriendOf(User other)
      public boolean isIndirectFriendOf(User other)

---

[6] As of this writing, the source code is available at http://mng.bz/KElg.

Summary

- You can visualize the structure and behavior of software using static and dynamic diagrams, such as UML object diagrams and sequence diagrams.
- An empty Java object takes 12 bytes of memory because of object headers.
- Asymptotic complexity measures time efficiency in a hardware-independent way.
- Big-O notation is the most common way to express an asymptotic upper bound to time complexity.

Answers to quizzes and exercises

POP QUIZ 1

Let's say that a contact comprises a name and a phone number. You usually access a contact list by name, in alphabetical order. That's a custom order based on the content of the object, so, despite its name ("list"), a contact list is better represented by a SortedSet, whose standard implementation is the class TreeSet.

In a real phone, a contact is a much more complex entity, including many attributes and being connected with different apps. As such, it's likely to be stored in some sort of database (for example, Android uses SQLite).

POP QUIZ 2

Here's a class diagram representing Java classes and methods:

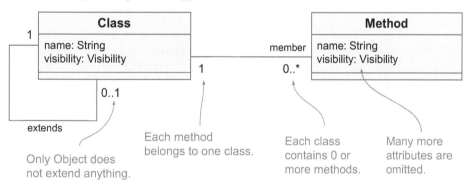

POP QUIZ 3

An android.graphics.Rect object occupies 12 bytes for overhead and 4*4 bytes for its four integer fields, for a total of 28 bytes. As usual in this book, this estimate ignores padding issues, which are likely to bring the actual size up to the next multiple of 8, which is 32.

POP QUIZ 4

Checking whether an array of even length n is a palindrome means checking whether a[i] equals a[n-1-i] for each i from zero to n/2. That's n/2 iterations, whose order of growth is in $O(n)$. (The constant factor $\frac{1}{2}$ is irrelevant to the asymptotic notation.)

EXERCISE 1

1. The complexity of the method is $O(n^2)$, that is, quadratic.

2. Here's a more efficient version that avoids the nested loop and the `if` statement:

```
public static int[][] identityMatrix(int n) {
    int[][] result = new int[n][n];        ❶ The matrix is initialized with zeros.
    for (int i=0; i<n; i++) {
        result[i][i] = 1;
    }
    return result;
}
```

3. The complexity of the new version is still quadratic because of the array allocation in the second line, which implicitly initializes all n^2 cells to zero.

EXERCISE 2

Here are the relevant lines from the source code of `LinkedList`:

```
public class LinkedList<E> extends AbstractSequentialList<E> ... {
    transient int size = 0;
    transient Node<E> first;
    transient Node<E> last;

    ...

    private static class Node<E> {
        E item;
        Node<E> next;
        Node<E> prev;
        ...
    }
}
```

A quick check reveals superclasses `AbstractSequentialList`, `AbstractList`, and `Abstract Collection`, in that order. Of those, only `AbstractList` contains an instance field, used to detect concurrent modifications to the list during an iteration:

```
protected transient int modCount = 0;
```

That said, a `LinkedList` with n elements occupies

- 12 bytes for overhead
- 3*4 bytes for the three fields `size`, `first`, and `last`
- 4 bytes for the inherited `modCount` field

In addition, for each element it occupies

- 12 bytes for object overhead
- 3*4 bytes for the three fields `item`, `next`, and `prev`

Summarizing, a `LinkedList` with n elements occupies $28 + n * 24$ bytes.

EXERCISE 3

The specifications are somewhat similar to the container scenario, except that you need to distinguish direct from indirect connections (aka friendships). A possible solution is to store direct connections explicitly and compute indirect connections on demand. You can then start the class as follows:

```
public class User {
   private String name;
   private Set<User> directFriends = new HashSet<>();

   public User(String name) {
      this.name = name;
   }

   public void befriend(User other) {
      directFriends.add(other);
      other.directFriends.add(this);
   }

   public boolean isDirectFriendOf(User other) {
      return directFriends.contains(other);
   }
```

Checking indirect connections requires a visit to an (undirected) graph. The simplest such algorithm is the *breadth-first search* (BFS), which maintains two sets of nodes:

- A *frontier* of nodes waiting to be visited
- A set of already *visited* (aka closed) nodes

Here's a possible implementation of a BFS:

```
public boolean isIndirectFriendOf(User other) {
   Set<User> visited = new HashSet<>();
   Deque<User> frontier = new LinkedList<>();

   frontier.add(this);
   while (!frontier.isEmpty()) {
      User user = frontier.removeFirst();
      if (user.equals(other)) {
         return true;
      }
      if (visited.add(user)) {        ❶ If not visited
         frontier.addAll(user.directFriends);     ❷ addAll inserts at the tail end.
      }
   }
   return false;
}
```

Further reading

You can find a thousand introductory books on Java programming. Here are my favorites:

- Cay S. Horstmann. *Core Java.* Prentice Hall, 2015.
  A two-volume behemoth, covering many parts of the API in detail, with a strong teaching emphasis

- Peter Sestoft. *Java Precisely*. MIT Press, 3rd edition, 2016.
  Not an actual introductory book, but rather a concise and comprehensive reference guide to the language and a limited selection of the API (including collections and Java 8 streams)

Regarding time complexity and big-O notation, any introductory book on algorithms features comprehensive explanations on the topic. This is the classic one:

- T. H. Cormen, C. E. Leiserson, R. L. Rivest, and C. Stein. *Introduction to Algorithms*. MIT Press, 2009.

Finally, for UML and related software engineering techniques, see the following:

- Martin Fowler. *UML Distilled*. Addison-Wesley, 2003.
  As its name suggests, this book condenses in fewer than 200 pages a solid introduction to UML notation, with special focus on class and sequence diagrams.
- Craig Larman. *Applying UML and Patterns*. Prentice Hall, 2004.
  Much wider in scope and page count than Fowler's book, this volume goes way beyond UML and serves as a systematic introduction to OO analysis and design. The second edition is also available as a free download.

Part 2

Software Qualities

In this part, we dive into various software qualities and optimize the heck out of them. In the first chapter of this part, you'll deal with efficiency, in terms of time and memory. Algorithms and data structures are the tools for this job.

Chapters 5 and 6 are focused on reliability, using techniques like design-by-contract and testing. Chapter 7 presents the best practices for writing readable code. Finally, in chapters 8 and 9, you'll sink your teeth into advanced programming techniques related to thread safety and reusability.

Need for speed:
Time efficiency

Achieving the maximum possible speed for a given computational task has fascinated programmers since the ancient times of punch-card programming. Indeed, you might say that a large part of computer science itself was born to satisfy this urge. In this chapter, I'll present three different container implementations that optimize speed in different ways. Why three? Can't I just present you with the *best* one? The thing is, there is no single best version, and that's one of the main takeaways from this chapter.

Basic programming classes and even introductory computer science curricula overlook this fact. The latter deal extensively with time efficiency, particularly in algorithm and data structure classes. Those classes and their textbooks focus on one problem at a time, be it visiting a graph or balancing a tree. When you consider a single algorithmic problem, with given inputs and desired outputs, you can compare any two algorithms for performance. You may find that the fastest possible procedure is the one with the least asymptotic worst-case time complexity. This is indeed how research makes progress on single computational questions.

On the other hand, many real-world programming tasks, including our container example, aren't like that. They don't accept an input, compute an output, and then terminate. They ask you to design a number of interacting methods or functionalities that you may use repeatedly any number of times. Different data structures may favor one method over another, reducing the complexity of the first and slowing down the latter. For this reason, often there's no all-around best solution, just different trade-offs.

This chapter features three implementations of the container class, all conforming to the API I established in chapter 1. They differ in their performance profiles, but none of them is always faster than the others, at least according to their worst-case complexity. But you'll also learn to measure the *average* performance of a given implementation when considering long sequences of operations. When you take average performance into account, the third implementation turns out to be the fastest in all but the most contrived scenarios, as the simple performance tests I present in section 3.4 will confirm.

Partial orders

In a multi-method context like ours, worst-case time complexity induces a *partial order* between implementations. A *partial order* is a relation between pairs of items, such that not every pair is comparable. For example, consider the relation "being descendant from" applied to pairs of people. A pair like (Mike, Anna) belongs to the relation if Mike descends from Anna. If two people a and b are unrelated, neither the pair (a, b) nor the pair (b, a) belongs to the relation, which means that the relation is a partial order. In a partial order, there might be items that are *not smaller* than any other. They are top items.

Economists call these items *Pareto optimal*, and call *Pareto front* the set of all Pareto optimal items. If we interpret "being descendant from" as "being smaller," the mythical Adam and Eve would be the only top elements, because they're not smaller than (that is, descendant from) any other person.

As a more computer-related example, the Java promotion rules between primitive types induce a partial order among them. In that order, "int" is smaller than (that is, convertible to) "long," whereas "boolean" and "int" are uncomparable.

If you're designing a class and you don't have specific information on how many times and in what sequence you'll invoke each method (that is, if you don't have a *usage profile*), the best you can do is to pick an implementation whose performance profile is Pareto optimal. In such an implementation, no method can be improved without degrading the performance of another. This chapter presents three Pareto optimal implementations for the water container problem.

POP QUIZ 1 Name a partial order that holds between classes in a Java program.

3.1 *Adding water in constant time* [Speed1]

In this section, I'll show you how to optimize the addWater method, whose complexity in our *Reference* implementation (chapter 2) is linear. It turns out that you can bring its complexity down to constant time without increasing the complexity of the other two methods in the class. You truly couldn't hope for anything better.

In *Reference*, the problem with addWater is that it needs to visit all containers that are connected to the current one and update their water amount. This is a waste, especially because *all connected containers share the same amount.* To prevent this waste, you move the amount field from the Container class to a new Group class. All containers belonging to the same group will point to the same Group object, containing the amount of water present in each of those containers.

In practice, the new Container class, called *Speed1*, has a single field:

```
private Group group = new Group(this);
```

Each container holds a reference to an object of a new class Group, which is the nested class shown in listing 3.1. You pass this to the constructor, so the new group starts with its first container inside. You'll find two instance fields in each Group object: one holding the amount of water in each container of the group, and the other storing the set of all containers in the group. In this way, each container knows its group, and the group knows all the containers it comprises.

The Group class is static because you don't want each group to be permanently linked to the container that created it. It's private because it shouldn't be exposed to the clients: they have no use for it, and they're not supposed to access it directly. Because the whole class is private, there's no point in applying visibility modifiers to its constructor and fields.

Listing 3.1 *Speed1*: The nested class Group

```
private static class Group {
   double amountPerContainer;
   Set<Container> members;        ❶ The set of all connected containers

   Group(Container c) {
      members = new HashSet<>();
      members.add(c);
   }
}
```

Figure 3.1 shows the situation after executing the first three parts of *UseCase*. Recall that those three parts create four containers (a, b, c, and d) and execute the following method calls:

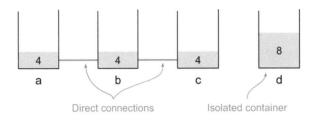

Figure 3.1 The situation after executing the first three parts of *UseCase*. Containers a through c have been connected together, and water has been poured into a and d.

```
a.addWater(12);
d.addWater(8);
a.connectTo(b);
b.connectTo(c);
```

The connectTo method is very similar to the one in *Reference*, and you can find it in the online repository for this book (https://bitbucket.org/mfaella/exercisesinstyle).

In figure 3.2, you can see the memory layout of *Speed1* at this point of *UseCase*. Because the containers have been connected in two groups, two objects of type Group exist, each holding a reference to the set of all containers belonging to the group, along with the water amount found in each of those containers.

Then, the read and write methods of Container operate straightfowardly on the Group object, as you can see in listing 3.2.

Listing 3.2   *Speed1*: Methods getAmount and addWater

```
public double getAmount() { return group.amountPerContainer; }

public void addWater(double amount) {
    double amountPerContainer = amount / group.members.size();
    group.amountPerContainer += amountPerContainer;
```

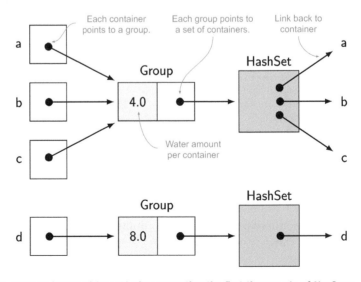

Figure 3.2 The memory layout of *Speed1* after executing the first three parts of *UseCase*

```
    }
```

3.1.1 Time complexity

Similarly to *Reference*, the `connectTo` method still needs to iterate over all containers in a group, leading to the time complexities in table 3.1. The table makes it clear that the bottleneck for this implementation lies in the `connectTo` method.

**Table 3.1 Time complexities of *Speed1*,
where n is the total number of containers**

Method	Time complexity
getAmount	$O(1)$
connectTo	$O(n)$
addWater	$O(1)$

Two steps in the `connectTo` method require linear time to complete:

1 Merging the elements of the two groups with `addAll`
2 Informing the elements of one of the groups being merged that their group has changed

The first step is easy to replace with a faster alternative. Switch from sets to linked lists and *voilà*: merging two collections becomes a constant-time operation. The second step is much more complicated to avoid. In fact, it's impossible to make `connectTo` run in constant time without raising the time complexity of `getAmount`. But if for some reason you really need a constant-time `connectTo`, you can employ the implementation from the next section.

3.2   Adding connections in constant time   [Speed2]

The aim of this section is to bring down the complexity of `connectTo` to constant time, leading to a new version of the container class, nicknamed *Speed2*. To achieve this objective, you'll use two techniques:

1 Represent groups of connected containers with a data structure that has a constant-time merge operation
2 Delay the update of water amounts until the latest possible time

For the first technique, you'll use a radically different way to represent a group of connected containers: a manually implemented circular linked list.

3.2.1 Representing groups as circular lists

A *circular linked list* is a sequence of nodes where each node points to the next one, in a circular fashion. There's no first or last node, no head or tail. An empty circular linked list contains no nodes at all, whereas in a list with a single node, that node points to itself as its successor.

In the water container application, each container is a node in a singly linked circular list, featuring an amount field and a single `next` reference, as shown in the following listing.

Listing 3.3   *Speed2*: Fields

```
public class Container {
    private double amount;
    private Container next = this;
```

POP QUIZ 2   What's the complexity of removing a given node from a singly linked circular list?

A nice property of circular linked lists, and the very reason you're using them here, is that if you're given any two nodes from two such lists, you can merge the lists in constant time, even if the lists are singly linked. You accomplish the merge by swapping the `next` references of the two nodes, as shown in figure 3.3.

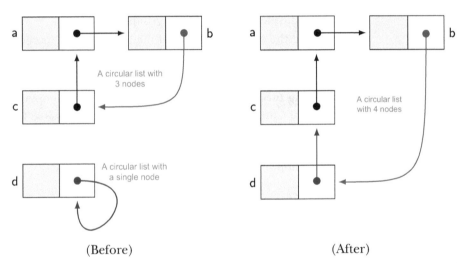

(Before)   (After)

Figure 3.3   Swapping the `next` pointers of two nodes (b and d) leads to merging two circular linked lists into one.

However, this technique only works if the two nodes belong to different lists. If they belong to the same list, swapping the references will produce the opposite effect: splitting the list into two separate lists. Therefore, this implementation suffers from the same limitation we observed for *Novice*: `connectTo` works correctly only if the two containers being connected are not connected yet, not even indirectly.

You may think it would be better for the `connectTo` method to *check* whether the two containers are already connected, before attempting to connect them. But doing so requires scanning at least one of the two lists, which is not a constant-time operation. You need to accept this lack of robustness to achieve the constant-time performance objective. You'll get your revenge in chapter 5, where you'll build bullet-proof container classes.

What about a plain old linked list?

Circular lists are not the only data structure to allow for constant-time merge. A plain old linked list also has this property, as long as the merge operation can directly access the first and last element of the two lists (aka their head and tail). To see this, pretend you could directly access the `head` and `tail` fields of two non-empty singly linked lists, `list1` and `list2`. Merging them by concatenation boils down to the following lines:

```
list1.tail.next = list2.head;
list1.tail = list2.tail;
```

After those two lines, `list1` represents the concatenation and `list2` is unchanged.

However, you can't use linked lists to connect water containers in constant time. To see this, recall that each container must have direct access to the head and tail of its list. When merging two groups, you would have to update all the involved containers so they'd reflect the new values for the head and tail after the merge. That update requires linear time.

TIP The standard Java implementation of linked lists (`LinkedList`) doesn't support constant-time concatenation. Calling `list1.addAll(list2)` iterates over all the elements of `list2`.

Figure 3.4 represents the memory layout at two moments during the execution of *Use-Case*, with the implementation of containers from this section (that is, *Speed2*). As you can see, the structure is exactly the same as in figure 3.3, except that the nodes in the lists are now water containers. On the left side of the figure, containers a, b, and c have been connected into a single group, so they're linked to each other in a circular fashion. Container d is still isolated, so its next reference points to itself.

The right side shows the effect of running the b.connectTo(d) instruction. Swapping the next references of b and d is sufficient to merge the two lists into one. Such swapping is the only content of the connectTo implementation in the following listing.

Listing 3.4 *Speed2*: Method `connectTo`

```
public void connectTo(Container other) {        ❶ Swaps the next fields
    Container oldNext = next;                       of this and other
    next = other.next;
    other.next = oldNext;
}
```

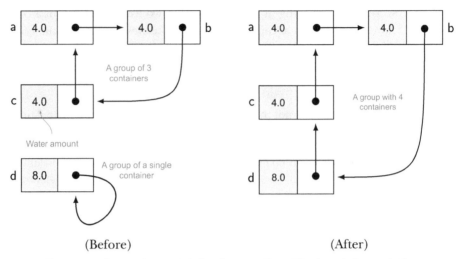

(Before)   (After)

Figure 3.4 **The memory layout of *Speed2* during the execution of *UseCase*, before and after b.connectTo(d). Swapping the next pointers of b and d leads to merging the two groups into one.**

3.2.2 *Delaying the updates*

To keep connectTo running in constant time, it doesn't update the water amounts in any way. After all, water amounts are only visible when getAmount is called. As a result, you can *delay* the update until the next call to getAmount. This approach is a standard trick in the programmer's toolbox, called *laziness* or lazy evaluation—a staple of functional programming. Laziness is the general idea of delaying a computation until you actually need it.

Laziness in the JDK

Standard Java collections are eager (the opposite of lazy). Java 8 introduced the streams library, a powerful framework for manipulating data sequences. Among other features, streams employ lazy evaluation. To appreciate the difference, start with a list of integers list. If you run

```
list.sort(null);
```

it will immediately sort the list, because the list is eager. (The null here signals that integers have a natural order, so no comparator is needed.) On the other hand, try converting that list to a stream and then sorting the stream:

```
Stream<Integer> stream = list.stream();
Stream<Integer> sortedStream = stream.sorted();
```

Contrary to the previous example, in this case, no sorting has taken place yet. The sorted method only sets a flag that *promises* to eventually sort the data. The library will actually sort the data when you apply a *terminal operation* to the stream, that is, when you convert the stream back into a collection or scan its elements in some way (by the `forEachOrdered` method, for example).

POP QUIZ 3 Think of two activities in your life that you perform eagerly (as soon as possible) and two activities that you delay as much as possible.

You use the same laziness with `addWater` so it updates only the current container, without actually distributing water among the group. Unfortunately, sooner or later you'll call `getAmount`, and you'll have to pay for all the laziness with a costly update operation, which distributes water amounts equally within a group. To improve clarity, you can delegate the update to a separate private method `updateGroup`. The resulting `addWater` and `getAmount` are shown in the following listing.

Listing 3.5 *Speed2*: Methods `addWater` and `getAmount`

```
public void addWater(double amount) {
    this.amount += amount;    ① Updates the local container only
}

public double getAmount() {
    updateGroup();    ② Support method responsible for distributing water
    return amount;
}
```

The update method, shown in listing 3.6, makes two passes over the circular list representing this group. In the first pass, it computes the total amount of water in the group and counts the number of containers in it. In the second pass, it uses the information it collected during the first pass to actually update the amount of water in each container to the new value.

Listing 3.6 *Speed2*: Support method `updateGroup`

```
private void updateGroup() {
    Container current = this;
    double totalAmount = 0;
    int groupSize = 0;

    do {                                        ① First pass:
        totalAmount += current.amount;            collect amount and count
        groupSize++;
        current = current.next;
    } while (current != this);
    double newAmount = totalAmount / groupSize;

    current = this;
    do {                                        ② Second pass:
        current.amount = newAmount;               update amounts
        current = current.next;
    } while (current != this);
}
```

In each pass, you need to visit each node in a circular list. To do so without circling forever, you can start from any node, follow the `next` references, and stop when you get back to your initial node.

A couple of questions come to mind:

1. Do you really need to invoke `updateGroup` every time `getAmount` is called? Perhaps you could use a boolean flag to remember whether this container is already updated and avoid unnecessary calls to `updateGroup`.
2. Can you move the `updateGroup` call from `getAmount` to `addWater`? It would be more reasonable to pay the price when writing, rather than reading.

Unfortunately, neither of these potential improvements is feasible—that is, assuming you want to keep the connection operation constant-time.

First, suppose you add an `updated` flag to all containers. Whenever a group is updated, its containers are flagged as updated. Subsequent calls to `getAmount` on those containers don't need to invoke `updateGroup`—so far, so good. Now, suppose you merge two groups with `connectTo`. The `updated` flags of their containers need to be reset, but you can't do this in constant time.[1] There goes your first improvement attempt.

Second, moving the `updateGroup` call from `getAmount` to `addWater` is fine, but only if you introduce a similar call in `connectTo` as well. Otherwise, reading the amount right after a group merge would give a stale result. This change also puts `connectTo` in linear-time complexity, which is against the objectives of this section.

The worst-case time complexity of the *Speed2* implementation is summarized in table 3.2. As expected, `connectTo` and `addWater` take constant time because we moved all the heavy lifting to `getAmount`, which requires linear time.

Table 3.2   Time complexities of *Speed2*, where n is the total number of containers

Method	Time complexity
getAmount	$O(n)$
connectTo	$O(1)$
addWater	$O(1)$

[1] To be fair, this would work if you moved the `updated` flag from single containers to a separate `Group` object, similar to *Speed1*. Still, even with this optimization, the worst-case complexity of `getAmount` would remain the same (linear).

3.3 The best balance: Union-find algorithms [Speed3]

It turns out that our little container problem is similar to the classic *union-find* setting. In that scenario, you want to maintain disjoint sets of elements, along with a distinguished element for each set called the set *representative*. You'll need to support the following two operations:

- Merge two sets (*union* operation)
- Given an element, find the representative from its set (*find* operation)

This section applies the union-find scenario to water containers, leading to an implementation nicknamed *Speed3*, which will turn out to be the best performing one in practice.

When applying the general union-find scenario to water containers, the sets you want to maintain are the groups of mutually connected containers. The representative for a group can be any container, and you'll use that container to store the official water amount for that group. When a container receives a `getAmount` call, you'll invoke a find operation to get the value from its group representative.

Many smart computer scientists have tackled this type of problem, eventually developing the following, provably optimal, algorithm. It suggests to represent a group as a *tree* of containers, where each container only needs to know its parent in the tree. The root of each tree is the representative for the group. Roots also should store the size of their tree, for reasons that will become clear shortly.

Parent pointer trees

A *parent pointer tree* is a linked data structure in which each node points to exactly another node, called its *parent*, except one special node, called the *root*, that points to no other node. Also, all nodes can reach the root by following the pointers. These constraints ensure that the pointers form no cycle, so trees are a special type of directed acyclic graph (DAG).

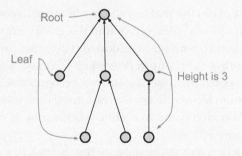

A parent pointer tree

Nodes having no children are called *leaves*. In a parent pointer tree, each node knows its parent, but the parent doesn't hold references to its children. As a result, you can navigate the tree only in the direction going from the leaves toward the root. The *height* of a tree is the length of the longest path from any node to the root.

Computer science trees are traditionally drawn with the root at the top and the rest growing downward; they're rooted in the sky.

POP QUIZ 4 You're writing a Java compiler and must represent the *subclass* relation between classes, which arranges classes in a tree. Do you employ a parent pointer or a children pointer tree?

According to the discussion of the tree algorithm, you end up with the fields shown in the following listing in each container.

Listing 3.7   *Speed3*: Fields, with no constructor needed

```
public class Container {
    private double amount;
    private Container parent = this;    ❶ Initially, each container is the root of its tree.
    private int size = 1;
```

You identify the root of a tree by having `parent==this`. You can see in listing 3.7 that each new container is initially the root of its tree, and the only node in it. You're using the fields `amount` and `size` for only the root containers. For the other containers, they're just wasting space. A memory-optimized implementation may want to do something about that.[2]

3.3.1   Finding the group representative

To get the desired performance, it's not enough to simply represent groups of containers as parent pointer trees. You must employ two techniques during tree operations:

1   During the find operation: the *path compression* technique
2   During the union operation: the *link-by-size* policy

I'll talk about the find operation and the path compression technique first. All operations on a `Container` need to find the group representative, because that's where the water amount information is located. Given the previous discussion on parent pointer trees, finding the group representative is easy. You just follow the parent references until you reach the root of your tree, recognizable by having `parent==this`. The path compression technique consists of *turning every node that you encounter into a direct child of the root*. You modify the tree while you navigate it, in such a way that future operations will be more efficient.

In practice, let's assign the root-finding task to a private support method called `find` `RootAndCompress` (listing 3.8). This method navigates the tree from this container up to the root of its tree, following the parent links. Along the way, it updates the parent reference of all encountered containers to point directly at the root. As a consequence,

---

[2]   Exercise 3 in chapter 4 asks you to address this issue and then offers a possible solution.

whenever you call it again on any of those objects, it will terminate in constant time, because it will immediately find the root.

For example, consider three containers x, y, and root that have been connected together in such a way that root is the group representative, y is its child, and x is the child of y, as in figure 3.5 (Before).

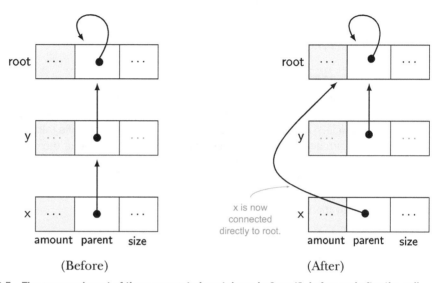

(Before)	(After)

Figure 3.5   The memory layout of three connected containers in *Speed3*, before and after the call x.findRootAndCompress(). After the call, container x has become a direct child of root. The amount and size values are omitted as unimportant.

A call to x.findRootAndCompress() must return a reference to root, as well as flatten the path connecting x to root, turning every intermediate container on the path from x to root into a direct child of root. In this example, the only container that can be flattened is x itself, because y is already a direct child of root. The desired situation after the call is depicted in figure 3.5 (After). You can elegantly accomplish the seemingly complex flattening task using the three-line recursive implementation shown in the following listing.

Listing 3.8   *Speed3*: Support method findRootAndCompress

```
private Container findRootAndCompress() {
    if (parent != this)        ❶ Checks if this is the root of its tree
        parent = parent.findRootAndCompress();   ❷ Recursively finds the root and
    return parent;                                   set it as the parent of this
}
```

Recursive methods can be tricky to follow, so let's analyze the behavior of the previous listing step by step. Whenever you call findRootAndCompress on a root container, it simply returns the container itself (this). If you call the method on a container that's further down the tree, the method invokes itself on its parent. If its parent is still not the root of the group, the method will again invoke itself on its parent, and so on, until eventually the method will be called on the root. At that point, a cascade of `returns` will start from the root and propagate to the original caller. Along the way, the method will update all `parent` references to point directly to the root.

Going back to the three-container example, you can follow the execution of

```
x.findRootAndCompress();
```

on the UML *sequence diagram* in figure 3.6. If you're not familiar with this type of diagram, check out the sidebar.

UML sequence diagrams

Sequence diagrams like the one in figure 3.6 show interactions between objects in time. Each object is represented by a box connected to a dashed vertical line called its *lifeline*. Time flows from top to bottom, and method calls (aka *messages*) are depicted as arrows from the lifeline of the caller to the lifeline of the callee. A message starts the execution of a method. Graphically, this is represented by a thin, empty, vertical activation box drawn on top of the callee's lifeline. If you want to emphasize the return value from a method (as I did in figure 3.6), you can add a dashed arrow from the activation box back to the caller.

Starting from the call `x.findRootAndCompress()`, figure 3.6 shows the sequence of actions that ensue: `findRootAndCompress` calls itself on `y` and then on `root`. At that point, a reference to `root` is returned all the way to the original caller, and along the way, all `parent` references are updated to `root` itself. As discussed earlier, this leads to the final memory layout in figure 3.5(After), with `x` now connected directly to `root` as a consequence of the flattening.

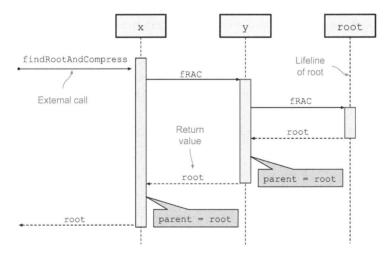

Figure 3.6   A sequence diagram for the call `x.findRootAndCompress()`, in the three-container scenario depicted in figure 3.5. The callouts are not standard UML. `fRAC` is short for `findRootAndCompress`.

Once you've implemented `findRootAndCompress`, methods `getAmount` and `addWa` `ter` are quite straightforward: they obtain the root of their group and then read or update its `amount` field, as you can see in the following listing.

Listing 3.9 *Speed3*: Methods `getAmount` and `addWater`

```
public double getAmount() {
    Container root = findRootAndCompress();    ❶ Obtains the root and flattens
                                                  the path
    return root.amount;                        ❷ Reads the amount from root
}
public void addWater(double amount) {
    Container root = findRootAndCompress();    ❸ Obtains the root and flattens
                                                  the path
    root.amount += amount / root.size;         ❹ Adds water to root
}
```

3.3.2 Connecting trees of containers

The tree structure allows for a straightforward connection algorithm that involves finding the roots of the two groups being merged and turning one of the roots into a child of the other root, as in figure 3.7.

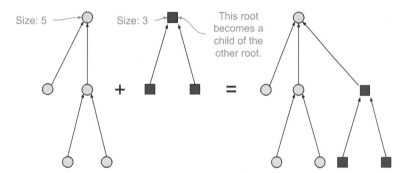

Figure 3.7 Merging two trees according to the link-by-size policy. The smaller tree gets attached to the root of the larger tree.

To limit the height of the resulting tree, you need to apply the following rule: attach the smaller tree (the one with fewer nodes) to the root of the larger tree. If the two trees have the same size, the choice is arbitrary. This is called *link-by-size policy* and is an important ingredient for obtaining the desired performance, as explained in the following section. Because of this policy, roots must know the size of their tree, hence the `size` field in every container.

Listing 3.10 shows a possible implementation of the `connectTo` method. It starts by identifying the roots of the two groups you're merging. Then, it checks whether those roots are the same—that is, if the two containers are already connected. Without this step, you would incur the same error (or rather, lack of robustness) of *Novice* and *Speed2*; connecting two containers that already belong to the same group would put the data structure into an inconsistent state. After that, the method computes the new water amount to be put in each container and merges the two trees according to the link-by-size policy I explained.

Listing 3.10   *Speed3*: Method `connectTo`

```
public void connectTo(Container other) {
    Container root1 = findRootAndCompress(),          ❶ Finds the two roots
            root2 = other.findRootAndCompress();
    if (root1==root2) return;                          ❷ This check is necessary!
    int size1 = root1.size, size2 = root2.size;
    double newAmount = ((root1.amount * size1) +
                    (root2.amount * size2)) / (size1 + size2);

    if (size1 <= size2) {                              ❸ The link-by-size policy
        root1.parent = root2;                          ❹ Attaches the first tree
        root2.amount = newAmount;                         to the root of the second
        root2.size   += size1;
    } else {
        root2.parent = root1;                          ❺ Attaches the second tree
        root1.amount = newAmount;                         to the root of the first
        root1.size   += size2;
    }
}
```

You now have all the information you need to perform the usual simulation of *Use-Case* and obtain the memory layout shown in figure 3.8, which refers to the situation after the first three parts of *UseCase*. At that point, b is the representative for the group comprising containers a, b, and c, whereas d is isolated and consequently its own representative.

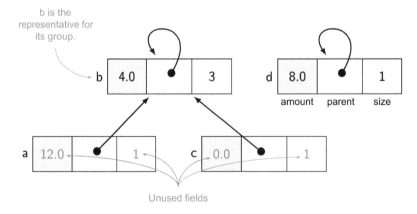

Figure 3.8 The memory layout of *Speed3* after executing the first three parts of *UseCase*. The `amount` and `size` fields of a and c are grayed out because they contain stale values that are irrelevant to the behavior of their objects. Only the fields of the group representatives are relevant and up-to-date.

3.3.3 *Worst-case time complexity*

As all container methods start by invoking `findRootAndCompress` (twice, in the case of `connectTo`), to compare *Speed3* with the previous container implementations you need to assess the worst-case complexity of that method. Since `findRootAndCompress` is a recursive method with no loops, its complexity is nothing other than the number of recursive calls it makes (aka the *depth* of the recursion), which in turn is equal to the length of the path from this container to the root of its tree. In the worst case, the method is called on a container that's the farthest away from the root, that is, as far from the root as the height of the tree. You still need to figure out the maximum height that a tree with a given number of nodes can reach. This is where the link-by-size policy enters the picture, ensuring that the height of a tree is *at most logarithmic with respect to its size*. For example, a tree representing a group of 8 containers can't be higher than 3 (recall that $3 = \log_2 8$ because $2^3 = 8$).

Figure 3.9 shows a sequence of union operations that build a tree with logarithmic height. The trick is to always merge trees with the same size. For every such merge, the height of the resulting tree increases by one, but the number of nodes doubles. Hence, the height is constantly equal to the base-2 logarithm of the size.

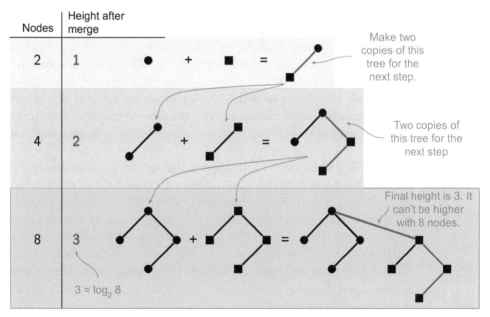

Figure 3.9 A sequence of union operations building a tree whose height is logarithmic in its size. This is the maximum height achievable with a given number of nodes.

You've seen how some `findRootAndCompress` calls require logarithmic time. Because all three of the public methods call that method, you'll obtain the worst-case time complexities shown in table 3.3.

Table 3.3   Worst-case time complexities of *Speed3*, where n is the total number of containers

Method	Time complexity
getAmount	$O(\log n)$
connectTo	$O(\log n)$
addWater	$O(\log n)$

Notice that, even if one specific call to x.findRootAndCompress() takes logarithmic time, the path compression technique ensures that future calls to the same method on the same container, as well as any other container sitting along the path from x to the root of its tree, will be executed in constant time. This observation suggests that it's somewhat misleading, albeit formally correct, to attribute logarithmic complexity to the three container methods, because that cost only applies to the *first* call on a given container. In the next section, I'll address this concern by switching to a different type of complexity analysis. For the moment, I'll use the worst-case complexities reported in table 3.3 to compare the performance of the three implementations I've presented in this chapter.

Figure 3.10 provides a graphical representation of the complexity of methods getAmount and connectTo in the three versions from this chapter. As anticipated, none of them is always better than the others. *Speed1* is the only one with guaranteed constant time for getAmount. Symmetrically, *Speed2* features the best performance for connectTo. *Speed3* strikes a balance between the two methods, attributing the same logarithmic complexity to both. When comparing any pair of implementations, one method improves its performance, and the other method worsens it. As I explained at the beginning of this chapter, you can describe this in fancier jargon as being Pareto optimal.

According to figure 3.10, to choose one of the implementations from this chapter, you should analyze the application context and figure out how often clients will call each method. If they'll make most calls to getAmount, you should choose *Speed1*. Conversely, if clients are more likely to invoke connectTo, you should pick *Speed2*.

In the next section, you'll find out that this type of worst-case analysis is in fact quite unfair to *Speed3*, whose performance really shines if you replace worst-case complexity analysis with *amortized complexity* analysis. This doesn't mean that the worst-case analysis is wrong, just that with *Speed3* the worst case happens so rarely that the corresponding performance is hardly relevant.

3.3.4   *Amortized time complexity*

Whereas standard analysis focuses on a single run of an algorithm, amortized analysis takes into account *sequences* of runs. This kind of analysis is the most appropriate for algorithms that perform extra operations so that future calls may be more efficient. Those extra operations work as an *investment*: they're an immediate cost for a future benefit. Single-run analysis would account for the cost but not for the benefit. By

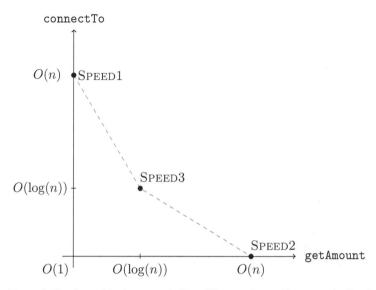

Figure 3.10 A graphical representation of the worst-case time complexity of methods `getAmount` and `connectTo` in implementations *Speed1*, *Speed2*, and *Speed3*. The dashed line connecting the three implementations represents the Pareto front.

considering sequences of operations, amortized analysis manages to measure both the cost and its future benefit.

In our case, the "compress" part of `findRootAndCompress` is the extra cost. You don't need it to find the root, but it makes future calls faster.

To perform amortized analysis, you have to decide on a sequence of operations of arbitrary length m, performed on a set of n containers. Being interested in the long-run cost, we can assume that m is bigger than n. Next, you have to choose how many of those m operations are `connectTo`, `getAmount`, or `addWater`. Notice that only $n - 1$ calls to `connectTo` are significant: after that, all containers will be connected in a single group. So, it makes sense to analyze sequences composed as follows:

1. They comprise at least n operations.
2. They contain $n - 1$ calls to `connectTo`.
3. All the other operations are either `getAmount` or `addWater`.

Now, in line with standard complexity analysis, you can ask what the order of growth is of the number of basic steps that any such sequence performs (that is, the worst case among all the sequences satisfying your assumptions). The actual analysis is way beyond the scope of this book, and I refer you to the *Further reading* section at the end of the chapter for details. In fact, even *stating* the complexity upper bound is somewhat complex! The most accurate upper bound for a sequence of m operations is not one of the easy functions, being slightly more than constant but way less than quasilinear ($m \log m$). As shown in table 3.4, you can write it as $O\big(m * \alpha(n)\big)$, where α is the *inverse Ackermann function*.

Table 3.4   Amortized time complexity for *Speed3*, where $\alpha(\cdot)$ is the inverse Ackermann function

Scenario	Amortized time complexity
A sequence of m operations on n containers	$O(m * \alpha(n))$

The Ackermann function

Wilhelm Ackermann originally proposed the eponymous function $A(k, j)$ in 1928. He was a student of renowned mathematician David Hilbert and an accomplished researcher himself. It was the first known example of a function that's algorithmically computable, but not computable through a limited set of operations called *primitive recursive*. The key property of this function is that it grows extremely fast, even when its arguments have small values. For example, $A(2, 1) = 7$, $A(3, 1) = 2047$, and $A(4, 1) > 10^{80}$.

The *inverse* Ackermann function $\alpha(n)$ is defined as the smallest integer k such that $A(k, 1) \geq n$. As $A(k, 1)$ grows extremely rapidly, small values of k are sufficient to make it bigger than n. In particular, $\alpha(n)$ is at most 4 for all values of n smaller than 10^{80}, which is the estimated number of atoms in the known universe.

As explained in the sidebar, the inverse Ackermann function is essentially constant, so the upper bound $O(m * \alpha(n))$ is equivalent to $O(m)$ for all practical purposes. Because we're discussing the complexity of a sequence of m operations, the $O(m)$ upper bound means that, in the long run, each operation takes constant time. You couldn't hope for anything better. In fact, the experiments I present in section 3.4.1 show that, in this case, the amortized analysis is much more relevant than the standard worst-case analysis, putting *Speed3* way ahead of the competition in a typical scenario.

3.3.5   *Amortized analysis of resizable arrays*

Amortized analysis of union-find trees is too complex to follow all the details, so let's do it on a simpler but highly relevant case: automatically resizable arrays like the Java classes `Vector` and `ArrayList`, and C# `List`. Those classes offer a handy service: store a variable-sized collection in contiguous memory, allowing for constant-time random access to any item in the collection. To do so, they store the collection in an array and resize it when needed. Unfortunately, you can't expand arrays in place.[3] In case of expansion, the class needs to allocate a new, larger array and then copy the content of the old array onto the new one. How expensive is this operation? What's the resulting complexity for adding a new element to the collection, given that any addition may trigger a costly resizing operation? Amortized complexity is the right tool for answering these questions. Indeed, the following is how Oracle's documentation puts it, when presenting the `ArrayList` class:

> *The add operation runs in* amortized constant time; *that is, adding n elements requires O(n) time.*

---

[3]   Actually, lower level languages allow this. Check out the `realloc` function from the C standard library.

Let's see why that's the case by analyzing the current OpenJDK implementation of `ArrayList`.[4] You can easily discover that the initial capacity of an empty `ArrayList` is 10 cells, and that the private method `grow` is responsible for expanding the underlying array. Inside that method you'll find the following crucial lines:

```
int newCapacity = oldCapacity + (oldCapacity >{}> 1);
...
elementData = Arrays.copyOf(elementData, newCapacity);
```

The `>>` operator is the bitwise right shift, an efficient way to divide an integer by two, so the net effect of the first line is to increase the capacity by 50%. Every time the array needs to be enlarged, it isn't enlarged by a single element, but by 50%. This strategy is essential to keep the (amortized) complexity in check. Then, the method reallocates the array to the new capacity with a call to `Arrays.copyOf`, a static utility method that allocates a new array and copies the contents of an existing array into it.

Now, consider a sequence of n insertions (method `add`) into a new `ArrayList`, and let's compute their total complexity. You need to know how many times the underlying array will be reallocated. Call this number k. Each reallocation multiplies the capacity by 1.5. As the initial capacity is 10, after k reallocations the capacity is $10 * 1.5^k$. To accommodate n insertions, we want this capacity to be at least n:

$$10 * 1.5^k \geq n.$$

That is, $k \geq \log_{1.5} \frac{n}{10}$. That's the logarithm to base 1.5. Don't worry, it'll go away soon; it's sufficient to know that $1.5^{\left(\log_{1.5} x\right)} = x$. Because k is by definition an integer, k is the smallest integer greater than or equal to $\log_{1.5} \frac{n}{10}$.[5] You can simplify calculations by relaxing the constraint that k be an integer and setting $k = \log_{1.5} \frac{n}{10}$. It's an approximation that doesn't bear on the final result.

In a sequence of n insertions, the first 10 will be fast (cost 1) because the initial capacity of an empty `ArrayList` is 10. The 11th insertion triggers the first call to `grow`, bringing the capacity to 15. The cost of this call is also 15, because `Arrays.copyOf` (see the previous code lines) needs to copy the 10 values from the old array to the new one and *initialize the five extra cells to* `null`. Summarizing, you can then express the cost of n insertions as follows:

$$\text{cost}(n) = \underbrace{1 + 1 + \ldots + 1}_{10 \text{ adds}} + \underbrace{15}_{\texttt{grow}} + \underbrace{1 + 1 + \ldots + 1}_{5 \text{ adds}} + \underbrace{22}_{\texttt{grow}} + 1 + 1 + \ldots,$$

---

[4] Currently available at http://mng.bz/j5m8.

[5] Actually, no integer can be *equal* to $\log_{1.5} \frac{n}{10}$. Do you know why?

which you can rearrange as follows:

$$
\begin{aligned}
\text{cost}(n) &= 10 + (15 + 5) + (22 + 7) + (33 + 11) + \dots \\
&= 10 + (15 * 1 + 5 * 1) + (15 * 1.5 + 5 * 1.5) + \left(15 * (1.5)^2 + 5 * (1.5)^2\right) + \dots \\
&= 10 + \sum_{i=0}^{k} \left(15 * (1.5)^i + 5 * (1.5)^i\right) \\
&= 10 + 20 \sum_{i=0}^{k} (1.5)^i
\end{aligned}
$$

You can then employ the standard formula for the sum of the first k powers of a constant a:

$$
\sum_{i=0}^{k} a^i = \frac{a^{k+1} - 1}{a - 1}
$$

If you apply that formula to $a = 1.5$ and $k = \log_{1.5} \frac{n}{10}$, you'll get

$$
\begin{aligned}
\text{cost}(n) &= 10 + 20 * \frac{1.5^{\left(\log_{1.5} \frac{n}{10} + 1\right)} - 1}{1.5 - 1} \\
&= 10 + 20 * \frac{1.5 * 1.5^{\left(\log_{1.5} \frac{n}{10}\right)} - 1}{0.5} \\
&= 10 + 20 * 2 * \left(1.5 * \frac{n}{10} - 1\right) \\
&= 10 + 60 * \frac{n}{10} - 40 \\
&= 6 * n - 30 \\
&= O(n).
\end{aligned}
$$

Summarizing, the cost of n insertions is linearly proportional to n, which means that the average long-run cost of a single insertion is constant. This calculation certifies that the calls to `grow` become more costly as fast as they move apart along the sequence of insertions. If you spread those costs over a long sequence of insertions, the average burden on each operation is constant (6 in this formula).

Insertion into `ArrayLists` isn't all roses. The same analysis showing that the long-run cost of each insertion is constant also highlights that the performance of a sequence of insertions is very uneven. Most insertions are extremely cheap, but every once in a while an insertion triggers a full copy of all previously inserted elements (a copy of their references, that is). The networking jargon gives us a nice way to put this: insertion into an `ArrayList` is a high-throughput operation (long-run constant time) plagued by high jitter (time variability). In contrast, insertion into a `LinkedList` has a similar throughput but essentially no jitter, because every insertion takes the same amount of time (the time needed to allocate a new node in the list).

3.4 *Comparing implementations*

In the previous sections, we developed three container implementations that optimize performance in different ways. We estimated that performance using worst-case and amortized complexity analysis. Worst-case analysis considers a single method, assuming the worst possible input, whereas amortized analysis considers arbitrarily long sequences of operations involving different methods. In both cases, only the order of growth is reported (see section 2.3 for details), which is both a blessing, because it facilitates comparisons, and a curse, because it's detached from actual running times. If you're a skeptic like me, you'll want to experimentally check that these theoretical performance measures correspond to actual running times.

3.4.1 *Experiments*

Let's start with a simple experiment, where the three implementations from this chapter challenge *Reference* on the following test case:

1 Create 20,000 containers and add some water to each one (20k constructor calls and 20k `addWater` calls).
2 Connect the containers in 10,000 pairs, add some water to each pair, and query the amount in each pair (10k `connectTo`, 10k `addWater`, and 10k `getAmount`).
3 Connect pairs of containers until all containers are connected into a single group. After each connection, add some water and query the resulting amount (10k `connectTo`, 10k `addWater`, and 10k `getAmount`).

I chose the total number of containers by trial and error so the running times would be long enough to show clear distinctions between implementations, and short enough to run the experiment repeatedly in a short amount of time. Table 3.5 reports the running times I get on my laptop. As expected, all classes from this chapter greatly outperform *Reference*, by as much as two orders of magnitude. In particular, our best attempt, *Speed3* is 500 times faster. On the other hand, *Speed2* is an order of magnitude slower than *Speed1* and *Speed3* (but still significantly faster than *Reference*). As I noted before, *Speed2* is a rather odd implementation that only makes sense if `getAmount` queries are rare compared to the other operations. That's not the case for the tested scenario.

Table 3.5   First experiment: Running times in milliseconds for a balanced use case involving 20,000 containers

Version	Time (msec)
Reference	2300
Speed1	26
Speed2	505
Speed3	6

To confirm these observations, you can run a modified use case, where you remove all calls to `getAmount` except for one, at the end. This strange scenario is designed to favor *Speed2* in the strongest possible way. When running the experiment on my lap-top, I get the running times shown in table 3.6. As you can see, *Speed2* now matches the performance of *Speed3*, whereas the other three implementations are essentially unaf-fected by the change, demonstrating that the amount query is a very cheap operation in all other versions. This second experiment confirms that *Speed3* is, in practice, the best choice overall as far as performance is concerned.

Table 3.6   Second experiment: Running times in milliseconds for a use case involving 20,000 containers and a single call to `getAmount`

Version	Time (msec)
Reference	2300
Speed1	25
Speed2	4
Speed3	5

Benchmarking

Comparing the performance of Java programs, or those in any other language executed by a VM, requires special caution. Both the compiler and the VM can make significant changes to the program, concealing what you're actually measuring. For example, these are two common optimizations:

- The compiler can drop certain lines of code if it realizes that they have no visible effect.
- The VM can switch back and forth between interpreting bytecode and compil-ing it to native code (this is called *just-in-time* compilation).

You can try to dodge these optimizations with suitable workarounds, such as the following:

- Make sure that each operation eventually contributes to a visible effect, like a printout or a file write.
- Run the code you're benchmarking multiple times before you start measuring time. These so-called *dry runs* induce the VM to compile the performance-critical sections and produce more meaningful timings.

In addition, Java comes with a standard benchmarking framework, called *Java micro-benchmarking harness* (JMH), that gives you fine-grained control over compiler and VM optimizations.

3.4.2   *Theory vs. practice*

When comparing the three implementations in this chapter, standard worst-case com-plexity analysis stops at table 3.7 and declares them essentially uncomparable: each is superior to the others in some use cases, but none of them is always optimal. More specifically, *Speed1* is the fastest when connections don't change often, and you add, remove, and query water amounts frequently. *Speed2* is optimal when you add new connections all the time and add and remove water constantly, but you seldom query the current water level in any container. Finally, *Speed3* appears like a compromise version, where all operations are not particularly fast and require about the same time. As such, it seems suitable for scenarios where you don't have a clear idea of how clients will use the class (aka the usage profile). Amortized analysis and actual experiments reveal that *Speed3* is in fact the fastest version in all but the most contrived examples (such as the second experiment).

Table 3.7   The worst-case time complexity of the three versions from this chapter and *Reference* from chapter 2

Version	getAmount	addWater	connectTo
Reference	$O(1)$	$O(n)$	$O(n)$
Speed1	$O(1)$	$O(1)$	$O(n)$
Speed2	$O(n)$	$O(1)$	$O(1)$
Speed3	$O(\log n)$	$O(\log n)$	$O(\log n)$

This doesn't mean you should throw worst-case complexity analysis out the window. It's still the most useful formal framework for comparing algorithms for an isolated, one-shot task. Besides, the asymptotic notation (big-O and the like) that comes with it is a powerful abstraction that applies to all kinds of performance analysis, such as amortized analysis or average-case analysis.

You shouldn't forget the worst-case qualifier, and keep in mind that sophisticated algorithms, like union-find, may make time investments that repay over time and only show their strength over long sequences of operations.

You've learned in this chapter that, when designing a class supporting an ongoing interaction with a method's clients, it may

Average-case analysis...

...is still another kind of complexity analysis. Instead of focusing on the worst possible input for a given algorithm, it estimates the average complexity over all possible inputs, assuming that all inputs can occur with the same probability.

not be enough to consider the complexity of each method separately. First, interactions between the performance of different methods may occur. As in our example, it might be possible to shift the computational burden from one method to another—that is, make one method faster at the expense of another. Second, it might be possible to make time investments that speed up future executions of one or more methods.

In the first case (interactions between methods), you need to pair complexity analysis with a usage profile to guide you toward the best solution. A usage profile is a characterization of how the clients will interact with a class. Typical information includes the relative frequency and the order in which you'll invoke the class methods. Such information can tell you which method is the most critical and warrants the maximum performance.

In the second scenario, amortized analysis like the one we performed on *Speed3* is a formal way to ascertain the value of a time investment in the long run. Both techniques are heavy on the brain and light on the fingers—no need to create the software and run it. In practice, the easiest (though not the quickest) path is to implement and profile different solutions. This path is also the most accurate, as long as the operating conditions remain similar to those used for profiling.

3.5   *And now for something completely different*

In this section, I'll apply the performance techniques I've covered so far to a different example. In fact, starting from this chapter, every chapter will feature this structure:

1 You'll tackle the familiar water container example, slowly and in detail.

2 You'll face a different example, but I'll only get you started on it, leaving some details to you.

3 At the very end of each chapter, you'll find a couple more exercises to help you really absorb the subject.

The task you're facing in this section is the following: Design a class `IntStats` that computes summary statistics for a list of integers, providing three public methods:[6]

- `public void insert(int n)`—Adds an integer to the list; integers can be inserted in any order.

- `public double getAverage()`—Returns the arithmetic mean of the integers inserted so far.

- `public double getMedian()`—Returns the median of the integers inserted so far. Recall that the median is the value that lies in the middle of the ordered sequence of integers. For example, the median of 2, 10, 11, 20, 100 is 11, which is the middle element. The median of an even number of numbers is defined as the arithmetic mean of the two central elements in the sequence. For example, the median of 2, 10, 11, 20 is 10.5. The median of a sequence of integers can be a real number.

You'll have to deal with three different performance requirements, which I've described in the following subsections.

---

[6] Java 8 introduced a similar class called `IntSummaryStatistics`, but it doesn't compute the median.

3.5.1 *Fast insertion*

Design the class `IntStats` so that `insert` and `getAverage` take constant time.

The following implementation features constant-time insertion and average. For simplicity, computation of the median proceeds by sorting the list, so it requires quasilinear time $(O(n \log n))$. It's possible to implement `getMedian` in linear time, but the algorithms for doing so go beyond the scope of this book.[7]

```
public class IntStats {
    private long sum;                                ❶ The current sum of all integers
    private List<Integer> numbers = new ArrayList<>();

    public void insert(int n) {
        numbers.add(n);
        sum += n;
    }
    public double getAverage() {
        return sum / (double) numbers.size();
    }
    public double getMedian() {
        Collections.sort(numbers);                   ❷ Library method for sorting a list
        final int size = numbers.size();
        if (size \% 2 == 1) {                          ❸ Odd size
            return numbers.get(size/2);
        } else {                                      ❹ Even size
            return (numbers.get(size/2 -1) + numbers.get(size/2)) / 2.0;
        }
    }
}
```

3.5.2 *Fast queries*

Design the class `IntStats` so that `getAverage` and `getMedian` take constant time.

You can easily shift the computational burden from `getMedian` to `insert` by sorting the sequence after each insertion. As a consequence, insertion time grows from constant to quasilinear $(O(n \log n))$.

A slightly more interesting solution is to maintain the list sorted by inserting every new number in the right position:

```
public void insert(int n) {
    int i = 0;
    for (Integer k: numbers) {
        if (k >= n) break;                    ❶ Stops at the first number
        i++;                                     greater than or equal to n
    }
    numbers.add(i, n);                        ❷ Inserts n at position i
    sum += n;
}
```

---

[7] Search for "linear-time selection algorithms" online or in the algorithm books from the *Further reading* section at the end of this chapter.

The other two methods can stay the same as in the previous version, except that get
Median doesn't need to perform the sorting step because the sequence is already sorted.
In this way, insert takes linear time, whereas getAverage and getMedian need only
constant time.

Finally, by switching from a list to a balanced tree (similar to a TreeSet), you could
lower the complexity of insert from linear to logarithmic.

3.5.3   *Fast everything*

Design the class IntStats so that *all* three public methods take constant time.

Sorry, not possible. In fact, it's impossible to offer just insert and getMedian in
constant time. Having the median in constant time requires it to be always up-to-date.
So, every insert must update the median, which in turn requires searching for the next
larger or smaller element. You can do that with a simple linear-time search or with a
data structure that maintains the integers in order, as discussed in the "Fast queries"
section. In both cases, insertion is not constant-time anymore.

More formally, you can prove that if such a data structure existed, you could sort
arbitrary data in linear time, which is a well-known impossibility.

3.6   *Real-world use cases*

The type of reasoning I'm promoting in this chapter comes in handy in numerous
performance-critical applications. Here are some suggestions:

- You might want to consider time efficiency when working with modern machine
  learning algorithms. The process of training a model requires two important
  ingredients: *(a)* lots of data, and *(b)* experimentation to determine the optimal model, which involves trial and error. Staring at your monitor while a
  model is working to converge to a solution is neither cool nor productive. Popular deep-learning frameworks take advantage of modern computer architectures by expressing the operations as a model that performs as a computational
  graph during training. These graphs are distributed across multiple processors
  to be executed in parallel.
- Even if you think you can get away with a suboptimal offline system, like a
  sluggish deep-learning model, it's difficult to do so when responsiveness is
  involved. Searching for books about algorithms in an online store that returns
  results to your queries in 10 minutes would probably make you look some-
  where else. In fact, a slow system can be the least popular choice even if the
  recommendations it produces are much more relevant. (In practice, there's
  almost always a trade-off between the degree of accuracy and time efficiency.)
- There are other occasions when time efficiency can have instantaneous effects
  on the earnings of the company you work for. High-frequency trading of financial products executes literally in the range of microseconds, and efficient algorithms with extremely low latency characteristics are not simply desirable but
  necessary. As you can imagine, high-frequency trading occurs automatically,

and trading at a rate twice as slow as the competition wouldn't lead to a happy path for your company.

- A poorly designed high-frequency trading system that can drive a handful of people out of business is an unfortunate event, but consequences from the failure of a real-time system can be catastrophic. A real-time system is designed to respond to a physical process, and time efficiency becomes a constraint: either the system operates within some specified time boundaries or it's not considered operational at all.

  In electric power systems, the Automatic Generation Control runs in the data room of a control center and sends control signals to adjust the output of power plants to maintain the generation-load/consumption balance. Failure to produce correct signals in a timely fashion can lead to a catastrophic event, such as a blackout.

3.7   *Applying what you learned*

Consider the following functionalities that you may want to add to containers.

- `groupSize`—An instance method with no parameters that returns the number of containers connected directly or indirectly to this one
- `flush`—An instance method with no parameters and no return value that empties all containers connected directly or indirectly to this one

EXERCISE 1

Add the `groupSize` method to the three water container implementations from this chapter without adding fields or modifying any other method.

1. What's its worst-case asymptotic complexity in the three cases?
2. Can you modify *Speed2* so that `groupSize` takes constant time, without increasing the asymptotic complexity of the other methods?

EXERCISE 2

Add the `flush` method to the three water container implementations from this chapter without modifying any other method.

1. What's its worst-case asymptotic complexity in the three cases?
2. Can you modify *Speed2* so that `flush` takes constant time without increasing the asymptotic complexity of the other methods?

EXERCISE 3 (MINI-PROJECT)

1. Design two classes, `Grid` and `Appliance`, representing an electrical grid and an appliance that the grid can power. Each grid (or each appliance) is characterized by the maximum power it provides (or absorbs). You can connect an appliance to a grid using the `plugInto` method, and you can turn it on and off using the `on` and `off` instance methods. (Initially, any new appliance is turned off.) Connecting an appliance to another grid automatically disconnects it from the first one. If turning an appliance on

overloads its grid, the method `on` must throw an exception. Finally, the `residualPower` method of `Grid` returns the power that's still available on this grid.

Make sure your solution will work with the following use case:

```
Appliance tv = new Appliance(150), radio = new Appliance(30);
Grid grid = new Grid(3000);

tv.plugInto(grid);
radio.plugInto(grid);
System.out.println(grid.residualPower());
tv.on();
System.out.println(grid.residualPower());
radio.on();
System.out.println(grid.residualPower());
```

Desired output from the use case:

```
3000
2850
2820
```

2. Can you design those two classes so that all their methods run in constant time?

EXERCISE 4
1. If `ArrayList` enlarged the array by 10% when full, would the amortized complexity of `add` still be constant?
2. That would make resizing more frequent. By how much exactly?

Summary

- You can optimize the same class for performance in different ways.
- You can move around the most expensive calculations that a class needs to perform according to a usage profile.
- A circular linked list is a good data structure for merging two sequences starting from arbitrary elements.
- Parent pointer trees are the data structure of choice for union-find scenarios.
- Amortized analysis is the formal way to characterize the average performance of a class over a long sequence of operations.

Answers to quizzes and exercises

POP QUIZ 1
There are two partial orders between pairs of classes in a Java program: (a) being a subclass, and (b) being an internal class.

POP QUIZ 2
Removing a given node from a singly linked circular list takes linear time ($O(n)$). Starting from that node, you need to walk the entire list until you come back to the predecessor of the node you wish to remove. At that point, you update the `next` reference of the predecessor to jump over the node you want to remove.

POP QUIZ 3

For me, it's very easy to identify activities that I put off as long as possible: car washing and dental appointments come quickly to mind. It's harder to find tasks I'm eager to do: finishing this answer is not one of them.

POP QUIZ 4

A parent pointer tree is more appropriate. Compiling a class requires knowing its immediate superclass; for example, in each constructor, the compiler will insert an invocation to a superclass constructor. On the other hand, knowing the subclasses is irrelevant to compiling a given class.

EXERCISE 1

1. For *Speed1* (constant time):

```
public int groupSize() {
   return group.members.size();
}
```

For *Speed2* (linear time):

```
public int groupSize() {
   int size = 0;
   Container current = this;
   do {
      size++;
      current = current.next;
   } while (current != this);
   return size;
}
```

For *Speed3* (logarithmic worst-case time, constant amortized time):

```
public int groupSize() {
  Container root = findRootAndCompress();
  return root.size;
}
```

2. For the second part of the exercise, it's easy to improve the time complexity of `group Size` in *Speed2* by adding a `groupSize` instance field and keeping it updated during `connectTo`.

EXERCISE 2

1. For *Speed1* (constant time):

```
public void flush() {
   group.amountPerContainer = 0;
}
```

For *Speed2* (linear time):

```
public void flush() {
   Container current = this;
   do {
      current.amount = 0;
      current = current.next;
   } while (current != this);
}
```

For *Speed3* (logarithmic worst-case time, constant amortized time):

```
public void flush() {
    Container root = findRootAndCompress();
    root.amount = 0;
}
```

2. As for the second question, it's impossible to achieve constant-time `flush` in *Speed2* without increasing the complexity of any other method. To do so, `flush` would have to lazily mark the current container in a way that encodes the fact that its group has been flushed. However, this event may be followed by more `addWater`, more `connectTo`, and even more `flush` actions, so the special mark you insert would become a complex history of events that have happened to this container since the last call to `getAmount`. In other words, a constant-time (and hence local) implementation of `flush` requires storing an unbounded trace of events in each container that will need to be replayed when `getAmount` is called, thus raising its complexity beyond linear.

EXERCISE 3
1. and 2. It's possible to perform all operations in constant time by storing in the `Grid` its residual power and keeping it updated at all times. Notice how grids don't need to know their appliances. It's enough for each appliance to have a reference to the grid it's currently plugged into, or `null` if it's still unplugged. We end up with the following structure for grids:

```
public class Grid {
    private final int maxPower;
    private int residualPower;
    ...
```

and the following for appliances:

```
public class Appliance {
    private final int powerAbsorbed;
    private Grid grid;
    private boolean isOn;
    ...
```

Appliances must have a way to update the residual power of their grid when you turn them on and off. Rather than accessing the `residualPower` field directly, you can achieve this best through a `Grid` method that throws the required exception if the operation overloads this grid:

```
void addPower(int power) {
    if (residualPower + power < 0)
        throw new IllegalArgumentException("Not enough power.");
    if (residualPower + power > maxPower)
        throw new IllegalArgumentException("Maximum power exceeded.");
    residualPower += power;
}
```

Ideally, only appliances shoud be able to access that method, but controlling access in this way isn't possible in Java, as long as `Grid` and `Appliance` are separate top-level classes. To partially hide that method, you can put the two classes in their own package and give package (aka default) visibility to `addPower`, as I did.

I chose to throw `IllegalArgumentException` when the grid is overloaded, even though `IllegalStateException` describes the situation equally well. Indeed, the error condition is due to the value of an argument (`power`) being incompatible with the current state of an object field (`residualPower`). In these cases, Joshua Bloch recommends throwing `IllegalArgumentException` (see *Effective Java*, item 72) and resorting to `IllegalStateException` only when no other argument value would work.

You can find the full `Appliance` and `Grid` classes in the accompanying repository (https://bitbucket.org/mfaella/exercisesinstyle).

EXERCISE 4
1. The answer is positive. Enlarging the array by *any* percentage, including a meager 10%, leads to constant amortized complexity of insertions. To prove it, just replace the 1.5 factor you used in the calculations in section 3.3.5 with another enlarging factor, such as 1.1 for 10%.

Choosing the right percentage is a balancing act between time and space. The smaller the percentage, the larger that constant will be, and so the less time-efficient. On the other hand, a more conservative percentage saves space because the `ArrayList` capacity will generally be closer to its size.

2. As I explained in this chapter, enlarging by a factor of f causes $\log_f \frac{n}{10}$ reallocations in the course of n insertions. Accordingly, enlarging by 10% instead of 50% leads to the following increase in reallocations:

$$\frac{\log_{1.1} \frac{n}{10}}{\log_{1.5} \frac{n}{10}} = \log_{1.1} 1.5 \approx 4.25.$$

Enlarging by 10% causes 4.25 times more reallocations than enlarging by 50%.

Further reading

There are several standard algorithm books that cover union-find algorithms and amortized complexity.

- T. H. Cormen, C. E. Leiserson, R. L. Rivest, and C. Stein. *Introduction to Algorithms*. MIT Press, 2009.
- J. Kleinberg and E. Tardos. *Algorithm Design*. Pearson, 2005.
- For a quick overview of union-find algorithms, Kevin Wayne from Princeton maintains high-quality slides that summarize their history and properties, based on the *Algorithm Design* book. You can easily find them online.

In this chapter, I didn't discuss Java-specific performance tips and tricks, choosing instead to focus on high-level, mostly language-independent algorithmic principles. You can use the following book to fill this gap by learning about the many ways you can tune a VM to the needs of a concrete application.

A substantial part of the book is devoted to garbage collection, as that is an area where several competing algorithms offer different performance profiles, with no single algorithm being superior for all applications. Additionally, the book discusses a range of monitoring and profiling tools available for Java.

- Scott Oaks. *Java Performance: The Definitive Guide.* O'Reilly Media, 2014.

Precious memory: Space efficiency

This chapter covers

- Writing space-efficient classes
- Comparing the memory requirements of common data structures, including arrays, lists, and sets
- Assessing trade-offs between performance and memory footprint
- Exploiting memory locality to improve performance

Sometimes, programmers need to store their data in as little space as possible. Contrary to intuition, this rarely happens because the device they're targeting comes with little memory. Rather, it happens because the amount of data is huge. For example, video games are a type of software that often pushes the limits of the hardware. No matter how many GB of memory the next console boasts, soon games will run out of it and start packing data in weird ways.

In this chapter, assume your water-management program will deal with millions, perhaps even billions of containers, and you want to keep as many of them as possible in main memory. Clearly, you'll want to shrink the memory footprint of each container as much as possible. On the other hand, you don't need to worry about the memory that temporary local variables use because they live only the short time span of a method call.

For each implementation in this chapter, you'll compare its memory footprint with the one of *Reference*, discussed in chapter 2. In the meantime, recall the fields used in that class:

```
public class Container {
    private Set<Container> group;      ❶ Containers connected to this one
    private double amount;             ❷ Amount of water in this container
```

4.1   Gently squeezing   [Memory1]

You can do somewhat better than *Reference* with a few simple tricks. First, it's quite unlikely that you really need the resolution or range of double-precision numbers to represent the amount of water in a container, so you can save 4 bytes per container by downgrading the amount field from `double` to `float`. You need to downgrade the argument of `addWater` and the return type of `getAmount` accordingly, so you're slightly modifying the public API. Note that the resulting class is still 100% compatible with *UseCase* from chapter 1 because that use case passes water amounts as integers, and integer arguments are compatible with both `float` and `double` parameters.

Space-saving data types

Reduced-size data types play a limited role in the main Java API, but they're well supported in more specialized contexts where memory may be an issue. For example, Android provides a `FloatMath` class with common mathematical operations performed on `float`s instead of `double`s. Also, in the Java specification for smart cards (aka *Java Card*), most integers occurring in the API are encoded as either `short`s or `byte`s.

POP QUIZ 1   If your program contains 10 occurrences of the string literal `"Hello World"`, how much memory is devoted to those strings?

Regarding the `group` field, its `Set` type was chosen in the reference implementation because it clearly expresses the intent that groups are unordered and contain no duplicates. By giving up this clarity of intent and switching to an `ArrayList`, you can save a significant amount of memory. After all, an `ArrayList` is a thin wrapper around a plain array, so the net memory cost of an extra element is just 4 bytes. Your new `Container` class, nicknamed *Memory1*, should start as shown in the following listing.

> **Listing 4.1   *Memory1*: Fields and method `getAmount`—no constructor needed**

```
public class Container {
    private List<Container> group;      ❶ It will be initialized with an ArrayList.
    private float amount;

    public float getAmount() { return amount; }
```

Additionally, if many containers are never connected to a group, you can save space by instantiating the list only when actually needed (aka *lazy initialization*). In other words, the `group` field equal to `null` represents an isolated container. This choice allows you to provide no explicit constructor, although it also means that `connectTo` and `addWater` need to treat isolated containers as special cases, as you'll see in a minute.

In general, you should be careful when migrating from a `Set` to a `List` because you're losing the ability to automatically reject duplicate elements. Luckily, you weren't using that ability in *Reference* because the groups you merged using the `connectTo` method are guaranteed to be disjoint in the first place. The implementation for `connectTo` shown in the following listing is what you obtain.

Listing 4.2 *Memory1*: **Method `connectTo`**

```
public void connectTo(Container other) {
    if (group==null) {              ❶ If this is isolated, initializes its group
        group = new ArrayList<>();
        group.add(this);
    }
    if (other.group==null) {        ❷ If other is isolated, initializes its group
        other.group = new ArrayList<>();
        other.group.add(other);
    }
    if (group==other.group) return;  ❸ Checks if they're already connected

    int size1 = group.size(),        ❹ Computes the new water amount
        size2 = other.group.size();
    float tot1 = amount * size1,
          tot2 = other.amount * size2,
          newAmount = (tot1 + tot2) / (size1 + size2);

    group.addAll(other.group);       ❺ Merges the two groups
    for (Container x: other.group) { x.group = group; }
    for (Container x: group) { x.amount = newAmount; }
}
```

Finally, the `addWater` method also needs to take into account the special case of an isolated container, to avoid dereferencing a `null` pointer, as shown in the following listing.

Listing 4.3 *Memory1*: **Method `addWater`**

```
public void addWater(double amount) {
    if (group==null) {              ❶ If this is isolated, updates locally
        this.amount += amount;
    } else {
        double amountPerContainer = amount / group.size();
        for (Container c: group) {
            c.amount += amountPerContainer;
        }
    }
}
```

Let's end this section by taking a look at the memory layout of this implementation. As usual, assume you run the first three parts of *UseCase*, which consist of creating four containers (a to d) and running the following lines:

```
a.addWater(12);
d.addWater(8);
a.connectTo(b);
b.connectTo(c);
```

The scenario is illustrated in figure 4.1, and the corresponding memory layout of *Memory1* is depicted in figure 4.2. The layout is very similar to *Reference*, except for the ArrayList instead of HashSet, and except for the null value in container d, instead of a reference to a one-element HashSet. The third difference in comparison to *Reference*—water amounts of type float instead of double—doesn't show in the diagram.

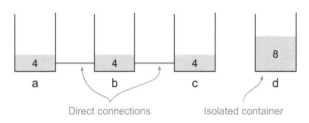

Figure 4.1   The situation after executing the first three parts of *UseCase*. You've connected containers a through c together and poured water into a and d.

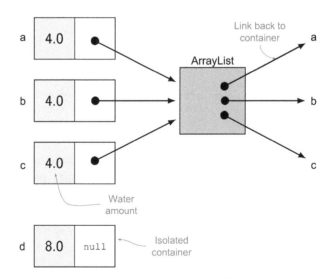

Figure 4.2   The memory layout of *Memory1* after executing the first three parts of *UseCase*

4.1.1   Space and time complexity

To estimate the memory footprint of a *Memory1* container, start by evaluating the size of an ArrayList, which is internally implemented as an array and a couple of book-keeping fields. The length of the internal array is called the *capacity* of the ArrayList, to distinguish it from its size, which is the number of elements actually stored in it. The memory requirements of an `ArrayList` come from the following features:

- 12 bytes for the standard object overhead
- 4 bytes for an integral field counting the number of structural modifications (insertions and deletions) ever performed on the list (This field is used to raise an exception if the list is modified during an iteration.)
- 4 bytes for the integral size field
- 4 bytes for the reference to the array
- 16 bytes for the standard array overhead
- 4 bytes for each array cell

The memory layout of an `ArrayList` is sketched in figure 4.3. Because an `ArrayList` with n elements contains at least n array cells, based on those features it occupies at least $40 + 4n$ bytes.

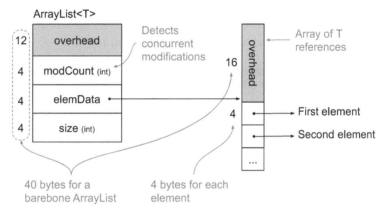

Figure 4.3 The memory layout of an `ArrayList`

In reality, the capacity of an `ArrayList` is often larger than its size. If you add an extra element to an `ArrayList` that's at full capacity, the class will create a larger array and copy the old one onto the new one. To improve its overall performance, the enlarged array will not be *tight*—just one cell longer than the old one. As I explained in detail in chapter 3 (section 3.3.5), the capacity actually will increase by 50%. As a result, at any given time the capacity of an `ArrayList` is between 100% and 150% of its size. In the following estimates, assume the average value is 125%.

Your results should look like the estimates in table 4.1. An isolated container (first scenario) carries no `ArrayList`. Only the container objects themselves take memory: 4 bytes for the `group` reference (which holds `null`) and 4 bytes for the `amount` field, plus the usual 12-byte object overhead. When you organize containers in 100 groups of 10 (second scenario), you have to add 100 `ArrayLists` to the footprint of 1,000 container objects.

Table 4.1   Memory requirements of *Memory1*

Scenario	Size (calculations)	Size (bytes)	% of reference
1000 isolated	$1000 * (12 + 4 + 4)$	20000	19%
100 groups of 10	$1000 * (12 + 4 + 4) + 100 * (40 + 10 * 1.25 * 4)$	29000	47%

As you can see from table 4.1, with a few simple changes to *Reference*, you can save a significant amount of space. In particular, the idea of allocating the lists when you first need them obviously brings about great savings in the first scenario, where all containers are isolated, so no list is ever allocated. The 50% savings in the second scenario are instead entirely due to having replaced HashSet with ArrayList.

Notice that the memory savings you've achieved in this section come at essentially no performance cost because the three operations keep the same complexity they have in *Reference*, as reported in table 4.2. On the other hand, the class is somewhat less readable than *Reference*. First, declaring the group field of type List hides the fact that groups are in fact unordered collections with no duplicates. Secondly, treating isolated containers as special cases is an unnecessary complication whose only aim is to save some space.

Table 4.2   Time complexities for *Memory1*, where n is the total number of containers. These complexities coincide with those of *Reference*.

Method	Time complexity
getAmount	$O(1)$
connectTo	$O(n)$
addWater	$O(n)$

The high memory overhead of HashSet and other standard collections is a well-known fact, so much so that several frameworks provide more space-efficient alternatives. For example, Android provides a class called SparseArray, representing a map with integer keys and reference values, which is implemented based on two same-length arrays. The first array stores the keys in ascending order and the second array stores the corresponding values. With this data structure, you pay for the improved memory efficiency with a worse time complexity: finding the value corresponding to a given key requires a binary search over the key array, which in turn requires logarithmic time. Exercise 2 at the end of this chapter invites you to further analyze the SparseArray class.

When you only need to store primitive values, several libraries, such as GNU Trove (https://bitbucket.org/trove4j/trove), provide specialized set and map implementations that avoid wrapping each value in the corresponding class.

4.2 *Plain arrays* *[Memory2]*

In your second attempt at saving memory, nicknamed *Memory2*, you'll replace the `ArrayList` representing a group with a plain array and keep its length exactly equal to the size of the group. The following listing shows what the beginning of the class should look like.

Listing 4.4 *Memory2:* **Fields and method** `getAmount`—**no constructor needed**

```
public class Container {
   private Container[] group;
   private float amount;

   public float getAmount() { return amount; }
```

As for *Memory1*, you may want to allocate the `group` array only when necessary, that is, when this container is connected to at least another one. The resulting memory layout in the usual scenario is shown in figure 4.4.

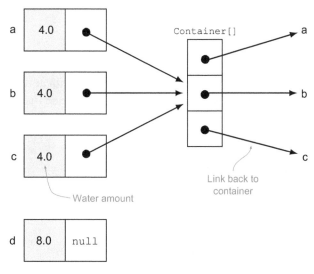

Figure 4.4 **Memory layout of** *Memory2* **after executing the first three parts of** *UseCase*

The `connectTo` method is quite similar to the one in *Memory1*, just slightly more cumbersome, because of its lower level of abstraction. For example, merging two `ArrayList`s is a simple matter of invoking the `addAll` method, whereas merging two arrays requires reallocating one of them and then iterating over the other.

Listing 4.5 *Memory2:* **method** `connectTo`

```
public void connectTo(Container other) {
   if (group==null) {          ❶ If this is isolated, initializes its group
      group = new Container[] { this };
   }
```

```
if (other.group==null) {                    ❷ If other is isolated,
  other.group = new Container[] { other };    initializes its group
}
if (group == other.group) return;   ❸ Checks if they're already connected

int size1 =        group.length,    ❹ Computes the new water amount
    size2 = other.group.length;
float amount1    =        amount * size1,
      amount2    = other.amount * size2,
      newAmount = (amount1 + amount2) / (size1 + size2);

Container[] newGroup = new Container[size1 + size2];   ❺ Allocates new group

int i=0;
for (Container a: group) {       ❻ For each container in lst group...
    a.group = newGroup;          ❼ ...updates its group
    a.amount = newAmount;        ❽ ...updates its amount
    newGroup[i++] = a;           ❾ ...and appends it to newGroup
}
for (Container b: other.group) {      Does the same for 2nd group
    b.group = newGroup;
    b.amount = newAmount;
    newGroup[i++] = b;
}
}
```

Finally, the addWater method is almost identical to the one from *Memory1*, except for the type of the water amount variables—float instead of double—as shown in the following listing.

Listing 4.6 *Memory2*: Method `addWater`

```
public void addWater(float amount) {
    if (group==null) {
        this.amount += amount;
    } else {
        float amountPerContainer = amount / group.length;
        for (Container c: group) {
            c.amount += amountPerContainer;
        }
    }
}
```

4.2.1 *Space and time complexity*

A plain array containing references to n containers takes $16 + 4n$ bytes, leading to the estimates in table 4.3 for our standard scenarios. An isolated container (first scenario) allocates no group array, and its memory footprint is exactly as large as in *Memory1*: 20 bytes. When you organize the containers in 100 groups of 10 (second scenario), a 10-cell array represents each group, taking 16 bytes of array overhead and 4*10 bytes for its actual content.

The bad news is that the memory savings you achieve with *Memory2* are insignificant compared with the previous version of *Memory1*. Isolated containers occupy the

Table 4.3 Memory requirements of *Memory2*

Scenario	Size (calculations)	Size (bytes)	% of reference
1000 isolated	$1000 * (12 + 4 + 4)$	20000	19%
100 groups of 10	$1000 * (12 + 4 + 4) + 100 * (16 + 10 * 4)$	25600	42%

same amount of memory, and groups of containers, now represented by arrays, are only marginally more compact than `ArrayList`s. In fact, the bigger savings come from keeping the arrays *tight*, that is, exactly as long as they need to be, rather than relatively loose as an `ArrayList`.

It's a good time to recall and compare the memory requirements of the three standard data structures you've used so far to represent groups of containers: `HashSet` (*Reference* and *Speed1*), `ArrayList` (*Memory1*), and plain arrays (*Memory2*). I'm not including classes *Speed2* and *Speed3* in the comparison because they're based on custom data structures that aren't immediately available for general use.

Table 4.4 summarizes these memory requirements. The size estimate for a plain array of object references is easy to make: 16 bytes of overhead and 4 bytes for each reference. I carried out the size analysis of `ArrayList` in detail in section 4.1.1. Here, I'm assuming that its capacity is equal to its size. (In reality, the former can be up to 50% larger than the latter.) Similar simplifying assumptions apply to the size analysis for `HashSet`, which I presented in section 2.2.1.

Table 4.4 Memory requirements of common collections, assuming that the capacity of the `ArrayList` and the `HashSet` is equal to their size. The second column is tagged "barebone" instead of "empty" because it doesn't take into account the default initial capacity of that collection.

Type	Size (barebone)	Size (each extra element)
array	16	4
ArrayList	40	4
LinkedList	24	24
HashSet	52	32

As you can see from the table, an array and an `ArrayList` are very close in terms of memory requirements, but `ArrayList` is more useful, supporting automatic resizing and other utilities, and leads to more readable code because of its higher level of abstraction. Moreover, `ArrayList` plays nicely with generics, whereas arrays are at odds with them.

POP QUIZ 2 For a type parameter `T`, why isn't "`new T[10]`" a legal Java expression?

`HashSet` is in a different, much bulkier league, particularly because it wraps each inserted element into a new object. However, it provides unique services in optimal time:

- Membership query in constant time (method `contains`)
- Rejection of duplicate elements in constant time (method `add`)
- Removal of an arbitrary element in constant time (method `remove`)

If your application requires those services, and you're not memory-constrained, a `Hash Set` will generally more than repay for its larger memory footprint.

Regarding performance, the time complexity of *Memory2* turns out to be the same as *Memory1* and *Reference*, as reported in table 4.5. After all, *Memory2* is just a variation of *Memory1* with plain arrays instead of `ArrayLists`.

Table 4.5 Time complexities for *Memory2*, where n is the total number of containers. These complexities coincide with those of *Reference*.

Method	Time complexity
getAmount	$O(1)$
connectTo	$O(n)$
addWater	$O(n)$

You may be wondering why the smart resizing policy of `ArrayList`, which guarantees amortized constant-time insertions, doesn't provide any advantage to *Memory2*. The explanation is that it *does* provide some advantage in the performance of `connectTo`, but the other operations the method performs hide that advantage. In detail, *Memory1* merges two groups through the line

```
group.addAll(other.group);
```

where `group` and `other.group` are two `ArrayLists`. *Memory2* instead executes the line

```
Container[] newGroup = new Container[size1 + size2];
```

The first is generally more efficient than the second because the extra capacity of the first `ArrayList` may be enough to insert all the elements from the second `ArrayList` without any new allocation. However, both versions of `connectTo` then proceed to iterate over *all* the elements from *both* of the old groups. As a result, asymptotically speaking, the later loops overrule the early savings, leading to the same big-O complexity of $O(n)$ for both versions of `connectTo`.

There's one more reason to like *Memory2*: it's entirely self-contained, in that it does not mention any other class from the Java API. In special circumstances, this could be beneficial, because it means that this class can function in a context with a very limited runtime environment, as allowed by the module system introduced with Java 9.

4.3   *Forgoing objects*   *[Memory3]*

Even an empty Java object takes 12 bytes, so if we respect the use case from chapter 1, a container can't take less space than that. Now, assume you can change the API to whatever takes the least amount of space, while still offering the same services as the original class: get the current water amount in a container, change the current amount, and connect two containers. What's the least amount of space you need to store the information that's actually necessary to offer those services?

To significantly reduce space usage, you can't afford to keep an object for each container, but clients still need a way to identify a specific container. The solution is to give clients a *handle*, a piece of information that uniquely identifies a container. A reference to a container object is a perfectly fine handle, but it comes with the 12-byte overhead you're trying to avoid. What you're looking for is an alternative handle that does *not* come with a memory overhead.

4.3.1 *The object-less API*

Rather than providing one object for each container, to save space you can let the client identify each container with an integer ID—the client-side handle for a container. It's then just natural to store the required information (water amounts and mutual connections) in a space-efficient data structure that's indexed by integers. Is there any particular structure that comes to mind? That's right, arrays.

Consequently, instead of a constructor, the class will include a static method that returns the ID of a new container:

```
int id = Container.newContainer();
```

Then, instead of calling c.getAmount() on a container object, the client will call a static method accepting a container ID:

```
float amount = Container.getAmount(id);
```

Analogously, to connect two containers, clients will pass their identifiers to a static connect method:

```
Container.connect(id1, id2);
```

Clearly, this implementation is against all OO canons, and you should consider it only for the sake of pushing our assumptions to the limit.

To familiarize yourself with the resulting API, check out how the use case from chapter 1 (nicknamed *UseCase*) is transformed to employ integer IDs instead of container objects. Recall the first lines of *UseCase*:

```
Container a = new Container();
Container b = new Container();
Container c = new Container();
Container d = new Container();

a.addWater(12);
d.addWater(8);
a.connectTo(b);
System.out.println(a.getAmount() + " " + b.getAmount() + " " +
                   c.getAmount() + " " + d.getAmount());
```

When forgoing container objects, you identify each container using an integer, and the previous lines become the following:

```
int a = Container.newContainer(), b = Container.newContainer(),
    c = Container.newContainer(), d = Container.newContainer();

Container.addWater(a, 12);
Container.addWater(d, 8);
Container.connect(a, b);
System.out.println(Container.getAmount(a) + " " +
                   Container.getAmount(b) + " " +
                   Container.getAmount(c) + " " +
                   Container.getAmount(d));
```

Although I'm recommending plain arrays for memory efficiency reasons, in practice you're as likely to use them for *time* efficiency reasons, because arrays bring the benefits of *cache locality*. In short, data that's closer together in memory (as in an array) is faster to access than data that's randomly spread around (as in a linked list). This fact is due to the organization of the CPU cache, a memory buffer bridging the performance gap between the CPU and the main memory. The cache keeps at hand small chunks of adjacent data. Keeping two related data items closer together in memory improves the likelihood that loading one piece of data into the cache also will carry the second piece of data with it, thus speeding up the ensuing operations. For example, all fields of the same object are arranged close together in memory. Hence, accessing one field is likely to speed up access to all other fields of the same object.

The memory hierarchy

The memory of modern computers is organized into a hierarchy of levels, each one larger and slower than the one above it. The top level comprises the CPU registers, typically spanning a few hundred bytes. Registers are the only kind of memory that can keep up with the CPU's native processing speed: registers can be read or written in every single CPU cycle.

Below the registers lays the cache, divided into several levels and comprising a few megabytes. Reading from the top-level cache (that is, moving data from the top-level cache to a register) takes only a few cycles, whereas reading directly from main memory requires *hundreds* of cycles.

The cache is organized in *lines*, each comprising multiple machine words. Whenever the program addresses a new memory location, the cache loads a full line starting at the address of that location. If that location is the first element of an array, several more array elements will be automatically loaded into the same cache line, ready to be quickly moved to the registers, if requested.

For the sake of concreteness, consider the recent AMD Zen architecture for desktop CPUs. Its cache is divided into three levels, and each line is 64 bytes long. The following are the main characteristics of the memory hierarchy (see http://mng.bz/E1lX):

Level	Size (per core)	Latency (cycles)
Registers	128 bytes	1
L1 cache	32 KB	4
L2 cache	512 KB	17
L3 cache	2 MB	40
Main memory	16 GB (typical)	~300

POP QUIZ 3 If set is a HashSet, would you expect the call set.contains(x) to speed up a subsequent call set.contains(y)? What if set was a TreeSet?

In Java, you can store a collection of items in a cache-local way only via arrays or classes based on arrays, such as ArrayList. However, generic collections like ArrayList can hold only references, so the cache locality is limited to the references themselves and doesn't extend to the data they point to. For example, an ArrayList<Integer> holds an array of references to Integers. The references will be adjacent in memory, but the actual integer values won't. The same applies to a plain array of Integer objects, as shown in figure 4.5.

You need external libraries, such as the GNU Trove I mentioned, to combine the automatic resizing and other handy capabilities of ArrayList with the cache locality of an array of primitive values. For example, GNU Trove class TIntArrayList represents a resizable array of primitive integers.

4.3.2 Fields and the getAmount method

The new Container class, nicknamed *Memory3*, identifies both containers and groups of containers via integral IDs. It uses two class arrays (that is, static fields) to encode the required information:

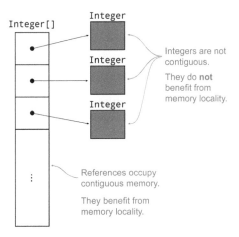

Figure 4.5 An array of Integer objects. The array itself occupies a contiguous chunk of memory, but the Integer objects the array points to are scattered in memory.

- The group array maps a container ID to its group ID.
- The amount array maps a group ID to the amount of water found in each container of that group.

Given a container ID, the getAmount method will access the group array to obtain the group ID for that container, and then the amount array to obtain the water amount in that group, as you can see in the following listing.

Listing 4.7   Memory3: Fields and method getAmount

```
public class Container {
   private static int group[] = new int[0];       ❶ From containerID to its group
   private static float amount[] = new float[0];   ❷ From groupID to
                                                      the per-container amount
   public static float getAmount(int containerID) {
      int groupID = group[containerID];
      return amount[groupID];
   }
}
```

It may seem odd to initialize those fields with zero-sized arrays, but there's a perfectly good reason to do it: if you do so, you don't have to treat the creation of the first container in any special way. You're improving uniformity and streamlining the code. In particular, you can always access group.length and amount.length because those arrays will never be null.

4.3.3   Creating containers with a factory method

Now, focus on the static method newContainer that replaces the constructor. A method returning a new instance of a class is often called a *factory method*. The newContainer method doesn't actually create an instance of an object because the whole point of *Memory3* is to avoid having an object for each container. However, by returning the ID of a new container, it fulfills the role of a factory method.

Factory methods vs. FACTORY METHOD

Any method that returns a new instance of a class is called a factory method. Compared to a constructor, a factory method has the following advantages:

- It's not bound to return an object of a specific class; any subtype of its declared return type would work.
  For example, the class EnumSet (an implementation of Set whose elements must belong to a given enumeration) provides new sets only through various static factory methods. For performance reasons, they return different implementations (subclasses of EnumSet) depending on the size of the underlying enumeration.
- Despite what I wrote earlier, a factory method is not forced to return an object that's actually new.
  It can cache or recycle objects, as long as doing so isn't cause for concern—perhaps because those objects are immutable. That's the case of the factory

method `Integer.valueOf`, which wraps a primitive integer into an immutable `Integer` object that may or may not be new.

On the other hand, FACTORY METHOD (spelled in all caps for clarity) is one of the original design patterns that the so-called Gang of Four defined. Naturally, the pattern features a factory method, but in a specific context: a class needs to provide an object to its clients, while leaving to its subclasses the ability to change the actual type of that object. For example, you can consider the `Iterable` interface with its `iterator` method an application of this pattern.

To implement `newContainer`, consider that this method needs to update the arrays to accommodate a new container and then return its ID. As every new container comes with its new group, you need to add an extra cell to both arrays. To do so, you use the static `Arrays.copyOf` method, which copies an array to a possibly different—smaller or larger—size. If the new size is smaller, the method discards the extra elements. If the new size is larger, as in the current case, it adds extra zeros, as is usual when you allocate a new array. The default zero value is just fine for the new `amount` cell because containers start empty. On the other hand, you need to explicitly set the new `group` cell to the ID of the new group, which you can take to be the smallest integer that's not yet the ID of a group—in other words, the size of the old `amount` array. You should end up with an implementation similar to the following listing.

Listing 4.8 *Memory3*: Method `newContainer`

```
public static int newContainer() {
    int nContainers = group.length,
        nGroups = amount.length;
    amount = Arrays.copyOf(amount, nGroups + 1);      ❶ Appends zero to amount
    group = Arrays.copyOf(group, nContainers + 1);    ❷ Appends zero to group
    group[nContainers] = nGroups;      ❸ Sets the group ID of the new container

    return nContainers;                ❹ Returns the ID of the new container
}
```

Additionally, there's no point in allowing clients to create `Container` objects, so you better forbid it. One way of doing so is by adding a private constructor with an empty body, thus preventing the compiler from adding the default constructor. The "Non-instantiable classes" sidebar compares different ways to achieve this effect.

Non-instantiable classes

Version *Memory3* of the container class holds only static members and is not meant to be instantiated. There are several ways in Java to prevent the client from creating objects of this class at compile time:

- Turning the class into an interface
- Declaring the class `abstract`

- Providing a `private` constructor (as the only constructor)

The first two techniques are not appropriate here because they invite the client to extend the class, whereas it's pointless to extend such a non-instantiable class. The third technique is the right choice because it prevents both instantiation and extension at the same time. Indeed, if you try to extend such a class, you'll realize that the constructor from the subclass has no way to make the mandatory call to a constructor from the superclass.

Moreover, the third technique is the way non-instantiable classes from the JDK work. Common examples include the so-called *utility classes* `Math`, `Arrays`, and `Collec tions`. Those classes have no state (no mutable fields) and are only meant to provide utility functions. *Memory3* is not a utility class because it stores information in its fields. It's a module providing its services outside the OO canon.

POP QUIZ 4 How do you design a class that can only be instantiated once (aka a *singleton*)?

Figure 4.6 shows the memory layout of this implementation after executing the first three parts of *UseCase*. Containers are organized in two groups, whose IDs are 0 and 1. The `group` array holds the group ID of each container, and the `amount` array holds the per-container water amount in each group.

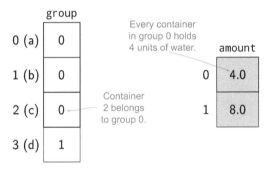

Figure 4.6 Memory layout of *Memory3* after executing the first three parts of *UseCase*

To keep the `amount` array at its optimal size, you need to ensure that there's no gap among the group IDs. Say there was a gap, and the group IDs for three groups were 0, 1, and 5. Those IDs correspond to indices in the `amount` array, so that array would need six cells for just three groups. More formally, you should maintain the following *class invariant*:

> If there are n groups overall, then their IDs are the integers from 0 to $n - 1$.

A class invariant is a property that holds at all times, except during the execution of a method of that class. So, methods from that class can count on invariants being true when they start, and they must ensure that those invariants are still true when they finish. (We'll return to this subject in chapter 6.)

The previous invariant makes sure that the `amount` array is as short as possible: exactly as long as the total number of groups. This property is easy to guarantee as long as groups are added but not removed. Unfortunately, each `connect` operation removes a group, by merging two groups into a single one. Hence, you need to perform some extra work to rearrange the group IDs after an operation has removed a group. A simple solution for removing a gap in the sequence of IDs is to move the gap to the end of the sequence, by assigning the missing ID (the gap) to the group currently holding the largest ID. That's the responsibility of the method `removeGroupAndDefrag`, described in the next section.

4.3.4 Connecting containers by ID

Next, let's examine the `connect` method, as shown in listing 4.9. At this point, its structure should be familiar to you, except for the following special features of *Memory3*:

- The size of a group isn't immediately available; the support method `groupSize` computes it by counting the number of occurrences of a given group ID in the `group` array.
- It merges two groups by assigning the ID of the first group to all containers in the second group.
- At the end, the support method `removeGroupAndDefrag` has to rearrange the group IDs.

Listing 4.9 *Memory3:* **Method** `connect`

```
public static void connect(int containerID1, int containerID2) {
    int groupID1 = group[containerID1],
        groupID2 = group[containerID2],
        size1 = groupSize(groupID1),    ❶ This method is presented later.
        size2 = groupSize(groupID2);
    if (groupID1 == groupID2) return;   ❷ Checks if they're already connected

    float amount1 = amount[groupID1] * size1,   ❸ Computes the new water amount
        amount2 = amount[groupID2] * size2;
    amount[groupID1] = (amount1 + amount2) / (size1 + size2);

    for (int i=0; i<group.length; i++) {   ❹ Assigns the first group ID
        if (group[i] == groupID2) {             to the members of the second group
            group[i] = groupID1;
        }
    }
    removeGroupAndDefrag(groupID2);
}
```

As usual, `connect` needs to compute the new amount of water in each container after the connection is made. To do so, it needs to know the size of the two groups being merged. However, the size of a group isn't stored anywhere, and you need to compute it by counting the number of containers sharing the given group ID. This is the purpose of the `private` support method `groupSize`, shown in the following listing.

> **Listing 4.10   *Memory3*: Support method `groupSize`**

```
private static int groupSize(int groupID) {
    int size = 0;
    for (int otherGroupID: group) {
        if (otherGroupID == groupID) {
            size++;
        }
    }
    return size;
}
```

Data streams

The `groupSize` method is the ideal occasion to show the potential benefits of the stream library that Java 8 introduced. You can convert the `group` array into a stream of integers (interface `IntStream`) and filter them according to a predicate (interface `IntPredicate`), leaving only the values that coincide with the given group ID. Finally, you can use the terminal operation `count` to count those values.

You also can use Lambda expressions, which Java 8 also introduced, to define the filtering predicate with a much shorter syntax than previously available (that is, instead of an anonymous class).

The result is the following one-liner, which replaces the whole body of `groupSize`:

```
return Arrays.stream(group)
             .filter(otherGroupID -> otherGroupID == groupID)
             .count();
```

I'll show you a more extensive application of streams in chapter 9.

Finally, as I explained earlier, the method `removeGroupAndDefrag` is responsible for removing a group while maintaining the class invariant.[1] To understand its inner workings, start by observing that when `connect` invokes `removeGroupAndDefrag` with argument k, no cell in the `group` array contains value k—no container belongs to group k anymore. Still, you can't just erase group ID k because that would leave a gap in the sequence of IDs, which is against the class invariant. Instead, you have to assign ID k to another group and update the two arrays accordingly. Say that before removal the group IDs span the range from 0 to $n - 1$. The simplest thing you can do is assign ID k to the group $n - 1$, then drop the ID $n - 1$ altogether.

Looking at listing 4.11, the `for` loop assigns group ID k to all containers previously associated with group $n - 1$. The `amount[groupID]` line copies the amount of the old group $n - 1$ to the new group k. The last `amount` line truncates the last cell from the

---

[1] The *defrag* name refers to the filesystem maintenance operation called *defragmentation*, which moves blocks around to make sure that files occupy contiguous space.

amount array, effectively erasing group $n - 1$ and restoring the class invariant. At the end, the group IDs span the range from 0 to $n - 2$, as desired.

Listing 4.11 *Memory3*: support method `removeGroupAndDefrag`

```
private static void removeGroupAndDefrag(int groupID) {
    for (int containerID=0; containerID<group.length; containerID++) {
        if (group[containerID] == amount.length-1) {
            group[containerID] = groupID;
        }
    }
    amount[groupID] = amount[amount.length-1];
    amount = Arrays.copyOf(amount, amount.length-1);
}
```

Figure 4.7 shows the step-by-step effect of running the following three lines from the revised use case I presented earlier:

```
Container.addWater(a, 12);
Container.addWater(d, 8);
Container.connect(a, b);
```

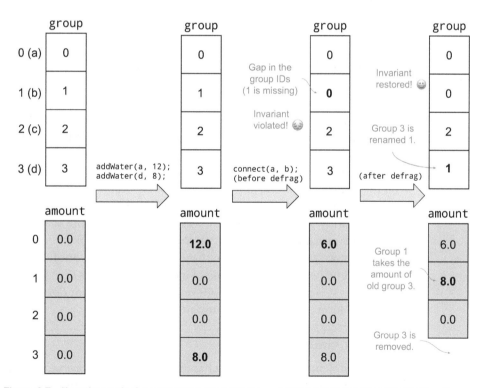

Figure 4.7 How the method `removeGroupAndDefrag` deletes a group while restoring the class invariant

In particular, the figure shows the situation toward the end of `connect`, before and after the call to `removeGroupAndDefrag` (last line in listing 4.9). Before the call, the invariant doesn't hold because group ID 1 is not assigned to any container. After the call, defragmenting has renamed group 3 as 1 and moved its amount to `amount[1]`, thus restoring the invariant.

You may be wondering what happens if the group to be removed is the very last (that is, if $k = n - 1$). A quick check reveals that you don't need to treat that case in any special way. Indeed, if $k = n - 1$, the `for` loop has no effect, because the condition in the `if` statement is always false. The next assignment (the `amount[groupID]` line) is also vacuous, and the last line (the `amount` line) simply drops the last cell from the `amount` array.

4.3.5   *Space and time complexity*

This implementation is based on two plain arrays whose sizes are kept respectively equal to the number of containers and to the number of groups. As a result, you can easily estimate the memory consumption, as shown in table 4.6.

Table 4.6   Memory requirements of *Memory3*

Scenario	Size (calculations)	Size (bytes)	% of reference
1000 isolated	$4 + 16 + 1000 * 4 + 4 + 16 + 1000 * 4$	8040	7%
100 groups of 10	$4 + 16 + 1000 * 4 + 4 + 16 + 100 * 4$	4440	7%

Dropping the container objects grants big memory savings and doesn't cost any performance—at least not in terms of asymptotic complexity, which stays the same as for *Reference*. In practice, all previous implementations of `connect(To)` and `addWater` iterate over only the groups being processed, whereas in *Memory3* those methods need to iterate over *all* containers. Indeed, both `connect` and `addWater` need to know the size of a group, which in turns requires iterating over the array of all containers (the `group` array). With many containers around, these loops may very well lower the effective performance, compared with *Reference*.

Moreover, we're focusing on the three public methods, but notice that the `newContainer` method, which plays the role of a constructor, takes linear time because of the calls to `Arrays.copyOf`. In all previous versions, starting from *Reference*, the constructor contains no loops, so it works in constant time.

4.4   *The black hole*   *[Memory4]*

The final implementation of this chapter, nicknamed *Memory4*, manages to use just 4 bytes for each extra container, at the expense of a higher time complexity. The idea is to employ a single static array, featuring one cell for each container and serving a dual purpose. For some indices, the array contains the index to the next container in the same group, as if groups were stored as linked lists. For containers that have no next container, because they're isolated or are simply the last one in their list, the array stores the amount of water in that container (and in each container of the same group).

I'm suggesting that you store both indices and water amounts in the same array. The first are integers, and the latter are naturally floating-point numbers. What type should the array be? Two options come to mind, leading to the same memory footprint (4 bytes per container):

1 *Array of type* `int`—When you have to interpret cell content as a water amount, you can divide it by a constant denominator, effectively implementing *fixed-point numbers*. For example, if you divide all water amounts by 10,000, you're providing them with five decimal digits after the decimal point.

2 *Array of type* `float`—When you have to interpret cell content as an array index, you must ensure that its value is a non-negative integer. After all, non-negative integers (up to a certain value) are a special case of floating-point numbers.

In the following listing, I'll go with option 2, which seems simpler, although you'll see in a minute that it comes with its share of caveats.

Listing 4.12   *Memory4*: Field—no constructor required

```
public class Container {
    private static float[] nextOrAmount;
```

When reading the content of a cell, how do you distinguish between *next* values and *amount* values? You can use an old trick from the bygone era when computer memory was *really* tight: encoding one of the two cases with positive numbers and the other case with negative numbers. More precisely, you'll interpret a positive number as the index of the next container, whereas a negative number stands for the *opposite* of the water amount in that container. For example, if `nextOrAmount[4] == -2.5`, it means that container 4 is the last in its group (or perhaps is isolated) and contains 2.5 units of water.

There's still a small catch: a zero value could be both an index and a valid amount value, but floats don't distinguish "plus zero" from "minus zero." You can avoid this ambiguity by assuming that zero is an amount, and never using zero as the index of the next container. Because you don't want to sacrifice cell zero, add 1 to all the indices you've stored in the array (aka a *bias*). For example, if container 4 is followed by container 7, you'll have `nextOrAmount[4] == 8`.

Figure 4.8 shows the memory layout of this implementation after executing the first three parts of *UseCase*. The value 2.0 in the first cell is a biased `next` pointer, indicating that the first container (that is, container a) is linked to container number 1 (that is, b). The value −4.0 in the third cell signifies that c is the last container in its group and that each container in the group holds 4.0 units of water.

Listing 4.13 presents the code for the `getAmount` method. It follows the `next` values, just like a linked list (second line of code), until it finds the last container in the list, identified by having a negative or zero value in it. That value is the desired water

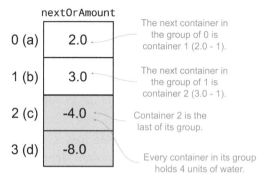

Figure 4.8   Memory layout of *Memory4* after executing the first three parts of *UseCase*. An array of four floats serves a dual purpose: linking containers belonging to the same group and storing the amount of water.

amount, with the opposite sign. Pay special attention to the −1 at the end of the third line of code, which removes the bias, and to the minus sign after `return`, which restores the proper sign for a water amount value.

Listing 4.13   *Memory4*: Method `getAmount`

```
public static float getAmount(int containerID) {
    while (nextOrAmount[containerID]>0) {      ❶ Looks for the last one in the group
        containerID = (int) nextOrAmount[containerID] -1;   ❷ Removes the bias
    }
    return -nextOrAmount[containerID];        ❸ Restores the correct sign
}
```

Using floats to represent array indices comes with a hidden drawback. In principle, array indices can span the whole range of non-negative 32-bit integers: 0 to $2^{31} - 1$ (approximately 2 billion, also known as `Integer.MAX_VALUE`). Floats have a much wider range, but a varying *resolution*. The distance between two consecutive floats changes with their size, as shown schematically in figure 4.9. When a float is small (close to zero), the next float is extremely close to it. When a float is large, the next float is farther away. At some point, that distance becomes larger than 1, and floats start skipping integer values.

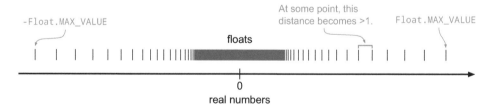

Figure 4.9   The relationship between real numbers and values of type `float`

For example, because of the wider range, a float can exactly represent 1E10 (10^{10}, that is, 10 billion), whereas an integer can't. Both types can represent 1E8 (100 million), but if a float variable contains 1E8 and you add 1 to it, it remains 1E8. Floats don't have enough significant digits to represent the number 100,000,001. The distance between 1E8 and the next float is larger than 1. Although 1E8 is well within the range of floats, it's outside their *uninterrupted integer range*, that is, the range of integers that can be represented exactly and without gaps. Table 4.7 summarizes the uninterrupted integer range of the most common numeric primitive types.

Table 4.7 Comparing the uninterrupted integer range of primitive types. The uninterrupted integer range is the set of (non-negative) integers that can be represented exactly and without gaps.

Type	Significant bits	Significant decimal digits	Uninterrupted integer range
int	31	9	0 to $2^{31} - 1 \approx 2 * 10^9$
long	63	18	0 to $2^{63} - 1 \approx 9 * 10^{18}$
float	24	7	0 to $2^{24} - 1 \approx 16 * 10^6$
double	53	15	0 to $2^{53} - 1 \approx 9 * 10^{15}$

POP QUIZ 5 Choose a data type and an initial value for variable x in such a way that the loop `while (x+1==x) {}` goes on forever.

Using floats as array indices isn't a terribly good idea and will work satisfactorily only as long as the indices stay below the uninterrupted integer range, which is much lower than `Integer.MAX_VALUE`. To see exactly how much lower it is, consider that non-negative integers have 31 significant bits, whereas non-negative floats only have 24 significant bits. Because $31 - 24 = 7$, the threshold for floats is $2^7 = 128$ times smaller than `Integer.MAX_VALUE`.

Funny things will happen if you create more than 2^{24} containers, and you'd be better off placing suitable runtime checks in the `newContainer` method. However, because this chapter is about memory consumption, let's stick to the plan and optimize only one code quality at a time, deferring such robustness considerations to chapter 6. You can find the rest of the source code for *Memory4* in the accompanying online repository (https://bitbucket.org/mfaella/exercisesinstyle).

4.4.1 Space and time complexity

The single static array from *Memory4* requires 4 bytes for the reference to the array, 16 bytes of standard array overhead, and 4 bytes for each actual cell. In this implementation, a given number of containers always takes the same amount of space, regardless of how they're connected. Table 4.8 provides the space estimates for our two usual scenarios.

These extreme memory savings come at a significant performance cost, as shown in table 4.9. Methods `connect` and `addWater` need to figure out the size of a group, given

Table 4.8   Memory requirements of *Memory4*

Scenario	Size (calculations)	Size (bytes)	% of reference
1000 isolated	$4 + 16 + 1000 * 4$	4020	4%
100 groups of 10	$4 + 16 + 1000 * 4$	4020	7%

the index of an arbitrary container in that group. This entails going back to the first container in a group and then visiting the whole virtual list of containers to appraise its length. Finding the first container in a group is tricky: the first container is the only element of the group that's not the target of any `next` pointer. To find it, you must visit the group list backwards, which requires quadratic time.

Table 4.9   Time complexities of *Memory4*

Method	Time complexity
getAmount	$O(n)$
connectTo	$O(n^2)$
addWater	$O(n^2)$

4.5   *Space-time trade-offs*

I'll start by summarizing the space requirements of the four container versions from this chapter and comparing them with *Reference* from chapter 2. (See table 4.10.)

Table 4.10   Memory requirements of all implementations from this chapter, plus *Reference*. Recall that *Memory3* and *Memory4* expose a different, object-less API.

Scenario	Version	Bytes	% of *Reference*
1000 isolated	Reference	108000	100%
	Memory1	20000	19%
	Memory2	20000	19%
	Memory3	8040	7%
	Memory4	4020	4%
100 groups of 10	Reference	61200	100%
	Memory1	29000	47%
	Memory2	25600	42%
	Memory3	4440	7%
	Memory4	4020	7%

As you can see from table 4.10, we managed to obtain significant memory savings by choosing suitable collections and encodings. To go beyond the barrier represented by the per-object overhead, we had to break the API established in chapter 1 and identify containers using integer IDs instead of container objects. All the implementations from this chapter also sacrifice readability and, as a consequence, maintainability. The quest for memory efficiency leads to using lower-level types (mostly arrays) instead of higher-level collections and special encodings, to the point of employing a float as an array index in *Memory4*. Most programming environments frown upon these techniques, but they come up in niche applications that are either severely memory-constrained, like some embedded systems, or need to keep a huge amount of data in main memory.

As I discussed in chapter 1, space and time efficiency are often at odds. This chapter and the previous one provide positive and negative examples of this rule of thumb, as highlighted in figure 4.10. The figure plots the space versus time requirements of the seven implementations from these chapters, plus *Reference* from chapter 2. Recall that *Memory3* and *Memory4* can achieve such noticeable memory savings at the cost of changing the API for containers.

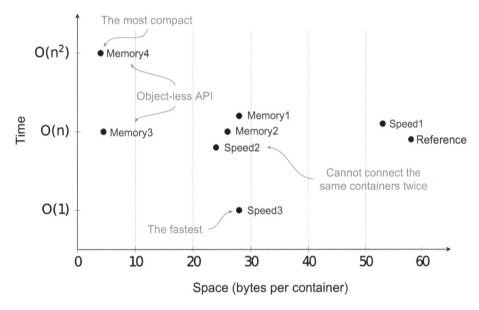

Figure 4.10 **Performance profiles of the implementations from chapters 3 and 4, plus *Reference*. For the space measure, you take the average number of bytes per container in scenario 2 (1000 containers connected in 100 groups of 10). For the time measure, you take the maximum complexity among the three class methods, with the caveat that you're measuring *Speed3* according to amortized complexity.**

The plot confirms that the most advanced implementations from the two chapters are indeed those that maximize the corresponding quality: *Speed3* has the maximum time performance, and *Memory4* the maximum space efficiency. Moreover, squeezing the memory requirements all the way to the approximately 4 bytes per container of *Memory4* raises the time complexity to a quadratic function. This is expected and in line with the typical trade-off between time and space.

On the other hand, *Speed3* excels in both time and space performance, exhibiting a memory footprint whose size is remarkably close to that of *Memory2*, which was the minimum we could achieve without sacrificing our standard API. Hence, in most practical circumstances, except the most memory-constrained, you really should consider *Speed3* to be the best data structure for the job.

4.6   *And now for something completely different*

It's time to apply space-saving techniques to a different scenario: meet *multi-sets*. A multi-set is a set that can contain duplicate elements. So, the multi-set $\{a, a, b\}$ is different from $\{a, b\}$, but it's indistinguishable from $\{a, b, a\}$ because the order of its elements doesn't matter.

Design a space-efficient multi-set implementation, called `MultiSet<T>`, supporting the following methods:

- `public void add(T elem)`—Inserts `elem` into the multi-set
- `public long count(T elem)`—Returns the number of occurrences of `elem` in the multi-set

Use the following questions as guidelines in comparing and choosing among different implementations:

1 Assume you insert n distinct objects multiple times, for a total of m insertions (so, m is at least as much as n). How many bytes does your implementation need for storing them?
2 What is the time complexity of `add` and `count` in your implementation?

It turns out there are two space-optimal implementations, depending on how many duplicates you expect.

4.6.1   *Low duplicate count*

If you expect few duplicates, you can use a single array of objects and append every inserted object at the end, both when it's the first appearance and when it's a duplicate.

As discussed in this chapter, using an `ArrayList` instead of a plain array makes perfect sense because it consumes only slightly more memory but greatly simplifies your implementation. Moreover, unlike arrays, `ArrayLists` work nicely with generics.

You should obtain something like the following:

```
public class MultiSet<T> {
   private List<T> data = new ArrayList<>();

   public void add(T elem) {
      data.add(elem);
   }
   public long count(T elem) {
      long count = 0;
      for (T other: data) {
         if (other.equals(elem)) {
            count++;
```

```
        }
    }
    return count;
}
}
```

Using the newer stream library, you can rewrite the `count` method as the following one-liner:

```
public long count(T elem) {
    return data.stream().filter(x -> x.equals(elem)).count();
}
```

The `add` method takes constant (amortized) time (recall section 3.3.5) and `count` takes linear time. The memory footprint after m insertions of n distinct objects is $56 + 4 * m$ bytes (independently of n), which breaks down as follows:

- 12 bytes for overhead of the `MultiSet` object
- 4 bytes for the reference to the `ArrayList`
- 40 bytes for a barebone `ArrayList` (see table 4.4)
- $4 * m$ bytes for the references to the elements of the multi-set

4.6.2 *High duplicate count*

If duplicates are common, you're better off using two arrays: one to hold the objects themselves and one to hold the number of repetitions for each object. If you're familiar with the collection framework, you'll recognize that this would be the perfect job for a `Map`. However, both standard implementations of `Map` (`HashMap` and `TreeMap`) are linked structures that take a lot more memory than two `ArrayLists`.

You end up with something like the following:

```
public class MultiSet<T> {
    private List<T> elements = new ArrayList<>();
    private List<Long> repetitions = new ArrayList<>();
    ...
```

I'll leave the rest of the implementation to you as an exercise. Just make sure that the i-th element of `repetitions` (the one you get from `repetitions.get(i)`) is the number of repetitions of the object `elements.get(i)`.

As far as performance is concerned, insertion needs to scan the first array to figure out whether the object is new or a duplicate. In the worst case, both methods `add` and `count` take linear time.

The resulting memory footprint after m insertions of n distinct objects is $100 + 28 * n$ bytes (independently of m) because of the following contributions:

- 12 bytes for overhead of the `MultiSet` object
- $2 * 4$ bytes for the references to the two `ArrayLists`
- $2 * 40$ bytes for two barebone `ArrayLists`
- $4 * n$ bytes to store references to each unique element (the first array)

- $(4 + 20) * n$ bytes to store a `Long` counter for each unique element (the second array) (Each `Long` object takes $12 + 8 = 20$ bytes.)

This two-array solution is the most memory-efficient if $100 + 28 * n < 56 + 4 * m$, that is, if on average each object is present at least seven times $(m > 11 + 7 * n)$.

4.7   Real-world use cases

In chapters 3 and 4, I discussed the two major factors that affect the efficiency of an algorithm: time and space. We've seen that it's possible to solve a problem using different approaches (for example, using an `ArrayList` instead of a `HashSet` to store a group of containers). As it turns out, choosing one approach over another results in a trade-off between time and space efficiency. The best choice depends on the context of the problem you need to solve. Let's look at a couple of use cases where space efficiency is important.

- In machine learning, everything revolves around datasets. Datasets are commonly represented as a dense matrix of rows of historical instances that include properties of interest, called *features* or *variables*. Consider a more complicated dataset consisting of a directed graph where the nodes are web pages and directed edges represent links between them. Theoretically, it's entirely possible to represent this dataset using an adjacency matrix. An adjacency matrix is a square matrix where rows and columns represent the nodes of the graph (web pages) and matrix values indicate whether an edge (link) exists from one web page to another (value 1) or not (value 0). If the graph is sparse, most of the matrix cells remain unused, leading to a waste of memory. In this case, you may have to consider using a representation that's memory-efficient but sacrifices time efficiency.
- Smartphones these days sport almost as much memory as a standard laptop, but that wasn't true when Google was designing the Android OS in the early 2000s. Android is also meant to run on other devices that have a lot less memory than a modern phone. Therefore, you can find several traces of memory-efficiency concerns throughout its API. For example:
  - The `android.util` package contains several classes providing memory-efficient alternatives to the standard Java collections. For example, `SparseArray` is a memory-efficient implementation of a map (aka an associative array) from integer keys to objects. (By the way, exercise 2 in this chapter asks you to analyze this class.)
  - All Android classes pertaining to graphics use single-precision `float` values instead of `double`s for coordinates, rotation angles, and so on. For example, see the class `android.graphics.Camera`.
- XML is widely used to exchange data between heterogeneous systems. It's a common pattern that an application parses the XML, stores the contents in a

relational database, and finally stores the XML itself as a BLOB. Subsequent business logic and queries are performed using the relational schema, and the event of requesting to retrieve the original XML is rare. Therefore, it might be more appropriate to design a space-efficient process that compresses the XML documents before storing them in the database.

4.8   Applying what you learned

EXERCISE 1
Read the description of a multi-set in section 4.6. The Google Guava library (https:// github.com/google/guava) contains a `Multiset` interface, and various implementations thereof, in the package `com.google.common.collect`. The main methods of `Multiset<E>` are the following:

- `public boolean add(E elem)`—Inserts `elem` into the multi-set and returns `true` (for compatibility with the `Collection` interface)
- `public int count(Object elem)`—Returns the number of occurrences of `elem` in the multi-set.

Check out the source code for the `HashMultiset` class and answer the following questions.
1. What's the time complexity of its `add` and `count` methods?
2. Would you say this class is optimized for space, time, or a compromise between the two?

Hint: You'll need to peek at the source code of both `HashMultiset` and its abstract superclass `AbstractMapBasedMultiSet`.

EXERCISE 2
The Android class `android.util.SparseArray` is a memory-efficient implementation of an array of objects, whose indices can be arbitrary integers instead of a contiguous interval starting at 0. As such, it's a replacement for `Map<Integer,Object>`. Internally, it uses two arrays: one for the indices (aka the *keys*) and one for the objects (aka the *values*).

Check out the source code for the `android.util.SparseArray` class (http://mng.bz /DNZA) and answer the following questions:
1. How much memory does an empty `SparseArray` created with `new SparseArray()` need?
2. How much memory does a `SparseArray` need that contains 100 objects with contiguous indices 0–99 (not counting the memory occupied by the objects themselves)?
3. How much memory does a `SparseArray` need that contains 100 objects with random integer indices?

EXERCISE 3
In section 3.3, you learned that in *Speed3* only containers that are representatives for their group use their `amount` and `size` fields. For the other containers, those fields

are irrelevant. Refactor *Speed3* to lessen this memory inefficiency, without changing its public API.

Hint: Consider that container objects are created before they're connected, that clients can hold references to them, and that objects can't dynamically change their type in Java.

EXERCISE 4 (MINI-PROJECT)

The class `UniqueList<E>` represents a fixed-size indexed list without duplicates and exposes the following public interface:

- `public UniqueList(int capacity)`—Creates an empty `UniqueList` with the specified capacity.
- `public boolean set(int index, E element)`—Inserts the given element at the given index and returns `true`, provided the index lies between 0 and `capacity - 1` and the element isn't present at another index. Otherwise, it doesn't change the list and returns `false`.
- `public E get(int index)`—Returns the element at the given index, or `null` if the index is invalid or empty (unassigned).

With that interface in mind, do the following:

1. Implement the `UniqueList` class in a space-efficient way.
2. Implement the `UniqueList` class in a time-efficient way.

Summary

- High-level collections like `HashSet` generally improve performance and code readability but incur greater memory overhead than low-level alternatives.
- When in desperate need of space, you may avoid object overhead by switching to integer IDs.
- Storing data in contiguous memory improves performance because of cache locality.
- Floating-point numbers have a wider range than integers but varying resolution.

Answers to quizzes and exercises

POP QUIZ 1

Only one copy of each string literal is actually stored in memory, thanks to a mechanism known as *string interning*.

As to the memory taken by a single "Hello World" string, before Java 9 it would have been represented as UTF-16: 2 bytes per character. Starting from Java 9, the *compact string* functionality recognizes that this particular string contains only ASCII characters and switches to a one-byte-per-character encoding. In both cases, the characters are stored in a byte array. On top of the actual characters, you have to add

- 12 bytes of `String` object overhead
- 4 bytes to cache the string hash code
- 4 bytes for the reference to the byte array
- 1 byte for the flag that specifies the encoding (traditional or compact)
- 16 bytes of overhead for the byte array

In sum, a single copy of "Hello World" (11 characters) takes

$$11 + 12 + 4 + 4 + 1 + 16 = 48 \text{ bytes.}$$

POP QUIZ 2

Two contrasting language design choices limit the cooperation between arrays and generics:

- The compiler erases unbounded type parameters and replaces them with `Object`.
- Arrays store their static type (and use it to check every array write).

As a consequence, if `new T[10]` was legal, the newly created array would behave just like `new Object[10]`. But that's not what the programmer would expect—hence the decision to declare the first expression illegal.

POP QUIZ 3

Yes, a call to `set.contains(x)` may have a slight positive impact on a subsequent call to `set.contains(y)` because the first call loads into the cache a part of the array of buckets of that `HashSet`. (See figure 2.7 to recall the internal structure of a `HashSet`.) If objects `x` and `y` have similar hash codes, the second call may find the reference to the bucket of `y` in the cache.

The same conclusion applies to a `TreeSet`, for a different reason. A `TreeSet` is an entirely linked data structure, where searching for an element involves following a path in a tree. The second call, `set.contains(y)`, may benefit from finding in the cache the first nodes in the path leading to `y`. (All paths start from the same root node, so at least that node is likely to still be in the cache.)

POP QUIZ 4

Singleton classes are a common way to offer a single point of access to some low-level service. You create a singleton class by declaring a private constructor as the only constructor and providing a public method that always returns the same instance. That instance is normally stored in a private static field of the class.

If the single instance is created on demand upon the first method call (*lazy initialization*), you have to be extra careful about thread-safety issues. This is known as the *safe initialization* problem, and you can read more about it in the book *Java Concurrency in Practice*, by Brian Goetz and others (see the *Further reading* list for chapter 8).

POP QUIZ 5

You can choose type `float` or `double` for variable `x`, and an initial value beyond the uninterrupted integer range of that type; for example, `float x = 1E8`.

This is one of the many fun quizzes in the book *Java Puzzlers*, by Joshua Bloch and Neal Gafter.

EXERCISE 1

Start your exploration from the concrete class `HashMultiset`, which extends `AbstractMapBasedMultiset` and uses the support class `Count` (in the `super` line), representing an integer that can be modified in place—a mutable version of `Integer`.

```
public final class HashMultiset<E> extends AbstractMapBasedMultiset<E> {

    public static <E> HashMultiset<E> create() {   ❶ Factory method
        return new HashMultiset<E>();
    }

    private HashMultiset() {   ❷ Private constructor
        super(new HashMap<E, Count>());   ❸ Calls the superclass constructor
    }
```

As you can see, a public factory method creates an empty `HashMultiset` (`public static` line), which invokes a private constructor (`private` line), which in turn forwards a new `HashMap` to a superclass constructor (`super` line). Next, take a look at the relevant portion of the superclass `AbstractMapBasedMultiSet`, where you'll find the actual instance field (`backingMap` in the following snippet) that supports the whole implementation:

```
abstract class AbstractMapBasedMultiset<E> extends AbstractMultiset<E>
                                        implements Serializable {
    private transient Map<E, Count> backingMap;
```

These snippets are sufficient to infer that the internal structure of a `HashMultiset` is a map from objects to integers, that a `HashMap` implements, storing the number of occurrences of each element. Just like `HashSet` is a time-efficient implementation of `Set`, so is `HashMap` with respect to `Map`.[2] Both classes focus on time efficiency at the expense of memory occupancy. You can now answer the two questions posed by the exercise:

1. The methods `add` and `count` have constant time complexity because they make a constant number of calls to the basic methods of `HashMap`, which in turn have constant time complexity. The usual caveats of hashed data structures apply: the hash function the `hashCode` method provides must spread objects uniformly over the range of integers.

2. The class `HashMultiset` is optimized for time efficiency.

EXERCISE 2

First, consider the instance fields of `SparseArray`, listed in the following code fragment. The `mGarbage` field is a flag used to delay the actual removal of an element until its absence is made visible (a form of *laziness*, as discussed in chapter 3).

---

[2] Internally, a `HashSet` is in fact a `HashMap` where all keys share the same dummy value.

```
public class SparseArray<E> implements Cloneable {
    private boolean  mGarbage = false;
    private int[]    mKeys;
    private Object[] mValues;
    private int      mSize;
```

Next, the following are the two (abridged) constructors involved when you make a call like `new SparseArray()`. The `mValues` line is an Android-specific way of efficiently allocating an array.

```
    public SparseArray() {
        this(10);    ❷ Default initial capacity: 10 items
    }
    public SparseArray(int initialCapacity) {
        ...
        mValues = ArrayUtils.newUnpaddedObjectArray(initialCapacity);
        mKeys = new int[mValues.length];
        mSize = 0;
    }
```

The previous snippets are sufficient to answer the questions:

1. You have learned in this chapter and in chapter 2 about the size of objects and arrays. You should be able to figure out the size of all fields of `SparseArray`, except the `mGarbage` field because I haven't specifically discussed the `boolean` primitive type. Even if you can encode its value in a single bit, its memory footprint is dependent on the VM. In the current version of HotSpot, each `boolean` takes one byte, which is the smallest unit of memory the CPU can address. As usual in this book, I'm ignoring the issue of padding, which inflates objects to align them to addresses that are multiples of 8.

That said, an empty `SparseArray` requires

- 12 bytes for the `SparseArray` object overhead
- 12 bytes for the fields `mKeys`, `mValues`, and `mSize`
- 1 byte for the `mGarbage` field
- 16 bytes of array overhead for `mKeys`
- 10*4 bytes for the initial `mKeys` array of length 10
- 16 bytes of array overhead for `mValues`
- 10*4 bytes for the initial `mValues` array of length 10

for a grand total of 137 bytes.

2. A `SparseArray` with 100 objects indexed from 0 to 99 needs its two arrays `mKeys` and `mValues` to have a length of (at least) 100. You can adapt the calculations for question 1 and obtain a result of 857 bytes.

3. The values of the indices have no effect on the structure of a `SparseArray`. That's exactly the meaning of "sparse" in its name. As a result, the memory footprint in this scenario is the same as in question 2: 857 bytes.

EXERCISE 3

To achieve maximal space efficiency, normal containers should only hold a `parent` field, of type `Container`. For group representatives (that is, tree roots), that field points to a special object holding the `amount` and `size` fields. The type of that support object must be a subclass of `Container`, and you'll need a downcast to convert it from its apparent `Container` class to its effective subclass.

This solution shrinks the memory footprint of normal containers, but it increases the size of group representatives because it adds an extra object that you didn't need in *Speed3*. It improves space efficiency only when most containers are connected to one another, forming few groups.

You can find the source code for this exercise in the online repository (https://bit bucket.org/mfaella/exercisesinstyle) as class `eis.chapter4.exercises.Container`.

EXERCISE 4

1. Container version *Memory2* shows that the memory savings you obtain by a plain array compared to an `ArrayList` are insignificant, so for the space-efficient version of `UniqueList`, you should use an `ArrayList`. However, that means that checking whether an element belongs to the list will take linear time.

Two issues complicate the implementation:

- You can only use methods `set` and `get` from the `List` interface with an index that's already occupied. The constructor needs to initially fill the list with the required number of `null` values.
- Methods `set` and `get` throw an exception if the index is out of range, whereas the specifications for this exercise require special return values (`false` and `null`, respectively). That's why you need to manually check that the index is in range.

The resulting code looks like this:

```
public class CompactUniqueList<E> {
   private final ArrayList<E> data;

   public CompactUniqueList(int capacity) {
      data = new ArrayList<>(capacity);
      for (int i=0; i<capacity; i++)  {    ❶ Fills with nulls
         data.add(null);
      }
      assert data.size() == capacity;    ❷ Sanity check
   }

   public boolean set(int index, E element) {
      if (index<0 || index>=data.size() || data.contains(element))
         return false;
      data.set(index, element);    ❸ Would throw an exception on illegal index
      return true;
   }

   public E get(int index) {
      if (index<0 || index>=data.size())
```

```
        return null;
    return data.get(index);   ❹ Would throw an exception on illegal index
    }
}
```

2. In a time-efficient implementation, we'd like all operations to run as fast as possible, ideally in constant time. In this case, you can cause that to happen by storing the elements in two data structures at the same time: a *list* for fast indexed retrieval and a *set* for fast rejection of duplicates. Here are the fields:

```
public class FastUniqueList<E> {
    private final ArrayList<E> dataByIndex;
    private final Set<E> dataSet;
```

The constructor and the `get` method are very similar to the previous case, and you can find them in the online repository (https://bitbucket.org/mfaella/exercisesinstyle). Only the `set` method shows the interplay of the two fields.

```
    public boolean set(int index, E element) {
        if (index<0 || index>=dataByIndex.size() || dataSet.contains(element))
            return false;
        E old = dataByIndex.set(index, element);   ❶ Returns the object
        dataSet.remove(old);                              previously at this index
        dataSet.add(element);
        return true;
    }
```

Further reading

I don't think you'll find books entirely devoted to memory-saving techniques. Squeezing more data into less space usually leads to cumbersome encodings and obscure programs, such as *Memory4*, and code clarity is much more precious than memory in most circumstances.

What you can do to limit memory consumption while keeping the code readable is choose more space-efficient data structures, as you did in *Memory1* when switching from `HashSet` to `ArrayList`. To learn more about the time and space complexity of standard algorithms and data structures, check out the textbooks I mentioned at the end of chapter 3.

You can find additional useful advice in the following books:

- Scott Oaks. *Java Performance: The Definitive Guide.* O'Reilly Media, 2014.
  Among a plethora of performance-enhancing techniques, this book allots a chapter to memory best practices, including tools to ascertain which objects are occupying the most memory and various memory-saving tips.
- E. White. *Making Embedded Systems.* O'Reilly Media, 2011.
  The aptly titled *Doing More with Less* chapter from this book contains useful memory-saving advice for embedded programming, focused on shrinking both the code segment and the data segment of a program.

Self-conscious code: Reliability through monitoring

This chapter covers

- Writing method specifications in contract form
- Enforcing contracts at runtime
- Using assertions
- Checking class invariants as a lightweight alternative to postconditions

Software reliability refers to the extent to which the system performs as expected, in a variety of operating conditions. In this chapter, we'll explore the main coding techniques you can use to prevent or expose unexpected program behaviors. But first, let's discuss how you can *define* the expected behavior of a piece of software, aka its *specification*. In line with the structure of this book, I'll focus on the behavior of a single class, such as `Container`. A popular way to organize specifications of OO programs and classes therein is through the *design-by-contract* methodology.

117

5.1   Design by contract

In ordinary language, a contract is an agreement in which each party accepts obligations in exchange for some benefits. In fact, what's an obligation for one party is the benefit of another. For example, a phone plan is a contract between a carrier and the phone owner. The carrier is obliged to render the phone service, and the owner is obliged to pay for it, so each party benefits from the other party's obligations.

The design-by-contract methodology suggests attaching contracts to software artifacts, particularly individual methods. A method contract comprises a *precondition*, a *postcondition*, and possibly a *penalty*.

5.1.1   Pre- and postconditions

The precondition states the requirements for the method to correctly function. It talks about the legal values for the parameters and about the current state of this object (for an instance method). For example, the precondition of a square-root method might state that its argument should be non-negative.

It's the caller's responsibility to respect the precondition of the method being called. In the analogy with an ordinary contract, the precondition is an obligation for the caller and a benefit for the callee. The method itself can either passively assume that the precondition holds or actively check whether it holds, and react accordingly.

The precondition should include only properties that are under the full control of the caller. For example, a method that takes a file name as an argument and opens that file can't list among its preconditions that the file exists, because the caller can't be 100% sure that it does. (Another process can erase that file at any time.) The method can still throw an exception in that case, but that exception will be of the *checked* variety, forcing the caller to handle it.

Conversely, the postcondition states the effect of the method and describes its return value and all the changes performed on the state of any object. In most well-designed classes, changes should be limited to the current object, but this isn't always the case. For example, the connectTo method in our running example must modify multiple containers to achieve its intended effect.

Pure methods and side effects

A method whose only effect is to return a value is called *pure*. Any other consequence, be it printing on screen or updating an instance field, is called a *side effect*. When called twice on the same arguments, a pure method returns the same result, a property known as *referential transparency*. (Recall that the current object is an implicit input to an instance method.) Functional languages, such as Haskell or Scheme, are based on the notions of pure functions and referential transparency. However, any useful program must eventually interact with its runtime environment, so functional languages wrap those necessary side effects into specially identified modules.

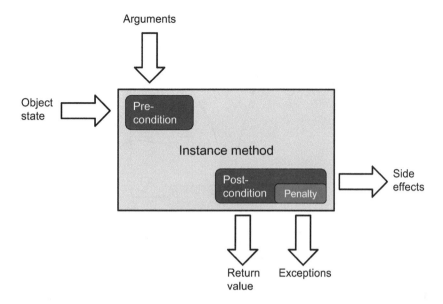

Figure 5.1 The high-level structure of a contract for an instance method. All consequences of a method besides its return value are called side effects.

The postcondition also should specify what happens when the caller violates a precondition: this is referred to as a *penalty*. In Java, the typical penalty consists of throwing an unchecked exception. Figure 5.1 is a graphical depiction of the contract for an instance method.

POP QUIZ 1 What's wrong with throwing a *checked* exception as a penalty?

For example, here's the contract for the `next` method of the `java.util.Iterator` interface:

1. *Precondition*—This iterator hasn't reached the end. Equivalently, a call to `has Next` would return `true`.
2. *Postcondition*—It returns the next item in the iteration and advances the iterator by one position.
3. *Penalty*—If the precondition is violated, the method throws `NoSuchElement Exception` (an unchecked exception).

Calling `next` when the iterator has already reached the end violates the precondition and is an error on the side of the client. (The error is outside the `next` method.) Conversely, an implementation of `next` that doesn't advance the iterator to the next item is violating the postcondition. In this case, the error lies inside the method itself.

Figure 5.2 depicts the detailed data dependencies involving various parts of the contract. The precondition dictates the legal values for the arguments and for the state of this object before the call. That's why two arrows are coming into the "precondition"

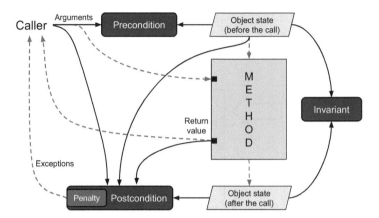

Figure 5.2   Detailed structure of a contract for an instance method. Solid arrows represent data dependencies pertaining to the contract (what the contract talks about). Dashed arrows are standard runtime interactions that occur regardless of the contract (what actually happens at runtime).

box. For example, the precondition of `Iterator::next` mentions only the state of the iterator because that method takes no arguments.

Because the postcondition describes all the changes that the method brings about, it may refer to the following data:

- The return value (as the main effect of the method)
- Both the old and new state of this object: the old state as an input that can influence the behavior of the method, and the new state as another effect of the method
- The value of the arguments, as inputs
- Other side effects that globally available objects or static methods produce, such as a call to `System.out.println`

Figure 5.2 omits the last case and depicts the others as incoming arrows into the "postcondition" box. For example, the postcondition of `Iterator::next` refers explicitly to the return value, and implicitly to both the old and new state of the iterator, when it says that "it returns the next item and advances the iterator by one position."

5.1.2   *Invariants*

Besides method contracts, classes can have associated *invariants*. An invariant is a condition, regarding the class fields, that's always true, except while an object is undergoing change due to a method of the class.

Invariants are *static consistency rules*: they refer to the state of the objects at a single instant in time. On the other hand, postconditions are *dynamic consistency rules* because they compare the state of the object(s) before and after a method call.

As the name implies, invariants must hold both before and after a method is called. Accordingly, in figure 5.2, invariants have incoming arrows from the old and new state of the object.

The initial state of each object, which a constructor establishes, must satisfy the invariants, and all public methods are responsible for preserving their validity. Private methods don't have this obligation because their role is to support public methods. As a result, when a private instance method runs, it's typically within the context of some ongoing public instance method that invoked it, either directly or indirectly. Because the current object may be undergoing change, the private method may find it in an intermediate state that violates an invariant, and may also leave it in an inconsistent state. It's only at the end of the public method that the state of the object must be consistent again, and invariants must be restored.

5.1.3 *Correctness and robustness*

You can refine software reliability into two qualities: correctness and robustness. The difference between them lies in the type of environment you assume for your system. When evaluating correctness, you imagine your system in a *nominal* environment, that is, an environment satisfying the system expectations. In such a friendly context, method preconditions are honored, external inputs arrive in a timely manner and in the right format, and all resources that the system needs are available. If the system is correct, it will behave according to plan in all friendly environments.

In principle, correctness is a Boolean property: either it holds or it doesn't. Partial correctness doesn't make a lot of sense. However, it's usually impractical to devise perfectly formal and complete specifications, and as soon as specifications become blurry, so does correctness. In the little controlled world of the container example, we'll put forward clear specifications and make sure the class is correct with respect to them. Then, we'll explore techniques that maximize our *confidence* in its correctness. Those techniques will be useful in real-world scenarios when you don't have months to spend over a single class, as I had when writing this book.

On the other hand, robustness refers to system behavior under exceptional or unanticipated environments. Typical cases include the host machine running out of memory or disk space, external inputs being in the wrong format or outside the legal range, methods being called in breach of their preconditions, and so on. A robust system is expected to react *gracefully* in such situations, where the appropriate definition of *grace* is highly dependent on the context.

For example, if a crucial resource is unavailable, the program might try to wait a little and request it again, a couple of times, before giving up and terminating. If the problem persists, and, more generally, whenever termination is the only way out, the program should clearly inform the user about the nature of the problem. In addition, it should strive to minimize data loss so the user can later resume their task as smoothly as possible.

> **POP QUIZ 2** If a program prints some output on paper, what's a graceful reaction to the printer being out of paper?

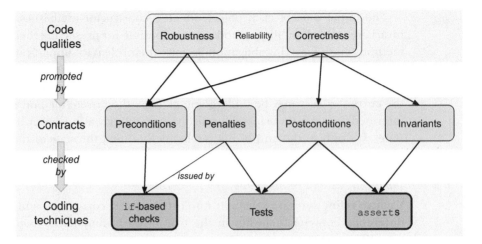

Figure 5.3   Relationship between reliability attributes, contract-based specifications, and coding techniques

Figure 5.3 summarizes the relationships between the two software qualities that constitute reliability, the various types of specifications I discussed earlier, and the three coding techniques you'll use in this chapter and the next.

Correctness is defined with respect to a contract, comprising pre- and postconditions, and optionally to a set of class invariants. The penalty is not directly related to correctness because it only springs into action when the caller violates a precondition. As such, it's a robustness issue.

Three coding techniques help implement and enforce contracts:

- Plain `if`-based checks make sure the caller is invoking a method in the proper way, obeying its preconditions, and issue a corresponding penalty otherwise.
- Java `assert` statements are useful to keep postconditions and invariants in check, particularly in safety-critical software.
- Finally, tests increase your confidence in the reliability of your software, mostly by checking postconditions and triggering penalties.

In this chapter and the next, I'll delve into the best practices regarding each of these techniques. For the moment, notice that the first two are *monitoring* techniques, active during regular operation of your software. Testing instead is performed before operation and separately from it.

5.1.4   *Checking contracts*

Many programming errors have to do with violating method preconditions. To expose these problems as early as possible, methods should check their preconditions at runtime and throw a suitable exception if they're not met. This is sometimes called *defensive programming*. Two standard exception classes are commonly used for this purpose:

- `IllegalArgumentException`—The value of an argument violates the precondition.

- `IllegalStateException`—The current state of this object is incompatible with the instance method being called or with the value of the arguments. For example, attempting to read from a file that already has been closed might throw this exception.

Assertions represent a related but more specific checking mechanism. An assertion is a statement of the following form:

```
assert condition : "Error message!";
```

When executed, the line evaluates the Boolean condition and throws an `Assertion Error` if the condition is false. The error message string is passed into the exception being thrown and will be printed out if the exception isn't caught. In other words, the assertion is quite similar to the following statement:

```
if (!condition) {
   throw new AssertionError("Error message!");
}
```

At this point, an assertion looks like a shorter version (aka *syntactic sugar*) of a regular `if`-based check. However, one crucial feature distinguishes the two: by default, the JVM does *not* execute assertions. You have to explicitly activate them with the "-ea" command-line option or via the corresponding IDE setting. When you have assertions turned off, the program doesn't incur the performance overhead due to evaluating the corresponding Boolean conditions.

A standard `if`-based check is always executed, but if an assertion performs that check instead, you'll be able to turn it on or off at each execution. The usual practice is to turn on assertions during development and then revert to the default "off" state for production. It seems that assertions win all the way: they're more succinct, and you have more control over them. Should you use them for *all* runtime error checking? It turns out that in some cases the flexibility that comes with assertions becomes a liability. In those cases, you want some checks to stay in place at all times, even during production.

C# assertions

C# assertions differ from Java's in two respects: you realize them by invoking static methods `Debug.Assert` and `Trace.Assert`, and their execution is controlled at compile time, instead of runtime. The compiler ignores calls to `Debug.Assert` when it compiles the program in release mode, whereas it always compiles and executes calls to `Trace.Assert`.

Design by contract provides simple guidelines for identifying which checks should always be on:

- Precondition checks on public methods should always be on, so you should use regular `if`-based checks for them.

- All other checks should be on only during development. These include post-condition and invariant checks, and precondition checks on nonpublic methods. Use assertions there.

The rationale is the following. Precondition violations are due to the caller not respecting the method contract. On the other hand, a postcondition or invariant violation is due to an issue within the class itself. Consider the following key assumption:

> Development and testing ensure that each single class is free from internal issues.

By an *internal issue*, I mean a bug that manifests itself even if the class clients respect all the rules that the contracts put forward. For the moment, take this assumption at face value; I'll discuss its plausibility in a second. If the previous assumption holds, the only way the program can misbehave is by a class misusing another class. In a properly encapsulated system, this can happen only via public methods. Hence, to expose these bugs, precondition checks on public methods are sufficient, and you should leave them on. Notice that checking preconditions at runtime doesn't fix the problem, it merely exposes it as early as possible during the execution so you can more accurately characterize the root cause.

How reasonable is the no-internal-issue assumption? That ultimately depends on the quality and intensity of the development process. The higher the quality and intensity, the more likely the assumption is to hold. By quality of the development process, I mean whether the developers follow the industry's best practices. Intensity (or effort) refers to the number of people and amount of time used to develop, and especially test, each class. For example, you can only expect small classes to be entirely free from internal issues. For good reason, writing small classes is one of the sacred best practices in OOP.

5.1.5   *The broader picture*

Figure 5.4 puts the techniques presented in this chapter and the next into a wider perspective. This book focuses on programming styles and techniques that even a single programmer can employ in their daily activities. Beyond that, at least two more types of intervention can contribute to software quality in general, and to reliability in particular.

First, there's human oversight: having a fellow developer look at your code and evaluate it according to company standards. You can arrange this in periodic reviews or sometimes as a continuous interaction between two colleagues, a practice known as *pair programming*.

Then, some software tools can automatically check a variety of code properties, enriching the scrutiny that the compiler already performs. You can divide such tools roughly into three categories, from the most basic to the most advanced:

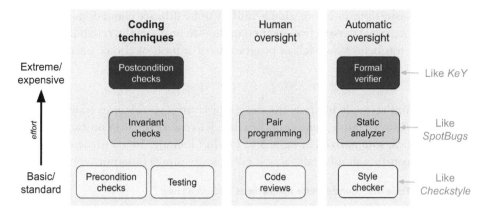

Figure 5.4 A broad view on quality-enhancing techniques.

- *Style checkers*—These tools only perform relatively superficial checks targeting readability and uniformity (discussed in chapter 7). In turn, those qualities also indirectly benefit reliability and maintainability.

  Example feature: Check that the indentation is correct and uniform (same number of extra spaces for each nesting level)

  Example tool: CheckStyle[1]

- *Static analyzers*—These tools are capable of performing a semantic analysis similar to the compiler's type-checking phase. Style checkers and static analyzers are also known as *linters*.

  Example feature: Checks whether an anonymous class contains an uncallable method (a method that doesn't override another method and that other methods of that class don't use)

  Example tools: SpotBugs,[2] SonarQube[3]

- *Formal verifiers*—These tools, mostly born out of academic research, understand a program at a deeper level than the typical compiler. That is, they can simulate the execution of the program on entire sets of values, a process known as *symbolic execution.*

  Example feature: Check whether an integer variable can ever become negative[4]

  Example tool: KeY[5]

It's usually up to your organization to choose the set of quality practices and tools it deems appropriate to the task at hand. What's suitable for developing a videogame is

---

[1] As of this writing, available at https://checkstyle.sourceforge.io.

[2] As of this writing, available at https://spotbugs.github.io.

[3] As of this writing, available at www.sonarqube.org.

[4] Technically, this property is undecidable. A formal verifier will *attempt* to prove or disprove it, but it's not guaranteed to succeed.

[5] As of this writing, available at www.key-project.org.

vastly different from what a military or healthcare client demands. Now, let's go back to our usual perspective, focused on how to improve the reliability of a single unit of code, even before your fellow programmers or tools of choice have a chance to look at it.

5.2   *Designing containers by contract*

You're ready to apply the design-by-contract guidelines to water containers and their *Reference* implementation. But first, let's figure out the contracts for the container methods, summarized in table 5.1. I didn't include the constructor in the table because its contract simply states that it creates an empty container.

Table 5.1   Contracts for the methods of `Container`

Method	Precondition	Postcondition	Penalty
getAmount	None.	Returns the current amount in this container	None
connectTo	Argument is not `null`.	Merges the two groups of containers and redistributes water	NPE[†]
addWater	If argument is negative, there's enough water in the group.	Distributes water equally to all containers in the group	IAE[‡]

† NPE = `NullPointerException`

‡ IAE = `IllegalArgumentException`

As you can see from table 5.1, the contracts are just a structured way to present the expected behavior of a method, explicitly distinguishing the assumptions from the guarantees. Compared to the method descriptions I provided in chapter 1, these contracts add the description of the preconditions and the corresponding penalties:

- `connectTo` requires its argument to be non-null and is expected to throw `Null PointerException` (NPE) otherwise
- `addWater`, when used with a negative argument, say $-x$, requires the total amount of water in the containers connected to this one to be at least x, or else it will throw `IllegalArgumentException` (IAE).

Those are two standard classes of exceptions, both of which are *unchecked* and subclasses of `RuntimeException`.

The precondition requiring an argument to be non-null is extremely common, as is the confusion about which type of exception is the most appropriate in this case. The sidebar sheds some light on the issue.

NullPointerException vs. IllegalArgumentException

Should you throw NPE or IAE when you receive a forbidden `null` argument? It's perhaps a tribute to programmers' attention to detail that such a question spurred a sequence of StackOverflow questions and answers, as well as being covered by the well-known *Effective Java* book.

Here are the main arguments in favor of the two options. In favor of NPE:

- It makes immediately clear what actual value caused the issue.

In favor of IAE:

- It makes immediately clear that the issue is a precondition violation.
- It's clearly distinguished from a JVM-generated NPE.

Although the arguments for IAE are arguably stronger, convention favors NPE, as witnessed by the authoritative *Effective Java* book (see item 72 in the third edition) and the following utility methods, from the `Objects` class:

```
public static Object requireNonNull(Object x)
public static Object requireNonNull(Object x, String message)
```

Those methods throw an NPE if `x` is `null`, and otherwise return `x` itself. They have served as the suggested way to enforce non-null parameters since Java 7.

Next, consider class invariants. Ideally, invariants should exactly describe what object states are consistent with the contracts. In more detail, they should tell us which values for the fields we can obtain after a series of legal operations. For *Reference*, this leads to the following invariants:

I1. For each container, the `amount` field is non-negative.

I2. Each container belongs to exactly one group.

I3. For each container, the `group` field is not `null` and points to a group containing `this`.

I4. All containers belonging to the same group share the same `amount` value.

Consider how these invariants relate to the contracts in table 5.1. Invariant I1 is intuitively obvious: a container can't include a negative amount of water. The precondition of `addWater` is in charge of defending this invariant against external attacks, that is, attempts to decrease water levels below zero. Invariants I2 and I3 are a consequence of our policy regarding groups of containers: they all start with a single container, then they're merged pairwise. The constructor establishes these invariants, and the `connectTo` method must preserve them by correctly merging groups. Finally, invariant I4 states the relationship between groups and amounts. It's the responsibility of `addWater` and `connectTo` to maintain it, as expressed by their postconditions.

It's an interesting exercise to verify that the four invariants, I1–I4, are *complete*, in the sense that you can build any pool of containers satisfying them from scratch by a legal sequence of constructor and method calls. Moreover, removing any one of the four invariants voids this property.[6]

POP QUIZ 3   Is this a valid invariant for the `Container` class: "Passing zero to `addWater` leaves all containers unchanged"?

Now that we've clearly laid out the contracts and invariants, you can use them to harden *Reference* for correctness and robustness. The path for preconditions and post-conditions is pretty clear: we'll check them at the beginning and end of their method, using `if`-based checks or assertions, according to the guidelines I presented earlier. Regarding invariants, we need to address the issue of when to check them, that is, how often and at which program points. Recall that invariants are supposed to hold at the beginning and end of each (public) method. At one extreme, we might check all invariants at all of those moments. At the other extreme, we might skip all invariant checking because *properly checking pre- and postcondition automatically ensures that invariants hold*. The weakness of the latter approach lays in the word *properly*. Indeed, in the following section, we'll implement a version of `Container` where each method carefully checks its pre- and postconditions, and you'll witness how tricky and expensive it is to perform these checks thoroughly. Then, in section 5.4, we'll replace postconditions with invariants, which are generally easier to check.

All versions of `Container` in this chapter are based on the same fields as *Reference*, repeated here for convenience:

```
public class Container {
    private Set<Container> group;
    private double amount;
```

❶ Containers connected to this one
❷ Amount of water in this container

5.3   *Containers that check their contracts*   *[Contracts]*

In this section, we'll develop a version of `Container` whose methods check both their precondition and their postcondition at each invocation.

5.3.1   *Checking the contract of addWater*

Let's start with the `addWater` method. You've already seen its contract in table 5.1, but I'll repeat it here for convenience:

- *Precondition*—If the argument is negative, there's enough water in the group.
- *Postcondition*—Distributes water equally to all containers in the group.
- *Penalty*—Throws an `IllegalArgumentException`.

The method has a simple precondition that you can check using a standard `if` statement, according to the guidelines I discussed earlier.

You should check the postcondition using assertions so that you can easily turn those checks off in production. So far, I've expressed the postcondition of `addWater` in rather

---

[6] For example, if you remove invariant I1, you admit an isolated container holding a negative amount of water. You can't obtain that scenario with a legal sequence of constructor and method calls.

vague terms. What does it mean to equally distribute the added water? Clearly, at the end of the method, all containers in the group must have the same amount of water. However, that's not the end of the story. The total amount in the whole group should be equal to the old total amount, plus the newly added water. To check this property, you have to store some information at the beginning of the method. Then you use it at the end to compare the way the object state was supposed to change with the way it actually changed.

This situation suggests structuring the method into the following four steps:

1. Check the precondition with a plain `if`.
2. Store the current group amount in some temporary variable so you can check the postcondition later.
3. Perform the actual water-adding operation.
4. Check the postcondition using the data you stored in step 2.

Moreover, keep in mind the following design objective: when assertions are turned off, you want all the time and space overhead of checking postconditions to go away. Consistent with that objective, you should only perform steps 2 and 4 when assertions are enabled. That's easy for step 4: just invoke `postAddWater` as the condition of an assertion. Step 2 is trickier because it's not naturally expressed as an assertion. To turn it into an assertion, you can wrap the assignment into a dummy comparison (see listing 5.1) that's always true. In this case, you can assert that the old group amount is positive. With this trick, the only residual overhead, even when assertions are disabled, is the allocation of the `oldTotal` variable on the stack.[7]

POP QUIZ 4 How do you set a Boolean flag to `true` only if assertions are enabled?

The following listing shows a possible implementation that delegates steps 2 and 4 to two novel support methods.

Listing 5.1 *Contracts*: Method `addWater`

```
public void addWater(double amount) {
    double amountPerContainer = amount / group.size();
    if (this.amount + amountPerContainer < 0) {       ❶ Checks the precondition
        throw new IllegalArgumentException(
                "Not enough water to match the addWater request.");
    }
    double oldTotal = 0;      ❷❶ Saves the postcondition data
    assert (oldTotal = groupAmount()) >= 0;      ❷❶ Dummy assert

    for (Container c: group) {      ❸ The actual update
        c.amount += amountPerContainer;
    }
    assert postAddWater(oldTotal, amount) :      ❹ Checks the postcondition
                "addWater failed its postcondition!";
```

[7] If you don't like the dummy assert trick, an alternative is to set a flag to `true` if assertions are enabled (how? see pop quiz 4), and use regular `if`s to skip certain operations when assertions are disabled.

```
        }
```

The implementation of `addWater` in listing 5.1 delegates two tasks to new support methods: `groupAmount` computes the total amount of water in a group of containers; `postAddWater` is responsible for checking the postcondition of `addWater`. The code for `groupAmount` is trivial, simply adding up the values of all `amount` fields in the current group, as shown in the following listing.

Listing 5.2   *Contracts*: Support method `groupAmount`

```
private double groupAmount() {    ❶ Returns the total amount in the group
    double total = 0;
    for (Container c: group) { total += c.amount; }
    return total;
}
```

The method `postAddWater`, in turn, splits its task into two parts: first it checks that all containers in the current group hold the same amount of water; then it verifies that the total amount in the group is equal to the old amount plus the newly added amount. (The following version of `postAddWater` is tentative—a better version follows.)

Listing 5.3   *Contracts*: Tentative version of support method `postAddWater`

```
private boolean postAddWater(double oldTotal, double addedAmount) {
    return isGroupBalanced() &&
         groupAmount() == oldTotal + addedAmount;    ❶ Exact comparison
}                                                         of doubles

private boolean isGroupBalanced() {    ❷ Checks that all the group
    for (Container x: group) {              shares the same amount
        if (x.amount != amount) return false;
    }
    return true;
}
```

As you can see, checking the postcondition requires more lines of code than the original nonhardened method! The sheer number of lines may lead you to surmise that you're more likely to make a mistake in coding the postcondition check than in writing the original method. Is there a point to this effort? If the check ends up simply repeating the same calculations that the method performed, the effort is clearly pointless. However, if you can find a different, and hopefully simpler, way to check that the outcome is correct, then the two different algorithms are checking each other. Even a mistake in the postcondition routine is an opportunity to refine your understanding of the class at hand.

Now you run this version of `addWater` on a simple example, with assertions on, and... it breaks! The VM reports failure in the postcondition of `addWater`. Here's the code fragment that generates the assertion failure—can you spot the problem?

```
Container a = new Container(), b = new Container(), c = new Container();
a.connectTo(b);
b.connectTo(c);
a.addWater(0.9);
```

The problem lies with the comparison between two double values in `postAddWater` (listing 5.3). If you don't use floating-point numbers on a regular basis, it's easy to forget that they don't behave like ideal real numbers. As a result, sometimes $(a/b) * b$ comes out different from a.

For example, the number 0.9 is not exactly representable in base 2. Its binary expansion is periodic, so it will be stored in an approximate way. When you divide it by 3 and add it to the three containers, more approximations are performed. In the end, when you sum back the amounts from each container in the group, the total comes out slightly different than expected. Summarizing, you're computing the amount of water in the group in two different ways, and then comparing them using `==`. Because of approximations, the two sides won't be exactly equal. Detailed calculations are beyond the scope of this book but within the reach of the resources listed in the *Further reading* section at the end of this chapter. Suffice it to say, in the current situation you get the following values after the call to `addWater`:

expected amount:　0.9

actual amount:　　0.8999999999999999

This suggests that you should almost always do floating-point comparisons with some tolerance for error. How much tolerance depends on the range of numbers you expect to handle. In this case, say the unit for liquids is liters (gallons would work just fine), and our containers will handle tens or hundreds of liters. In this scenario, it's safe to assume you're not interested in single drops of water, so it's reasonable to employ a tolerance of, say, $0.0001 = 10^{-4}$ liters—roughly equal to the amount of water in a drop. You end up with the following improved version of `postAddWater`.

> **Listing 5.4 *Contracts*: support methods `postAddWater` and `almostEqual`**

```
private boolean postAddWater(double oldTotal, double addedAmount) {
    return isGroupBalanced() &&
            almostEqual(groupAmount(), oldTotal + addedAmount);
}

private static boolean almostEqual(double x, double y) {
    final double EPSILON = 1E-4;   ❶ Tolerance for rounding errors
    return Math.abs(x-y) < EPSILON;
}
```

POP QUIZ 5 What happens if you pass "not-a-number" (`Double.NAN`) to `addWater`?

5.3.2 *Checking the contract of connectTo*

Next, let's examine the `connectTo` method and its contract:

- *Precondition*—Argument is not `null`
- *Postcondition*—Merges the two groups of containers and redistributes water
- *Penalty*—Throws `NullPointerException`

This kind of precondition is so common that the JDK provides a standard way to handle it with the `Objects.requireNonNull(arg,msg)` static method. As I explained earlier, that method throws an NPE with a custom message if `arg` is `null`, otherwise returning `arg` itself.

Properly checking the postcondition, in contrast, poses significant challenges. Start by translating the postcondition into a list of practical checks to be performed on the instance fields. Call G the set of containers that `this.group` points to at the end of `connectTo(other)`. The postcondition requires that the following properties hold:

1. G is not `null`, and its elements are all the containers that belonged to the two old groups of `this` and `other`.
2. All containers in G must point back to G via their `group` reference.
3. All containers in G must have the same `amount` value, equal to the total amount in the two old groups divided by the number of containers in G.

To check property 1, you need to store the old groups of `this` and `other` before the merge, that is, at the beginning of `connectTo`. The method could modify those groups, so you need to store a copy of those sets. Property 2 doesn't need any information beforehand; to verify it, it's sufficient to iterate over all containers in G and check that their `group` field points back to G. Finally, checking property 3 requires you to know the value of the `amount` fields before the merge, or at least the sum of those values over all containers connected to `this` or `other`. Summarizing, you need to store the following information, as it stands before the merge:

- A copy of the groups of `this` and `other`
- The total amounts of water in those groups

Introduce a nested class `ConnectPostData` to keep this information together, as shown in the following listing.

Listing 5.5   *Contracts*: Nested class `ConnectPostData`

```
private static class ConnectPostData {      ❶ Stores data needed to check
    Set<Container> group1, group2;            the postcondition
    double amount1, amount2;
}
```

You can now draft the code for `connectTo`, following the same four-step structure as `addWater`. As before, you should try to keep the overhead to a minimum when you have assertions disabled. In listing 5.6, the only overhead that sticks even when you have assertions disabled is the allocation of the `postData` local variable (in the fifth line). You achieve this effect by embedding the call to `saveConnectPostData` into a dummy assert statement that always succeeds (in the sixth line).

The code that actually makes the connection is the same as for *Reference*, so I've omitted it from the following listing for readability.

Listing 5.6 *Contracts*: Method `connectTo` (abridged)

```
public void connectTo(Container other) {
    Objects.requireNonNull(other,           ❶ Checks the precondition
            "Cannot connect to a null container.");
    if (group==other.group) return;

    ConnectPostData postData = null;        ❷ Prepares the postcondition data
    assert (postData = saveConnectPostData(other)) != null;   ❸ Dummy assert

    ...  ❹ The actual operation goes here (same as Reference)

    assert postConnect(postData) :          ❺ Checks the postcondition
            "connectTo failed its postcondition!";
}
```

Methods `saveConnectPostData` and `postConnect`, respectively, store the needed information and use that information to check whether the postcondition holds. They are shown in the following listing.

Listing 5.7 *Contracts*: Methods `saveConnectPostData` and `postConnect`

```
private ConnectPostData saveConnectPostData(Container other) {
    ConnectPostData data = new ConnectPostData();
    data.group1 = new HashSet<>(group);     ❶ Shallow copy
    data.group2 = new HashSet<>(other.group);
    data.amount1 = amount;
    data.amount2 = other.amount;
    return data;
}
private boolean postConnect(ConnectPostData postData) {
    return areGroupMembersCorrect(postData)
        && isGroupAmountCorrect(postData)
        && isGroupBalanced()
        && isGroupConsistent();
}
```

In the name of readability, the `postConnect` method delegates its task to four different methods, whose roles I've summarized in table 5.2.

You've already seen the code for `isGroupBalanced` earlier (listing 5.3). Let's have a quick look at the code to check whether the old groups were properly merged (listing 5.8). It first checks that the new group contains all the members from the two old groups (second and third lines). To make sure that the new group doesn't contain any

Table 5.2   The four methods used to check the postcondition of `connectTo`

Method	Property checked
`areGroupMembersCorrect`	The new group is the union of the two old groups.
`isGroupConsistent`	Each container in the new group points back to the group.
`isGroupAmountCorrect`	The total amount in the new group is the sum of the amounts in the old groups.
`isGroupBalanced`	All containers in the new group have an equal amount of water.

extra members,[8] it checks that the size of the new group is equal to the sum of the sizes of the two old groups (fourth line).

Listing 5.8   *Contracts*: Support method `areGroupMembersCorrect`

```
private boolean areGroupMembersCorrect(ConnectPostData postData) {
    return group.containsAll(postData.group1)
        && group.containsAll(postData.group2)
        && group.size() == postData.group1.size() +
                           postData.group2.size();
}
```

Automatically checked contracts

In this book, I present contracts as a discipline for structuring your designs around clearly defined APIs. Some programming languages and tools take this concept to the next level by allowing you to formally define contracts with an ad-hoc language and have a specialized tool automatically check them, either statically (at compilation time) or dynamically (at runtime).

For example, the Eiffel programming language supports pre- and postconditions via the `require` and `ensure` statements. Not surprisingly, Bertrand Meyer, who was also responsible for the design-by-contract methodology, invented Eiffel. The language even allows postconditions to access the old value of a field on entry to the current method. Then, you can instruct the compiler to translate those contract annotations into runtime checks.

Java doesn't offer native support for contracts, but several tools try to fill this gap, such as KeY (www.key-project.org) and Krakatoa (http://krakatoa.lri.fr). Both support specifications written in the Java Modeling Language and provide semi-automatic static contract verification.

---

[8] It may be argued that the size check is redundant. Indeed, if all containers respect the invariants before the call to `connectTo`, there's no way for `connectTo` to reach any other container that's not in one of the two groups being merged. Even a faulty implementation can produce a *smaller* new group but not a *larger* one.

5.4 *Containers that check their invariants*   *[Invariants]*

The previous section shows how complicated it may be to properly check postconditions. A handy alternative is to periodically verify invariants instead. Recall the invariants I established for *Reference* earlier in this chapter:

I1. For each container, the `amount` field is non-negative.

I2. Each container belongs to exactly one group.

I3. For each container, the `group` field is not `null` and points to a group containing `this`.

I4. All containers belonging to the same group share the same `amount` value.

If the class is correct and its clients use it in the right way (that is, while respecting the preconditions of all methods), all postconditions and invariants will hold. A programming error in a method may trigger a postcondition violation. In turn, a postcondition violation may cause an invariant to fail. Assuming that preconditions are respected, a postcondition violation precedes and causes any invariant violation. On the other hand, a postcondition violation doesn't necessarily show up as an invariant violation.

For example, assume that `addWater` contained the following error: when asked to add x liters of water, it adds only $\frac{x}{2}$ liters instead. Because the method leaves all objects in a legal state, this implementation would pass all invariant checks. That's because invariants are *static consistency rules* that only look at the current state of the object(s). On the other hand, it would miserably fail the postcondition verification that *Contracts* performs.

To summarize, checking postconditions, as we did in the previous section, is generally safer but more expensive. Conversely, checking invariants is easier but also somewhat riskier: some programming errors that a postcondition check may catch might pass the invariant audit.

When are you supposed to check invariants? As I said, in principle you could check them at the beginning and end of all methods, and at the end of all constructors. This is a standard, albeit drastic, solution that you can apply in all contexts. On the other hand, you may want to be a little more subtle, and avoid unnecessary checks, by focusing on those methods that could actually break an invariant.

Assume that you trust the constructor to initially establish all invariants. The constructor from *Reference* is so simple that you can easily count on that. Which methods can break invariants? Invariants are properties of objects' states, so only methods that modify the value of the fields can potentially break an invariant.

Let's examine the three public methods of *Reference*:

- `getAmount` is clearly a read-only method, and therefore it can't break any invariant.
- `addWater` modifies the `amount` field, so it could in principle break invariants I1 and I4 of all the containers it touches.

■ Finally, `connectTo` is the most critical method, because it modifies both fields of many containers. If improperly coded, it could break all invariants for many containers.

Table 5.3 summarizes these observations.

Table 5.3   What each method modifies and which invariants it could break

Method	Modified fields	Invariants it could break
getAmount	None	None
connectTo	amount and group	I1, I2, I3, I4
addWater	amount	I1, I4

One way to avoid unnecessary work is to check an invariant only *at the end of the methods that could break it*. We'll implement these checks using assertions, essentially treating invariants as postconditions of those methods. This simplification is safe, in the sense that you're still able to attribute an invariant violation to the method that caused it. Indeed, since the state of our objects starts in an invariant-abiding condition and is properly encapsulated (that is, private), only public methods can be responsible for tarnishing it. As soon as one public method messes up, you'll witness the error as an assertion failure coming from that method.

According to table 5.3, we can focus on methods `connectTo` and `addWater`. Both of these methods modify the state of multiple objects, so we should check the invariants of all the objects they touch. This is particularly cumbersome for method `connectTo`: according to its contract, an invocation like `a.connectTo(b)` is supposed to modify the state of all containers that, at the start of the method, are connected to either a or b. However, at the point when we plan to check the invariants, that is, at the end of the method, we don't know which containers were previously connected to either a or b, unless we implicitly trust the correctness of the method itself.

5.4.1   *Checking the invariants in connectTo*

As I illustrated in the previous discussion, when it comes to checking the invariants at the end of `connectTo`, you have two options:

1. At the beginning of the method, store (a copy of) the current groups of `this` and `other` so that you can then properly check the invariants on *all* relevant objects.

2. Only check the state of the objects belonging to the single group obtained at the end of the method.

Option 1 is safer, but it resembles the heavy work you ended up doing in the previous section to check the postcondition of `connectTo`. I advise you to pursue option 2, instead, which is more practical and gives partial trust to the method. It assumes that it correctly merges the two preexisting groups into a single one, and it checks all the other properties that the invariants cover.

You should end up with something akin to the following listing, where the invariant-checking task is delegated to a private support method. I'm omitting the central part of `connectTo`, as it's exactly the same as in *Reference*.

Listing 5.9 *Invariants*: Method `connectTo` (abridged) and its support method

```
public void connectTo(Container other) {
    Objects.requireNonNull(other,              ❶ Checks the precondition
                          "Cannot connect to a null container.");

    ...   ❷ The actual operation goes here (same as Reference)

    assert invariantsArePreservedByConnectTo(other) :
            "connectTo broke an invariant!";   ❸ Checks the invariants
}


private boolean invariantsArePreservedByConnectTo(Container other) {
    return group == other.group &&
            isGroupNonNegative() &&
            isGroupBalanced() &&
            isGroupConsistent();
}
```

By choosing option 2, you don't have to save the state of any object at the beginning of `connectTo`. You can just check the precondition (in the second line), perform the connection operation (same as *Reference*), and finally check the (simplified) invariants (in the `assert` line).

Three more support methods are involved in checking the invariants. You've already seen an implementation of `isGroupBalanced` in the previous section. You can see now that it's checking invariant I4. The other two invariant-checking methods are detailed in the following listing.

Listing 5.10 *Invariants*: Two invariant-checking support methods

```
private boolean isGroupNonNegative() {   ❶ Checks invariant I1
    for (Container x: group) {
        if (x.amount < 0) return false;
    }
    return true;
}
private boolean isGroupConsistent() {    ❷ Checks invariants I2, I3
    for (Container x: group) {
        if (x.group != group) return false;
    }
    return true;
}
```

To see that we aren't catching all invariant violations, consider the scenario in figure 5.5. On the left side (Before), three containers are connected into two groups: a is isolated, whereas b and c are connected. We don't care about water amounts in this example; assume they're equal in all containers. This state of affairs satisfies all invariants.

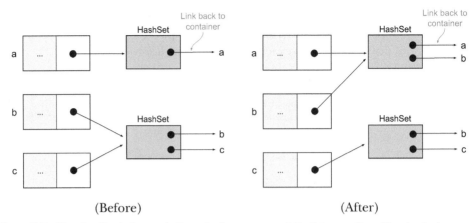

(Before)   (After)

Figure 5.5 The situation before and after a faulty `a.connectTo(b)` operation. The checks in *Invariants* don't catch this type of fault. Water amounts are omitted as unimportant.

Now, imagine that a faulty implementation of `a.connectTo(b)` brings about the situation on the right side (After). Instead of joining all of the containers in a single group, that implementation updates the group of `a` to include `a` and `b`, and container `b` now points to its new group. Meanwhile, container `c` and its group are left untouched. As a consequence, container `c` still "believes" it belongs to a group including `b` and `c`.

This fault breaks invariant I2 because `b` belongs to two different groups, but *Invariants* doesn't detect the problem. Indeed, by choosing option 2 that I described earlier, you'll check only that the two containers being connected (`a` and `b`) point to the same group and that the `group` field of all containers in that group actually points to that group (method `isGroupConsistent`).

The fault in figure 5.5 would be detected if we chose option 1 instead of option 2. Also, *Contracts* would detect it as a postcondition violation.

5.4.2 Checking the invariants in addWater

The implementation of `addWater` follows the same scheme as `connectTo`. As I discussed earlier and summarized in table 5.3, it's enough to check the validity of invariants I1 and I4 because they're the only ones that `addWater` could possibly invalidate.

As you can see in the following listing, invariant verification is delegated to a private support method that invokes two other methods that you've already encountered in the previous sections.

Listing 5.11 *Invariants*: Method `addWater` and its support method

```
public void addWater(double amount) {
    double amountPerContainer = amount / group.size();

    if (this.amount + amountPerContainer < 0) {      ❶ Checks the precondition
        throw new IllegalArgumentException(
            "Not enough water to match the addWater request.");
    }
```

```
    for (Container c: group) {
        c.amount += amountPerContainer;
    }
    assert invariantsArePreservedByAddWater() :      ➋ Checks the invariants
            "addWater broke an invariant!";
}

private boolean invariantsArePreservedByAddWater() {
    return isGroupNonNegative() && isGroupBalanced();
}
```

5.5 And now for something completely different

Let's apply the techniques from this chapter to a different, drier example (no water involved). Consider a class `BoundedSet<T>`, representing a bounded-size set that keeps track of the order of insertion of its elements. In detail, a `BoundedSet` has a fixed maximum size, called its *capacity*, established at construction time. The class offers the following methods:

- `void add(T elem)`—Adds the specified element to this bounded set. If this addition brings the set size beyond its capacity, this method removes from the set the *oldest* element (the one that was inserted first). The addition of an element that already belongs to the set *renews* it (that is, it makes the element the newest one in the set).
- `boolean contains(T elem)`—Returns `true` if this bounded set contains the specified element.

This type of functionality is common when a program needs to remember a small number of frequently used items, as in a cache. Concrete examples include the Open Recent menu entry of many programs or the Recently Used Programs feature of the Windows Start menu.

5.5.1 The contracts

The first step toward a reliable implementation involves stating the method contracts in more detail, clearly distinguishing preconditions and postconditions. In this particular case, there's very little to add to the informal descriptions of the methods because those two methods have no preconditions: you can invoke them at any time with any argument (except `null`). You obtain the following contract for `add`:

- *Precondition*—Argument is not `null`.
- *Postcondition*—Adds the specified element to this bounded set. If this addition brings the set size beyond its capacity, this method removes from the set the *oldest* element (the one that was inserted first). The addition of an element that already belongs to the set *renews* it (that is, it makes the element the newest one in the set).
- *Penalty*—Throws `NullPointerException`.

For `contains`, you may want to explicitly say in the postcondition that this method doesn't modify its set:

- *Precondition*—Argument is not `null`.
- *Postcondition*—Returns `true` if this bounded set contains the specified element. It doesn't modify this bounded set.
- *Penalty*—Throws `NullPointerException`.

5.5.2   *A baseline implementation*

Before actively checking these contracts, start with a plain implementation of `Bounded Set`. In this way, you'll see more clearly the costs associated with those checks. First, choose the internal representation for a bounded set. A linked list is a handy choice because it allows you to keep the elements sorted by insertion time and efficiently remove the oldest element with the dedicated method `removeFirst`. However, this doesn't mean that insertion in a bounded set will occur in constant time. To renew an element that's already present, you need to scan the list, remove the element from its current position, and then add it to the front of the list, which takes linear time.

You get the following basic structure for the class:

```
public class BoundedSet<T> {
   private final LinkedList<T> data;
   private final int capacity;

   public BoundedSet(int capacity) {    ❶ Constructor
      this.data = new LinkedList<>();
      this.capacity = capacity;
   }
```

Next come the two methods. As you can see, the linked list allows you to write a very simple implementation, in exchange for limited performance (one of the typical trade-offs filling this book).

```
   public void add(T elem) {
      if (elem==null) {
         throw new NullPointerException();
      }
      data.remove(elem);      ❶ Removes elem if it's already there
      if (data.size() == capacity) {
         data.removeFirst();   ❷ If full, removes the oldest
      }
      data.addLast(elem);     ❸ Adds elem as the newest
   }
   public boolean contains(T elem) {
      return data.contains(elem);
   }
```

5.5.3 *Checking the contracts*

As we've done with water containers, let's design a hardened implementation of `Bounded Set` whose methods actively check their contracts.

Focus on the postcondition of `add`, which is the most interesting part of both contracts. Since `add` is supposed to modify the state of the bounded set in a specific and substantial way, the hardened `add` method needs to start by making a copy of the current state of the bounded set. At the end of `add`, a private support method will compare the current state of this bounded set with the copy made at the beginning of `add` and check that it's been modified according to the contract.

The modern suggested way to provide copy capability to a class is through a *copy constructor*,[9] that is, a constructor accepting another object of the same class. You can easily achieve that for `BoundedSet`:

```
public BoundedSet(BoundedSet<T> other) {      ❶ Copy constructor
    data = new LinkedList<>(other.data);
    capacity = other.capacity;
}
```

As I've discussed with regard to water containers, you should make sure that you only execute everything connected to the postcondition check, including the initial copy, when assertions are enabled. As before, you can achieve this objective by wrapping the initial copy in a dummy assert statement.

```
public void add(T elem) {
    BoundedSet<T> copy = null;
    assert (copy = new BoundedSet<>(this)) != null;     ❶ Dummy assert

    ...    ❷ The actual operation goes here.

    assert postAdd(copy, elem) :       ❸ Checks the postcondition
            "add failed its postcondition!";
}
```

Finally, the following code shows the private support method responsible for actually checking the postcondition. It first checks that the newly added element sits at the front of the current list. Then, it makes a copy of the current list so it can remove the newest element from both the current and old lists. At that point, it compares the position of all other elements before and after the call to `add`—they should be the same. You can handily delegate this check to the `equals` method of the lists.

```
private boolean postAdd(BoundedSet<T> oldSet, T newElement) {
    if (!data.getLast().equals(newElement)) {     ❶ newElement must be at the front.
        return false;
    }
    ❷ Removes newElement from both old and new
    List<T> copyOfCurrent = new ArrayList<>(data);
    copyOfCurrent.remove(newElement);
    oldSet.data.remove(newElement);
```

---

[9] Check out item 13 in *Effective Java* to learn why that's preferred over the `clone` method for new classes.

```
    if (oldSet.data.size()==capacity) {    ❸ If it was full, drop the oldest.
        oldSet.data.removeFirst();
    }
    ❹ All remaining objects should be the same, in the same order.
    return oldSet.data.equals(copyOfCurrent);
}
```

As with water containers, checking the postcondition takes more effort than the `add` operation that you're scrutinizing, both at coding time and at runtime. This confirms that you should reserve such checks for special circumstances, such as in safety-critical software or for particularly tricky routines.

5.5.4 Checking the invariants

Recall that an invariant is a static consistency property on the fields of a class that should hold at all times, except when an object is undergoing change because of a method. Given the chosen representation for bounded sets (the fields `data` and `capacity`), only two consistency properties characterize a valid bounded set:

    I1. The length of the list `data` should be at most equal to `capacity`.

    I2. The list `data` shouldn't contain duplicate elements.

Any list and any integer satisfying these two invariants are sound, and you could, in fact, obtain them by a legal sequence of operations on an initially empty bounded set. You should check these invariants in a private support method, like the following:

```
private boolean checkInvariants() {
    if (data.size() > capacity)    ❶ Invariant I1
        return false;
    ❷ Invariant I2 follows.
    Set<T> elements = new HashSet<>();
    for (T element: data) {
        if (!elements.add(element))    ❸ If add returns false, this element is a duplicate.
            return false;
    }
    return true;
}
```

Once again, focus on the `add` method. The method `contains` is a trivial one-liner that can't spoil the state of the object.

A hardened `add`, instead, can check the invariants at the end of each call. As usual, put such a check in an `assert` statement so you can easily turn on and off all reliability enhancements together (but remember, they'll be off by default).

```
public void add(T elem) {
    ...    ❶ The actual operation goes here.

    assert checkInvariants() : "add broke an invariant!";
}
```

Some potential bugs in `add` might pass unnoticed by the invariant check but be flagged by the more thorough postcondition check from the previous section. For example, imagine if `add` removed the oldest element even when the bounded set wasn't full.

The invariant check wouldn't notice the problem because this defect doesn't bring the bounded set into an inconsistent state. More precisely, the state of affairs after `add` is not inconsistent *in itself.* It's just inconsistent with respect to the *history* of that object, but invariants don't care about history. The postcondition, on the other hand, would catch this defect by comparing the state of the bounded set before and after the `add` operation.

5.6   *Real-world use cases*

Refactoring `addWater` to enforce the design-by-contract principles was not an easy job. In fact, it was necessary to write more code to implement precondition and postcondition checks than to perform the actual business logic. The key question is: Is it worth the trouble? Here are some real-world use cases for you to consider:

- Let's say you're working for a small startup that a bank has hired to develop software for handling ATM transactions. Deadlines are pushing very hard, as the bank has grown substantially and needs to replace its legacy transaction-handling software, which can't handle the expansion of the retail network. To meet the deadlines, the software leader in your team makes a catastrophic decision: focus on the business logic to be able to deliver a solution fast. Luckily, banks don't trust anyone. They have their own team of software testers who put everything under the microscope before deploying to production. It turns out that the elegantly crafted software your team has developed suffers from a minor bug: it's possible to withdraw more than you actually have in your bank account—and all that embarrassment is because the software skipped a precondition check. Software fails, and often it fails catastrophically. Paying the cost of reliability during development will prevent future despair.

- You might want to take a library you've developed in the past and refactor it to take advantage of the features of the underlying programming language's latest release. Or you may want to refactor the existing code to add some new features. The cost of poor design may not be obvious at the first library releases, but poor design accrues over time, and people have even come up with a term for the eventual cost of poor design: *technical debt.* As it accrues, technical debt might even impede future evolution of the library. Design by contract and the related programming techniques help control technical debt by promoting explicit specifications and reliability.

- When creating new software, developers often face the following dilemma: what programming language should we use? Obviously, the answer depends on many factors, and among them are the complexity of the underlying system and its reliability. It turns out that the more complicated the system design, the more difficult it is to make the system behave correctly and be robust under unexpected events. When reliability is a primary concern, one consideration is how much of a contract can your programming language express *in a way that you can check at compile time.* You may end up switching your programming paradigm so you can catch more defects at compile time. For example, functional programming is known to promote reliability but at the cost of a steeper learning curve and occasionally lower performance.

Let's not fool ourselves: failure is inevitable. That's why I defined robustness as *the capability of a system to react gracefully in situations that may lead to failure, rather than a system that's designed to avoid all possible causes of failure.* Modern distributed systems are prone to failure because of their inherent nature and are thus created with this principle in mind: partial failures, inconsistencies, and reordering of messages among the nodes are impossible to control. Instead, they're part of the design contract so you can handle them gracefully.

5.7   *Applying what you learned*

EXERCISE 1

1. Write down the contract for the method `add` from the `java.util.Collection` interface. (Yes, you can look at the Javadoc.)
2. Do the same for the method `add` from the `java.util.HashSet` class.
3. Compare the two contracts. How are they different?

EXERCISE 2

Implement the static method `interleaveLists`, defined by the following contract:

- *Precondition*—The method receives as arguments two `List`s of the same length.
- *Postcondition*—The method returns a new `List` containing all the elements of the two lists, in an alternating fashion.
- *Penalty*—If at least one of the lists is `null`, the method throws `NullPointer Exception`. If the lists have different lengths, the method throws `Illegal ArgumentException`.

Make sure that the precondition is always checked, and the postcondition is checked only if assertions are enabled. Try to minimize the overhead when you have assertions disabled.

EXERCISE 3

An object of type `java.math.BigInteger` represents an integer of arbitrary size, internally encoded by an array of integers. Check out its source code in OpenJDK (http://mng.bz/Ye6j) and locate the following private members:

```
private BigInteger(int[] val)
private int parseInt(char[] source, int start, int end)
```

1. Write down the contract of the private constructor. Make sure to include in the precondition all assumptions that the constructor needs to terminate regularly. Does the constructor actively check its precondition?
2. Do the same for the `parseInt` method.

EXERCISE 4

The following method supposedly returns the greatest common divisor of two given integers. (Don't worry; you don't need to understand it.) Modify it so it checks its postcondition when assertions are enabled, and try it on 1000 pairs of integers. (You can find the following code in the `eis.chapter5.exercises.Gcd` class in the online repository at https://bitbucket.org/mfaella/exercisesinstyle.)

Hint: Try to check the postcondition in the simplest possible way. You shouldn't have doubts about the correctness of the check itself.

```
private static int greatestCommonDivisor(int u, int v) {
    if (u == 0 || v == 0) {
        if (u == Integer.MIN_VALUE || v == Integer.MIN_VALUE) {
            throw new ArithmeticException("overflow: gcd is 2\^{}31");
        }
        return Math.abs(u) + Math.abs(v);
    }
    if (Math.abs(u) == 1 || Math.abs(v) == 1) {
        return 1;
    }
    if (u > 0) { u = -u; }
    if (v > 0) { v = -v; }
    int k = 0;
    while ((u & 1) == 0 && (v & 1) == 0 && k < 31) {
        u /= 2;
        v /= 2;
        k++;
    }
    if (k == 31) {
        throw new ArithmeticException("overflow: gcd is 2\^{}31");
    }
    int t = (u & 1) == 1 ? v : -(u / 2);
    do {
        while ((t & 1) == 0) { t /= 2; }
        if (t > 0) { u = -t; }
        else { v = t; }
        t = (v - u) / 2;
    } while (t != 0);
    return -u * (1 <{}< k);
}
```

Summary

- Software reliability starts with clear specifications.
- A standard form of specifications is in terms of method contracts and class invariants.
- You should check preconditions for public methods during all phases of the development process.
- You should check other preconditions, postconditions, and invariants only as needed, during development or in safety-critical software.
- Assertions allow you to enable or disable certain checks at any program run.

Answers to quizzes and exercises

POP QUIZ 1

Throwing a checked exception as a penalty forces the caller to deal with that exception, either by catching it or by declaring it in its `throws` clause. This is cumbersome because the penalty can simply be avoided by respecting the preconditions. Checked exceptions are intended for exceptional conditions that can't be avoided because they're outside the direct control of the caller.

POP QUIZ 2

A graceful reaction to running out of paper is to alert the user to the problem and give them the option to retry or abort the printing. In contrast, ungraceful reactions would be to crash the program or to silently ignore the print request.

POP QUIZ 3

The proposed property compares the state of an object before and after a method call. That's the job of a postcondition, not an invariant. Invariants can only refer to the current state of an object.

POP QUIZ 4

You initialize the flag with `false` and then set it to `true` using a dummy assertion:

```
boolean areAssertionsEnabled = false;
assert (areAssertionsEnabled = true) == true;
```

POP QUIZ 5

Recall that not-a-number (NaN) is one of the special values for floating point numbers, together with plus and minus infinities. NaN is subject to special arithmetic rules. Those that concern this quiz are the following:

- NaN / n gives NaN
- NaN + n gives NaN
- NaN < n gives `false`
- NaN == NaN gives `false` (You read this right!)

Looking at the code of `addWater` in *Contracts* (listing 5.1), you can see that passing NaN as the value of the `amount` parameter passes the precondition check because `this.amount + amountPerContainer < 0` evaluates to `false`. The subsequent lines set the amount field of all containers in the group to the value NaN. Finally, assuming you've enabled assertions, the method checks its postcondition through the method `postAddWater` (listing 5.4). There, NaN will fail both the `isGroupBalanced()` and the `almostEqual()` tests, and the invocation will terminate with an `AssertionError`.

If you have assertions disabled (as they are by default), the invocation to `getAmount` silently sets all containers in the group to holding NaN. These observations suggest that the contract of `addWater` should in fact be refined to tackle NaN and the other special values in a more reasonable way, such as by declaring them invalid through the precondition.

EXERCISE 1

1. The contract of an abstract method tends to be more involved than that of a concrete method. An abstract method has no implementation, so it's basically a *pure contract*. Therefore, its contract needs to be clear and detailed. The situation is even more sensitive in an interface like `Collection`, which, being the root of the collection hierarchy, must accommodate a large variety of specializations (precisely 34, among classes and interfaces).

The Javadoc for `Collection.add` contains a wealth of information. Start with the qualifier "optional operation." You can interpret it as specifying *two alternative contracts* for this method. First, an implementation can choose not to support insertions, like an immutable collection. In that case, it must respect the following contract:

- *Precondition*—No invocation is legitimate.
- *Postcondition*—None.
- *Penalty*—Throws `UnsupportedOperationException`.

If the class implementing `Collection` supports insertions, it must obey a different contract. Such a class can freely choose the precondition of `add`, to constrain the kind of insertions that are legitimate, but it must issue specific penalties when rejecting an insertion, as the following contract describes:

- *Precondition*—Implementation-defined.
- *Postcondition*—Ensures that this collection contains the specified element. Returns `true` if this collection changed as a result of the call.
- *Penalty*—Throws:
  - `ClassCastException` if the argument is invalid because of its type
  - `NullPointerException` if the argument is `null` and this collection rejects `null` values
  - `IllegalArgumentException` if the argument is invalid because of some other property
  - `IllegalStateException` if the argument can't be inserted at this time

Note how this contract doesn't specify under which conditions an insertion will change the underlying collection. That burden lies with the subclasses.

2. The class `HashSet` specializes the contract for `add` as follows:

- *Precondition*—None. (All arguments are legitimate.)
- *Postcondition*—Inserts the specified element in this collection, unless an element equal to it (according to `equals`) is already present. Returns `true` if this collection didn't contain the specified element before the call.
- *Penalty*—None.

3. The contract in `HashSet` specifies that this collection doesn't contain duplicate elements. Attempting to insert a duplicate is not an error: it doesn't violate the precondition and it doesn't raise an exception. It just leaves the collection unchanged.

EXERCISE 2

Here's the code for the `interleaveLists` method. Note how regular `if` statements check the precondition, whereas the postcondition is delegated to a separate method, only invoked when assertions are enabled.

```
public static <T> List<T> interleaveLists(List<? extends T> a,
                                          List<? extends T> b) {
  if (a==null || b==null)
      throw new NullPointerException("Both lists must be non-null.");
  if (a.size() != b.size())
      throw new IllegalArgumentException(
              "The lists must have the same length.");

  List<T> result = new ArrayList<>();
  Iterator<? extends T> ia = a.iterator(), ib = b.iterator();
  while (ia.hasNext()) {
      result.add(ia.next());
      result.add(ib.next());
  }
  assert interleaveCheckPost(a, b, result);
  return result;
}
```

Here's the code for the support method responsible for checking the postcondition:

```
private static boolean interleaveCheckPost(List<?> a, List<?> b,
                                           List<?> result) {
  if (result.size() != a.size() + b.size())
      return false;

  Iterator<?> ia = a.iterator(), ib = b.iterator();
  boolean odd = true;
  for (Object elem: result) {
      if ( odd && elem != ia.next()) return false;
      if (!odd && elem != ib.next()) return false;
      odd = !odd;
  }
  return true;
}
```

EXERCISE 3

First, note a few details about how these private members are documented. The official Javadoc page for `BigInteger` doesn't mention any private member. That's the default behavior for Javadoc, and you can change it using the `--show-members pri vate` command-line option. Still, in the source code, the constructor is equipped with a full comment in Javadoc style, whereas the method is preceded by a brief comment in free format. Apparently, the constructor is deemed important enough to warrant more detailed documentation. In chapter 7, you'll learn more about Javadoc and documentation guidelines. Now, let's extract the contracts from these comments and from the code.

1. Regarding the constructor, the Javadoc mentions that `val` should not be modified during the execution of the constructor. This property refers to multithreaded contexts, where the program may be executing other code at the same time as this constructor. As such, this requirement doesn't exactly fit in the classic form of contract presented in this chapter, as that's tailored to sequential programs.

On the other hand, a quick look at the constructor source code shows that the array `val` is also implicitly assumed to be non-null and non-empty, leading to the following contract:

- *Precondition*—`val` is non-null and non-empty.
- *Postcondition*—It creates the `BigInteger` corresponding to the integer encoded in `val` in two's-complement big-endian format.
- *Penalty*—Throws:
  - `NullPointerException` if `val` is `null`
  - `NumberFormatException` if `val` is empty (length 0)

The constructor is actively checking whether the array `val` is empty. There's no need to check for `val` being `null` because that case induces an NPE automatically.[10]

2. The comment preceding `parseInt` declares "Assumes `start < end`." That's one explicit precondition. Skimming through the method body, you'll also notice that the `source` argument must be non-null and that `start` and `end` must be valid indices in `source`. Finally, every character in the specified interval of `source` must be a digit. You can put these observations in contract form as follows:

- *Precondition*—`source` is a non-null sequence of digit characters; `start` and `end` are valid indices for `source`, and `start < end`.
- *Postcondition*—Returns the integer that the digits between the two indices `start` and `end` represent.
- *Penalty*—Throws:
  - `NullPointerException` if `source` is `null`
  - `NumberFormatException` if any character in the specified interval is not a digit
  - `ArrayIndexOutOfBoundsException` if `start` or `end` is not a valid index in `source`

The method actively checks that each character in the interval is a digit. It omits the check for `null` as redundant. The only precondition explicitly stated in the documentation is not checked: invoking the method with `start ≥ end` doesn't raise any exception, but, rather, returns the integer corresponding to the single character `source[start]`.

As a side remark, this method doesn't use any instance field, so it should be `static`.

---

[10] You may still prefer to check that explicitly to clarify your intent and equip the exception with a more specific error message.

EXERCISE 4

The code for this exercise is a slightly edited excerpt from the class Fraction[11] from the Apache Commons project. It employs a highly non-obvious algorithm by Donald Knuth. Since the method modifies its arguments, and you need those arguments to check the postcondition, you need to store their original values in two additional variables. Then, at the end of the method, you can check the postcondition using an auxiliary method.

```
private static int greatestCommonDivisor(int u, int v) {
    final int originalU = u, originalV = v;

    ❶ The original procedure goes here (modifies u and v).

    int gcd = -u * (1 <{}< k);
    assert isGcd(gcd, originalU, originalV) : "Wrong GCD!";
    return gcd;
}
```

For the auxiliary isGcd method, I said the simplest solution is preferable. In this case, you may simply apply the definition of "greatest common divisor," and check that

- gcd is indeed a common divisor of originalU and originalV
- every larger number is not a common divisor

```
private static boolean isGcd(int gcd, int u, int v) {
    if (u \% gcd != 0 || v \% gcd != 0)    ❶ Checks that gcd is a common divisor
        return false;
    for (int i=gcd+1; i<=u && i<=v; i++)    ❷ Checks any larger number,
        if (u \% i == 0 && v \% i == 0)          up to the minimum of u and v
            return false;
    return true;
}
```

This implementation of isGcd is very inefficient, being linear in the size of the smallest number between u and v. A more reasonable course of action would be to use Euclid's classic algorithm (https://en.wikipedia.org/wiki/Euclidean_algorithm) or invoke an already implemented GCD procedure, such as the BigInteger.gcd() method from the JDK.

Further reading

- Bertrand Meyer. *Object-Oriented Software Construction*. Prentice Hall, 1997.
  This book formally introduced the design-by-contract methodology and the programming language, Eiffel, designed to support it.
- J.-M. Muller et al. *Handbook of Floating-Point Arithmetic*. Birkhäuser, 2010.
  Want to impress friends and family with your mastery of everything floating-point? Study this volume of over 500 pages. It comes with a free PhD in computer science.

---

[11]   The fully qualified class name is org.apache.commons.lang3.math.Fraction.

- David Goldberg. "What Every Computer Scientist Should Know About Floating-Point Arithmetic." *ACM Computing Surveys*, 23, 1991.
  At 44 pages, this article delivers its promise, but it doesn't grant a PhD.
- Joshua Bloch. *Effective Java*. Addison-Wesley, 2017.
  The third edition of a celebrated book on Java best practices. Written by one of the designers of the Java platform.

Lie to me:
Reliability through testing

6

This chapter covers

- Designing a suite of unit tests
- Applying input coverage criteria
- Measuring code coverage
- Assessing and improving code testability

Even developers who've never heard of design by contract know what tests are: the final phase of every software development project, when evil people called testers try to expose your brilliant time-saving hacks and characterize them as "bugs." Jokes aside, tests have an increasingly central role in the modern software development process. One well-known point of view, called *test-driven development*, even suggests that tests should come before, rather than after, any production code. In that case, tests are used as executable specifications, and the rest of the system is written to pass those tests.[1]

The content of this chapter is independent of the specific view you hold on tests. You're just going to enrich *Reference* (or any implementation that conforms to its API) with a set of tests that's reasonable and tries to cover its functionalities as much as possible. In line with the theme of this book, I'll focus on *unit testing*, that is, testing

---

[1] You can learn about TDD from the book *Growing Object-Oriented Software, Guided by Tests*, mentioned in the *Further reading* section at the end of this chapter.

of a single class. Later, I'll critically analyze the water container API in the light of testability and suggest some improvements based on common best practices.

6.1   Basic testing notions

Testing is the primary validation activity in the software industry. As such, you can find a wealth of theories and techniques related to it. As with the other topics, in this book I can touch on only the basics of testing, and that's fine. Plenty of specialized resources are available for digging a lot deeper into this topic, some of which are listed in the *Further reading* section at the end of this chapter.

The objective of testing is to find and remove as many bugs as possible, thus increasing your confidence in the correctness and robustness of your program. More precisely, you can't really expect a complex program to ever become entirely bug-free, so testing should aim at identifying all large defects—those that are likely to occur soon and often during regular use. Testing seldom catches the subtler and more intricate bugs. Only an extended period of heavy use creates the right conditions for those bugs to emerge.

Like many aspects of software engineering, the ability to design good tests comes from practice at least as much as it stems from solid principles. Because I can't provide you with instant practice, I'll do the next best thing: present you with the principles while applying them to a concrete example.

6.1.1   Coverage in testing

You can increase the likelihood of catching all large defects by adopting a systematic approach to testing, guided by *coverage* considerations. Indeed, coverage is one of the main themes in test design, and it comes with several meanings. In general, by coverage I mean the extent to which the tests manage to stimulate different parts of the system. Two broad ways to measure coverage have been developed: code-based and input-based. *Code-based coverage* refers to the percentage of source code that a given set of tests execute at least once. As you'll learn in this chapter, you can measure that percentage in different ways. Code-based coverage is traditionally tied to *whitebox testing*, so called because it assumes we have inside knowledge of the software under test (SUT) and its source code.

Input-based coverage, on the other hand, ignores the internals of the program being tested and focuses only on its API. Roughly speaking, it suggests analyzing the set of possible input values to identify a smaller set of representative inputs. Input-based coverage is connected to *blackbox testing*, in the sense that it's independent from the source code of the SUT.

The two types of coverage complement each other, and in this chapter you'll exploit both of them. First, you'll deal with input-based coverage by designing test suites that try to provide a rich selection of input values. Then, you'll use a tool to measure the code coverage that those tests achieve. In other words, you'll use input-based coverage as the design objective and code-based coverage as a form of validation of the test plan itself.

6.1.2 *Testing and design-by-contract*

Before going into specifics, let's compare the objective of testing with the objective of the techniques I presented in the previous chapter, centered on the thorough verification of a contract.

Checking preconditions of public methods and reacting with the appropriate penalty is a basic form of defensive programming, and a generally accepted best practice. Testing doesn't replace it in any way, but, rather, reinforces it. Indeed, later in this chapter, you'll design some tests aimed at verifying that those defenses are in place.

Checking postconditions or invariants in-method is a completely different matter: the objective there is to detect problems *within* the class itself, and that's the same objective as for unit testing. Hence, those techniques can serve somewhat as an alternative to testing.

Compared with those other techniques, testing has the two following advantages that make it much more common in practice:

- Testing moves the invariant and postcondition checks *outside* of the class itself. That's a very convenient choice that keeps classes small and simple and clearly distinguishes responsibilities, among classes and among developers, allowing the organization to assign development and testing to different teams.
- Testing invites you to carefully design the set of input values that you'll provide to the SUT. This aspect is missing from the other techniques. In other words, implementing in-method postcondition or invariant checks is only half the story. Without a systematic strategy for calling specific methods with specific input values (which amounts to a testing plan), those checks may or may not reveal bugs at any stage of program development and production. Testing puts you in charge of the process, with coverage metrics supporting your confidence in the correctness and robustness of the SUT.

Figure 6.1, repeated from the previous chapter, puts tests in relation with code qualities and design by contract. Tests check that methods respect their postconditions, and that they react to invalid inputs (as defined by the preconditions) with the advertised penalties. In so doing, tests promote reliability by exposing defects and facilitating their removal.

In particularly critical code, it may be useful to enrich testing with some of the techniques from the previous chapter. For example, you can put invariant checks in place to be able to run the system in robust mode at any time. In this way, if an anomalous behavior survives testing and is discovered during production, you can more easily diagnose and fix it.

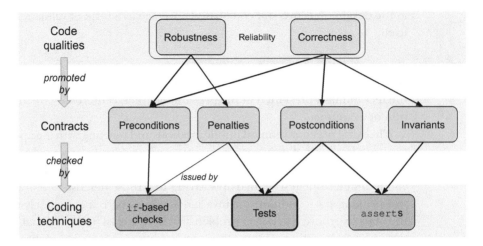

Figure 6.1   The relationship between reliability attributes, contract-based specifications, and coding techniques

POP QUIZ 1 Which parts of a method contract are relevant for testing that method?

Modern testing is based on the ability to quickly and repeatedly execute an evolving collection of tests. This automation process is supported by libraries and frameworks, the most popular of which is the xUnit family, including JUnit for Java and NUnit for .NET languages. If you're not familiar with JUnit, the next section provides a brief introduction to it.

6.1.3   *JUnit*

JUnit is the standard unit testing framework for Java. It provides free and open source facilities for writing and running a test suite. The following tests are based on JUnit 4.0, so I'll start with a quick overview of this framework.

JUnit makes heavy use of Java *annotations*. If you're not familiar with this Java construct, check out the sidebar.

Java annotations

An annotation is a tag that starts with the "@" symbol and that you can attach to a method right before its signature. The annotation most programmers are familiar with is @Override, as in the following fragment:

```
public class Employee {
  private String name, salary;
  ...
  @Override
  public String toString() {
    return name + ", monthly salary " + salary;
  }
}
```

```
    }
```

The @Override tag in the snippet signals to the compiler that the attached toString method is *intended* to be an override. In other words, the programmer is instructing the compiler to perform an extra check: if the target method is not overriding a superclass method, compilation will fail. Whereas @Override is an annotation with no arguments, other annotations may have any number of them. (You'll see an example shortly.)

In reality, annotations are a general mechanism for attaching metadata to program elements. Besides methods, you can also apply them to classes, fields, local variables, method parameters, and more. Annotations are passive elements that carry extra information about a program element. They can be transferred to the bytecode and read at runtime using reflection. Programmers can easily define their own custom annotations and write tools that interpret them to alter or enrich the execution of the program in various ways.

In JUnit, every test takes up a method, and a set of related tests form a class. Not all methods in a class must represent a test. You specify that a method represents a test by decorating it with the @Test annotation:

```
@Test
public void testSomething() { ... }
```

If a given test is supposed to raise an exception (this is common when testing for robustness), you tell JUnit which class of exception you expect by setting the value of the expected attribute of the @Test annotation:

```
@Test(expected = IllegalArgumentException.class)
public void testWrongInput() { ... }
```

As these examples indicate, test methods don't return a value. Test success or failure is determined by an appropriate *JUnit assertion*, not to be confused with the Java assert instruction. A JUnit assertion is one of a number of static methods that the framework offers to compare the expected result of an operation with the effective result. Whenever an assertion fails, it throws the Assertion

C# attributes

Attributes are the C# way to attach metadata to program elements. They work similarly to Java annotations, but you distinguish them by brackets instead of an at (@) symbol. For example, the analog to Java's @Deprecated annotation is C#'s [Obsolete] attribute.

Error exception, just like a Java assert instruction. JUnit will catch those exceptions, keep running all the other tests in the suite, and present a final report summarizing the outcome of each test.

The most common assertions are the following public static void methods from the org.junit.Assert class:

- assertTrue(String message, boolean condition)—The test succeeds if the condition is true. This is the most general JUnit assertion, allowing you to plug in any custom check returning a Boolean. The message string in this and the following methods will be attached to the exception thrown if the assertion fails, and later will be included in the final report.

- `assertFalse(String message, boolean condition)`—The opposite of the previous case: the test succeeds if the condition is false.
- `assertEquals(String message, Object expected, Object actual)`—The test succeeds if `expected` and `equals` are both `null`, or if they're equal to each other (according to their `equals` method). Similar assertions accept primitive types `long`, `float`, and `double`, instead of `Object`. However, the floating-point versions are deprecated[2] in favor of the following assertion.
- `assertEquals(String message, double expected, double actual, double delta)`—The test succeeds if the values `expected` and `actual` are within `delta` from each other; `delta` is the tolerance for the comparison. As I discussed in section 5.3, you shouldn't compare floating-point numbers exactly, but, rather, with some room for rounding errors. I'll come back to that point in a minute.

You can run JUnit from the command line, but it's much more common to launch it as part of an IDE so you can easily run and visually analyze tests.

6.2   *Testing containers*   *[UnitTests]*

It's time to go back to our containers. This section is a little different from most of the others because you won't be developing another version of the `Container` class, but, rather, a set of tests for its functionalities. Which version of `Container` are we testing, you may ask? Because we're using the blackbox approach, we're not targeting any specific implementation of `Container`. Instead, we're targeting its API, as established in chapter 1. A nice consequence is that you'll be able to run the tests against all implementations from this book that comply with that API, and that's exactly what you'll do in section 6.2.4. If you feel the need to have a concrete implementation in mind, just think of *Reference*.

You can find the code for the following tests in the `eis.chapter6.UnitTests` class in the online repository (https://bitbucket.org/mfaella/exercisesinstyle).

6.2.1   *Initializing the tests*

The following tests use the same API that normal clients use. As a consequence, we won't be able to directly check the internal state of the objects. The `getAmount` method is essentially the only feedback we have access to (and the only method that returns a value, by the way). We'll come back to this limitation later in this chapter.

All of our tests need to operate on one or more `Container` objects. Rather than creating these containers at the beginning of each test, you can avoid some code repetition by adding some `Container` fields to the class and initializing them in a method

---

[2]   Not only are they formally deprecated, they *always fail*.

you tag with the JUnit annotation `@Before`. When you tag a method with `@Before`, it will be executed before each test. We call such objects that multiple tests share *test fixtures*. Accordingly, our test class starts as follows:

```
public class UnitTests {
    private Container a, b;      ❶ Test fixtures

    @Before                      ❷ Instructs JUnit to execute this method before every test
    public void setUp() {
       a = new Container();
       b = new Container();
    }
```

For the sake of completeness, you can use the dual annotation `@After` to tag a method that you want executed after each test. This is useful if test fixtures need to release some resources upon dismissal. Moreover, you can attach annotations `@Before Class` and `@AfterClass` to static methods that you want executed once, before or after the whole sequence of tests in the current class. You may want to use them to set up and tear down computationally expensive fixtures that several tests share, such as database connections and network channels in general.

Now, you'll design your first `Container` test, checking that the constructor works as expected. Because the constructor has no inputs, invoke it just once and check the only property that the API allows you to verify: that a newly minted container is empty.

```
@Test
public void testNewContainerIsEmpty() {
    assertTrue("new container is not empty", a.getAmount() == 0);
}
```

In this case, it's OK to compare two floating-point numbers exactly because there's no reason for the class to approximate this value. In the previous snippet, I'm using `assertTrue` because I think it's more readable than the equivalent `assertEquals`, which looks like this:

```
assertEquals("new container is not empty", 0, a.getAmount(), 0);
```

Readable asserts with Hamcrest matchers

In the examples so far, I've been using the basic way to write JUnit assertions. A better alternative is to use the library *Hamcrest*, shipped with JUnit. This library allows you to express the condition being checked in a more readable way, by building a *matcher* object and passing it to the `assertThat` assertion.

For example, the basic assertion

```
assertEquals("new container is not empty", 0, a.getAmount(), 0);
```

you can rewrite as the following Hamcrest assertion:

```
assertThat("new container is not empty", a.getAmount(), closer(0, 0));
```

Besides being more readable, Hamcrest conditions lead to clearer diagnostic messages in case of failure. To witness this difference, assume that an empty container mistakenly started with 0.1 units of water. The first assertion, based on `assertEquals`, fails with the following message:

```
new container is not empty
expected:<0.0> but was:<0.1>
```

whereas the assertion using Hamcrest provides more details:

```
new container is not empty
Expected: a numeric value within <0.0> of <0.0>
     but: <0.1> differed by <0.0> more than delta <0.0>
```

I'll use Hamcrest matchers in this chapter's second example in section 6.4.

6.2.2 *Testing addWater*

Next, we'll test the behavior of the `addWater` method. Its inputs include its parameter and the current state of this container. Because these inputs can take a huge number of values, it's time to introduce a systematic way to choose the input values you'll send to the method under test. The standard blackbox technique is called *input domain modeling*.

INPUT DOMAIN MODELING

The input domain model approach helps you identify a restricted set of interesting values to subject your method to. It proceeds in the following three steps:

1 Identify a small number of relevant input *characteristics*. A characteristic is a feature that partitions the set of possible values into a finite (hopefully small) number of categories, called *blocks*. Relevant characteristics can be suggested by the type of an input or by the method contract. For example, a common characteristic for an integer input is to divide its values into three blocks: negative numbers, zero, and positive numbers.

2 Combine characteristics into a finite set of combinations. For example, figure 6.2 shows two characteristics for an input of type `int`. Together, they define six possible combinations, except that one of them is empty because zero is conventionally treated as an even number.

3 Pick an input value from each combination. Each of those values defines a test. The test consists of invoking the method with the chosen input value and comparing its output with the expected output according to the contract. (Note that the correct output may be an exception.)

You'll apply this technique now to `addWater`, and later to `connectTo`.

CHOOSING THE CHARACTERISTICS

The first way to identify relevant characteristics for your inputs is to simply observe their data type. Primitive data types come with standard characteristics:

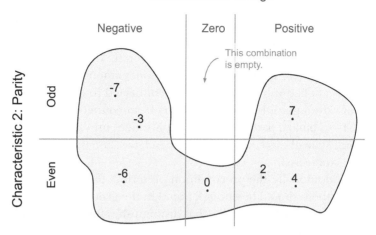

Figure 6.2 Two characteristics for an input of type `int`: sign and parity. Together, they partition integers into five sets, because the combination "sign zero, odd parity" is contradictory.

- For a numeric type, it's natural to distinguish zero from the other values because it exhibits special arithmetic properties.
- Similarly, an API often treats positive and negative numbers differently, with negative numbers frequently being unwelcome.
- You should single out the `null` value for every reference type, as it requires special treatment.
- Finally, a special case for strings, arrays, and collections is for them to be empty.

These observations about type-based characteristics are summarized in table 6.1 and only scratch the surface on the subject. Expert testers commonly use many more interesting standard characteristics. For example, strings can span the whole space of Unicode characters (technically, *code points*), and characters and alphabets that are less well known are often sources of errors.

Table 6.1 Standard characteristics for common types of inputs, aka *type-based characteristics*

Type	Characteristic	Blocks
int/long	Sign	{negative, zero, positive}
float/double	Sign and special values	{negative, zero, positive, infinity, NaN}
String	Length	{null, empty string, nonempty string}
array or collection	Size	{null, empty array/collection, nonempty array/collection}

POP QUIZ 2   What characteristic would you choose for a data type representing a date?

A more interesting and fruitful source for characteristics is the contract of the method under test. You can mine both its pre- and postcondition for relevant properties of the inputs. For example, let's take the contract of addWater. The postcondition tells us that addWater distributes the added water among all containers connected to this one. This applies only if a container is connected to this one, so as the first characteristic, let's distinguish isolated containers from connected ones. This characteristic—call it C1—is binary, partitioning the input values into two blocks: the values where the current state of this container is to be isolated, and the values where the current state is to be connected.

Additionally, the precondition prescribes that when the method argument is negative, there should be enough liquid in the group to satisfy the request. This suggests a characteristic—call it C2—that distinguishes four cases (hence, four blocks):

1. The argument is positive.
2. The argument is zero; because the number zero has special arithmetic properties, it's customary to single it out in tests.
3. The argument is negative, and there's enough water in the group (a valid negative).
4. The argument is negative, and there's not enough water in the group (an invalid negative).

Table 6.2 summarizes these two characteristics.

Table 6.2   The two characteristics chosen for testing addWater

Name	Characteristic	Blocks
C1	This container is connected to at least another.	{true, false}
C2	Relation between the argument and the amount in the current group	{positive, zero, valid negative, invalid negative}

CHOOSING THE BLOCK COMBINATIONS

Each characteristic partitions the input values into a small set of blocks. To find as many defects as possible, it's useful to test some or all *combinations* of blocks from different characteristics. In our case, the number of characteristics and the number of blocks within are so small that you can exhaustively test all eight combinations of blocks:

1. (C1=false, C2=positive)
2. (false, zero)
3. (false, valid negative)
4. (false, invalid negative)
5. (true, positive)
6. (true, zero)
7. (true, valid negative)
8. (true, invalid negative)

Unsurprisingly, this strategy is called *All Combinations Coverage*. Note that the two characteristics C1 and C2 are independent, so all eight combinations make sense. In other cases, this strategy gives rise to too many combinations. I've presented some alternative strategies that pick a more limited number of combinations in the sidebar.

Input coverage criteria

Researchers and practicioners have come up with many more input coverage criteria that in one way or another limit the total number of tests to be performed. The following are two that they commonly use:

- *Each Choice Coverage*—This criterion suggests that you include each block from each characteristic in at least one test.
  In the case of `addWater`, here's a selection fulfilling this criterion:
    1. (true, zero)
    2. (true, positive)
    3. (true, valid negative)
    4. (false, invalid negative)

  Many alternative solutions are possible, all with at least four tests, because the second characteristic C2 features four blocks.

- *Base Choice Coverage*—According to this criterion, you're supposed to choose a base combination of blocks and then vary one characteristic at a time, covering all possible values for that characteristic. In our case, you can choose
    1. (true, positive)

  as the base combination because it's in some sense the most typical. Altering the value of the first characteristic leads to the combination
    2. (false, positive)

  Whereas altering the second characteristic from the basic combination generates the following three combinations, which complete the selection:
    3. (true, zero)
    4. (true, valid negative)
    5. (true, invalid negative)

POP QUIZ 3 If you identify three independent characteristics, with n_1, n_2, and n_3 blocks, how many tests do you need to achieve All Combinations Coverage? What about Each Choice Coverage and Base Choice Coverage?

CHOOSING THE ACTUAL VALUES

The last step in the input domain model approach consists of choosing one set of concrete values for each combination of characteristics. Continuing the process for `addWater`, consider combination 7 from the following list:

1. (C1=false, C2=positive)   5. (true, positive)

2. (false, zero)   6. (true, zero)

3. (false, valid negative)   7. **(true, valid negative)**

4. (false, invalid negative)   8. (true, invalid negative)

Your objective in the final step is to devise a container c and a `double` value `amount` such that the following call,

```
c.addWater(amount);
```

falls in the number 7 combination of blocks, that is, C1=true and C2=valid negative. In plain words, the container c should be connected to at least another container, `amount` should be a negative number, and there should be enough water in c's group to fulfill the request. It's pretty straightforward to prepare this scenario using the API for containers. You should end up with a test method similar to the following:

```
@Test
public void testAddValidNegativeToConnected() {
    a.connectTo(b);    ❶ Sets up the desired scenario
    a.addWater(10);
    a.addWater(-4);    ❷ This is the line under test.
    assertTrue("should be 3", a.getAmount() == 3);
}
```

WHAT ARE WE ACTUALLY TESTING?

Because `addWater` returns no value, how do you know whether it actually worked? Easy—you call `getAmount` and compare the expected value with the actual value. But how do you know that `getAmount` correctly reports the current amount value? You don't. Even worse, how do you know that the following two lines set up the testing scenario correctly?

```
        a.connectTo(b);
        a.addWater(10);
```

Again, you can't be sure.

Although the previous test is directed at `addWater`, it's jointly testing `connectTo`, `getAmount`, and `addWater`! If something goes wrong, you have no way of knowing which of the three methods is at fault. In most cases, you can expect `getAmount` to be a simple getter, so it's much more likely for `addWater` or `connectTo` to be wrong. However, this is not always the case: in *Speed3* from chapter 3, the implementation of `getAmount` is about as complex as that of `addWater`. Both need to traverse a parent-pointer tree up to its root, as recalled in the following listing.

Listing 6.1   *Speed3*: Methods `getAmount` and `addWater`

```
public double getAmount() {
    Container root = findRootAndCompress();    ❶ Obtains the root
                                                   and flattens the path

    return root.amount;                         ❷ Reads the amount
}                                                  from the root
```

```
public void addWater(double amount) {
   Container root = findRootAndCompress();     ③ Obtains the root
                                                  and flattens the path
   root.amount += amount / root.size;          ④ Adds water to the root
}
```

There's no way out of this conundrum, unless you adopt a radically different approach and let the tests access the state of the containers directly (by opening up the visibility of the fields or by putting the tests inside the `Container` class). That would be a big step toward whitebox testing, rendering the tests implementation-specific and hence less useful. I'll expand on these observations in section 6.3, devoted to testability.

Listing 6.2 shows the code for the four `addWater` tests on an isolated container (C1=false). Note that for simplicity I'm comparing doubles exactly (no tolerance for rounding errors) because the water we're putting in stays in this container, so there's no reason for `addWater` to perform any rounding. The last of these tests is supposed to raise an exception because we're intentionally violating the precondition. You can tell JUnit which kind of exception to expect using the `expected` parameter of the `@Test` annotation.

Listing 6.2 *UnitTests*: Four tests for `addWater` on an isolated container

```
@Test
public void testAddPositiveToIsolated() {     ① Cl=false, C2=positive
   a.addWater(1);
   assertTrue("should be 1.0", a.getAmount() == 1);
}
@Test
public void testAddZeroToIsolated() {         ② Cl=false, C2=zero
   a.addWater(0);
   assertTrue("should be 0", a.getAmount() == 0);
}
@Test
public void testAddValidNegativeToIsolated() {  ③ Cl=false, C2=valid negative
   a.addWater(10.5);
   a.addWater(-2.5);
   assertTrue("should be 8", a.getAmount() == 8);
}
@Test(expected = IllegalArgumentException.class)
public void testAddInvalidNegativeToIsolated() {  ④ Cl=false, C2=invalid negative
   a.addWater(-1);
}
```

The two characteristics from table 6.2, namely container isolation and the relation between the current group water amount and the amount passed as argument, are a good starting point for a test suite, but you could certainly add others if more testing was deemed necessary. For example, every time a floating point value is provided as input, you should take into account the special values that such types support: positive and negative infinity, and not-a-number (NaN). First, you should enrich the contract of `addWater` by specifying the reaction to those special values (presumably, an exception).

Then, you might proceed to add a characteristic that takes those values into account, leading to more block combinations and more tests.

6.2.3   *Testing connectTo*

Let's move on to testing the `connectTo` method. The inputs to this method are its parameter and the current state of the two containers being connected. The only precondition is for the argument not to be null, so that's a property you should include in your analysis, as characteristic C3. You can overload C3 to also take into account another special value for the parameter: `this`. It turns out we hadn't really taken into account this case when laying out the contract of `connectTo`. Now we'll refine the contract and stipulate that attempting to connect a container with itself should result in a NOP.[3]

The effect of the `connectTo` method is to merge two groups of containers. Hence, it seems natural to distinguish different scenarios based on the size of the two groups before the merge operation. Groups can't be empty: by definition, an isolated container forms its own group, so we'll distinguish groups of size 1 from larger groups. We'll denote groups of a size greater than 1 with 2^+. Characteristics C4 and C5 capture these sizes. Notice that C5 ("size of the other group") includes the extra value "none," which applies when the method argument is `null` and says no other group exists.

Finally, another characteristic (C6) checks whether those two groups were the same (that is, the containers were already connected). Table 6.3 summarizes the identified characteristics.

Table 6.3   Characteristics chosen for testing `connectTo`

Name	Characteristic	Blocks
C3	Value of argument	{null, this, other}
C4	Size of this group	$\{1, 2^+\}$
C5	Size of the other group	{none, 1, 2^+ }
C6	The two groups coincide.	{true, false}

This time, the characteristics are not entirely independent of one another, in that not all combinations are feasible. The following constraints apply:

- When the argument of `connectTo` is `null` (C3=null), there's no other group, so C5=none and C6=false.
- If you try to connect a container with itself (C3=this), the other characteristic-sre have only two possibilities: they're equal to either (1, 1, true) or (2^+, 2^+, true).

---

[3]   NOP stands for No Operation. It started as a mnemonic for the machine code instruction that does nothing. It then spilled over to more generally signify a null operation.

- If you're connecting two distinct containers (C3=other), and they happen to be already connected (C6=true), the size of their common group can't be 1.

Luckily for us, these constraints bring the number of legal combinations from 36 down to the following nine:

1. (other, 1, 1, false)
2. (other, 2^+, 1, false)
3. (other, 1, 2^+, false)
4. (other, 2^+, 2^+, false)
5. (other, 2^+, 2^+, true)
6. (this, 1, 1, true)
7. (this, 2^+, 2^+, true)
8. (null, 1, none, false)
9. (null, 2^+, none, false)

We'll perform one test for each of these combinations, except the last, as there really is no point in distinguishing combination 9 from 8. In both cases, the expected behavior consists of simply throwing an NPE. You can generalize this observation: if a value for a characteristic violates the precondition and hence leads to an exception, it's usually sufficient to test it just once, rather than in all possible combinations.

Unsurprisingly, you run into the same observability problem that I discussed earlier. The main effect of `connectTo` is to merge two groups, but the API doesn't provide any means to directly inspect groups. There's no public method for checking whether two containers are connected. In fact, the only method returning *any* information on the state of the containers is `getAmount`. You can check that the information that `getAmount` returns is *consistent* with the two groups having been merged, but the tests have no way to ascertain whether the groups have actually been merged.

The following listing provides the code for the tests corresponding to `connectTo` combinations 1 to 3. Recall that all tests can use the fixtures I defined earlier: two empty and isolated containers called `a` and `b`.

Listing 6.3 *UnitTests:* **Three tests for** `connectTo`

```
@Test
public void testConnectOtherOneOne() {      ❶ CI=other, C2=I, C3=I, C4=false
    a.connectTo(b);              ❷ Line under test
    a.addWater(2);
    assertTrue("should be 1.0", a.getAmount() == 1);
}
@Test
public void testConnectOtherTwoOne() {       ❸ CI=other, C2=2+, C3=I, C4=false
    Container c = new Container();
    a.connectTo(b);
    a.connectTo(c);              ❹ Line under test
    a.addWater(3);
    assertTrue("should be 1.0", a.getAmount() == 1);
}
@Test
public void testConnectOtherOneTwo() {       ❺ CI=other, C2=I, C3=2+, C4=false
    Container c = new Container();
    b.connectTo(c);
    a.connectTo(b);              ❻ Line under test
```

```
        a.addWater(3);
        assertTrue("should be 1.0", a.getAmount() == 1);
    }
```

6.2.4 Running the tests

Table 6.4 summarizes the outcome of the 17 tests we devised, when run against four different implementations: *Reference* from chapter 2; the "fast" implementation, *Speed3* from chapter 3; and the two "robust" implementations I presented in chapter 5, nicknamed *Contracts* and *Invariants*.

Table 6.4 Number of passed tests for different implementations. Results don't depend on having assertions enabled or disabled.

	Reference	Speed3	Contracts	Invariants
constructor	1/1	1/1	1/1	1/1
addWater	**6**/8	**6**/8	8/8	8/8
connectTo	8/8	8/8	8/8	8/8
Failed tests	C2 = invalid negative	C2 = invalid negative	—	—

The first two implementations fail the two `addWater` tests, where we try to remove more water than is actually available (C2 = invalid negative). Indeed, those implementations don't check this condition and will happily support negative amounts of water in a container.

We intentionally engineered the other two implementations to faithfully respect their contract, so they pass all tests with flying colors. It may be worth noticing that passing these tests doesn't depend on enabling the assertions because standard `if`-statements that are always on check the preconditions.

6.2.5 Measuring code coverage

You can check the code coverage that these tests achieve using the JaCoCo tool, an open-source Java code coverage framework. It collects runtime information using a *Java agent*, that is, a piece of code that runs in the background on a JVM to inspect or modify the execution of a program. After the tool collects the information, it can produce reports in various formats, including rich and navigable HTML pages. Similarly to JUnit, JaCoCo is well integrated in the most popular IDEs, but you also can run it from the command line.

JaCoCo measures various types of code coverage criteria:

- *Instruction coverage*—Percentage of bytecode instructions executed.
- *Line coverage*—Percentage of Java source code lines executed. The compiler may compile a line into several bytecode instructions. A line is considered executed if at least one of those instructions is executed. Hence, line coverage always appears larger than instruction coverage.

- *Branch coverage*—Percentage of conditional branches executed. This refers to if and `switch` statements.

You can find instructions on how to run JaCoCo from the command line in the file `UnitTests.java`,[4] which also contains the tests developed in this chapter. After running the tests with JaCoCo, you get a coverage report whose content is summarized in table 6.5. It informs you that you managed to execute all bytecode instructions from the *Reference* and *Speed3* implementations—not a bad result!

Table 6.5 Code coverage measures for various implementations. Here, "assert on/off" refers to the Java `assert` statement, not to JUnit assertions.

Version	Instruction	Line	Branch
Reference	100%	100%	100%
Speed3	100%	100%	100%
Contracts (assert off)	38%	50%	25%
Contracts (assert on)	92%	100%	63%
Invariants (assert off)	51%	56%	29%
Invariants (assert on)	92%	100%	68%

By the way, having executed all bytecode instructions and having found no bugs doesn't mean that no bug exists. It may very well be that the inputs you provided weren't the right ones to expose an error. For example, a malicious coder could write addWater so that it crashes when π (that is, `Math.PI`) liters of water are added. It's very unlikely that any amount of blackbox testing would find that out. However, a detailed code coverage analysis would flag that case as unexplored, possibly exposing the trap.

For *Contracts* and *Invariants*, coverage depends heavily on whether you've enabled Java `assert` statements (via the -ea command-line option). When you haven't, the tests explore only about 50% of the source code lines and even less of the bytecode instructions because you aren't running the code pertaining to the postconditions and invariant checks. On the other hand, with asserts enabled, you reach 100% line coverage. You don't reach full instruction and branch coverage because all checks are passing, so the "failed check" branches aren't being executed. No amount of testing would improve that because the SUT is actually correct, so the testing can't reach those branches.

> **POP QUIZ 4** If your program contains `assert` instructions, should you test it with assertions enabled or disabled?

---

[4] You can find this file in the package eis.chapter6 from the online repository (https://bitbucket.org /mfaella/exercisesinstyle).

6.3   *Testability*   *[Testable]*

To test a program unit, you need to be able to provide inputs to it *(controllability)* and observe the effect of those inputs *(observability)*. Moreover, if the unit under test (UUT) depends on other units (such as a method invoking a method of another class), and your tests reveal a defect, you don't know whether that defect belongs to the UUT or to one of its dependencies. That's why proper unit testing requires you to *isolate* the UUT from its original dependencies.

The following subsections expand on these three aspects of testing and improve the testability of our running example. The improved version shares the same structure as *Reference*, whose fields I'll repeat here for convenience:

```
public class Container {
    private Set<Container> group;      ❶ Containers connected to this one
    private double amount;             ❷ Amount of water in this container
```

However, testability is a property of an API, so the improved version will have a slightly different (richer, actually) public interface.

6.3.1   *Controllability*

Controllability refers to the ease of providing arbitrary inputs to the UUT. The `Container` class is highly controllable because it receives inputs directly from its clients via its API.

Poorly controllable units receive their inputs from files, databases, network connections, or, even worse, GUIs. In those cases, testing requires an infrastructure that simulates the other end of the communication channel. I won't go into the details because they'd lead us astray from the running example, and entire books are devoted to the topic. As usual, you can find some suggestions in the *Further reading* section at the end of this chapter.

> **POP QUIZ 5** Suppose you add to the `Container` class a static method that reconstructs a set of container objects from a file (aka a *deserialization* method). How would adding this method affect testability?

6.3.2   *Observability*

The water container API I established in chapter 1 aims at simplicity and scores quite poorly on observability.

First, the methods `connectTo` and `addWater` don't return any value. Testability urges all methods to return some value, to get some form of immediate feedback from any invocation. For example, `connectTo` might return at least a Boolean value, indicating whether the two containers being connected were already connected or not (as shown in the following listing), similarly to the way the `add` method of `Collection` reports whether the insertion was successful.

Listing 6.4   *Testable*: Method `connectTo` (abridged)

```
public boolean connectTo(Container other) {
   if (group==other.group) return false;

   ...  ❶ The actual operation here (same as Reference)

   return true;
}
```

More interestingly, `addWater` might return the amount of water in this container after the present addition, as shown in the following listing.

Listing 6.5   *Testable*: Method `addWater`

```
public double addWater(double amount) {
   double amountPerContainer = amount / group.size();
   for (Container c: group) { c.amount += amountPerContainer; }
   return this.amount;
}
```

As to observing the current state of a water container, `getAmount` is the only method providing any feedback on the state of a container. This is a very limited perspective, like looking at a room through a keyhole. The connections are completely hidden, and you can infer them only by the way water is distributed among different containers. It would be straightforward to add further methods to the API, exposing more information and improving testability. For example, a natural addition would be a method that checks whether two containers are currently connected, as shown in the following listing. This check is very easy to perform in *Reference* because connected containers point to the same group object, leading to the following implementation.

Listing 6.6   *Testable*: Additional method `isConnectedTo`

```
public boolean isConnectedTo(Container other) {
   return group == other.group;
}
```

In fact, in chapter 7, you'll end up adding a number of such methods, albeit for a different reason: readability.

> **POP QUIZ 6**   Suppose you add to the `Container` class a public method returning the number of containers connected (directly or indirectly) to this one. How does the new method affect testability?

6.3.3   *Isolation: Severing dependencies*

The idea of unit testing is to check the behavior of a single unit (such as a class) *in isolation*. In this way, a failed test is sure to lead to a defect in that unit, with no need to go hunting for the bug in various classes. In this respect, the container example is an ideal test "unit," because it's perfectly isolated, not depending on any other class, except for the standard JDK.

Conversely, in most real-world scenarios, classes are interconnected in complex ways, making testing and the subsequent fault diagnosis more complicated. To mitigate these issues, you can use techniques such as *mocking* and *stubbing*, which involve replacing the actual dependencies with fake ones that are hopefully simple enough to be above suspicion. Libraries like Mockito and Powermock help automate such tasks.

A common way to improve testability in the presence of dependencies is to employ *dependency injection*. Simply put, if the class under test creates objects of another type (such as a `Container` creating a `HashSet`), the dependency injection scheme suggests having the client pass such objects from the outside.

In our scenario, instead of the current constructor from *Reference*:

```
public Container() {
    group = new HashSet<Container>();
    group.add(this);
}
```

you might have the following:

```
public Container(Set<Container> emptySet) {
    group = emptySet;
    group.add(this);
}
```

This new version is more testable because the testing suite can replace `HashSet` with a simple, perhaps fake implementation of the `Set` interface, ensuring that any defect the tests reveal is coming from the code in `Container` and not from `HashSet`. That course of action would be absurd in this specific context because `HashSet` is a trusted keystone of the JDK. Still, bear with me while we use our running example to explore the pros and cons of this technique.

The *injected* version of the constructor comes with two serious drawbacks:

- It exposes an implementation detail of the `Container` class, violating encapsulation. Not only does it show the client that new containers need a set, it even lets the client choose what kind of set to use! If you later decide to switch from the set-based representation of *Reference* to the tree-based representation of *Speed3*, you need to modify the public API of containers. This is a general issue with dependency injection: you must balance improved testability against decreased encapsulation.
- It puts a heavy burden on the caller: passing a new empty `Set` for every new container it wishes to create. The client has many ways it can mess up—for example, by passing a set that's not empty or the same set to more than one container.

You can easily improve on the second of these issues. For starters, you can check that the client-provided set is indeed empty, and abort otherwise. Moreover, to prevent the same empty set from being used to initialize multiple containers, you may *copy* the set argument, provided the implementation that the client chooses supports cloning.

```
public Container(Set<Container> emptySet) {
  if (!emptySet.isEmpty())
      throw new IllegalArgumentException("The set is supposed to be empty!");
  group = (Set<Container>) emptySet.clone();
  group.add(this);
}
```

Finally, reflection allows you to write a variant that both guarantees emptiness by construction and avoids cloning; you accept a Class object and use it to instantiate a new empty set, as you can see in listing 6.7. Notice how you can use generics to make sure the client-provided Class object refers to an implementation of Set<Container>. There's still a small catch: the set implementation the client chooses must provide a constructor with no arguments; otherwise, the method getDeclaredConstructor will throw an exception.

> **Listing 6.7 *Testable*: Constructor supporting dependency injection**

```
  public Container(Class<? extends Set<Container>{}> setType)
        throws ReflectiveOperationException {
    group = setType.getDeclaredConstructor()
                  .newInstance();
    group.add(this);
  }
```

In practice, rather than implementing dependency injection from scratch, you're better off employing one of the frameworks built for this purpose. The sidebar gives you some pointers.

Dependency injection frameworks

Java Enterprise Edition (now known as *Jakarta EE*) and a number of Java frameworks, such as Google Guice, a small library, and Spring, a large framework for enterprise applications, support dependency injection (DI). In all cases, the framework offers the following functionalities:

1. You label a method or constructor as requiring dependency injection. You usually achieve this with an annotation. For example, Spring uses @Autowired, whereas Guice and JEE use @Inject. This type of interaction, when you instruct a framework to invoke your code, is also known as *inversion of control*.
2. You bind concrete classes to the parameters that will be injected.
3. At runtime, the framework takes care of instantiating the appropriate concrete classes and transferring them to the corresponding method or constructor.

6.4   And now for something completely different

As usual, in this section I'll apply the techniques I've presented in this chapter to a different example. This time, it'll be the same as the example from chapter 5—the bounded set data structure—because this chapter is an ideal continuation of the previous one, and establishing clear contracts, as we did in the previous chapter, should precede any testing effort.

For water containers, I helped you design test cases and *then* I introduced testability issues and discussed related improvements to the API. For bounded sets, I'll do the opposite, which is closer to what you would (or should) do in practice:

- First, design (or improve) the API with testability in mind.
- Then, design a test suite.

Recall from chapter 5 that a `BoundedSet` is a set with a fixed capacity established at construction time, and the following functionalities:

- `void add(T elem)`—Adds the specified element to this bounded set. If this addition brings the set size beyond its capacity, this method removes from the set the *oldest* element (the one that was inserted first).

    The addition of an element that already belongs to the set *renews* it (that is, it makes the element the newest one in the set).
- `boolean contains(T elem)`—Returns `true` if this bounded set contains the specified element.

In chapter 5, we decided to represent a bounded set using a linked list and a capacity:

```
public class BoundedSet<T> {
    private final LinkedList<T> data;
    private final int capacity;
```

Now, let's analyze and enhance the testability of `BoundedSet`.

6.4.1 *Improving testability*

You can see that the bounded set API is poorly observable because the only method providing any information on its state is `contains`. You have no way of knowing the insertion order of its elements, or at least which element is the oldest and therefore the next one to be removed. In fact, not even the current size of the set is available.

As I explained in the section about observability, the first improvement involves adding a return value to the methods that lack it. For example, you may equip `add` with a return value of type `T`, representing the object that's been evicted from the set (if any). This kind of return value is similar to the way `Map.put(key, val)` returns the value previously associated with that key.

Check out the following updated contract for `add`. Besides describing its return value, it states that a `null` argument is not accepted; otherwise, the `null` return value would be ambiguous:

- `T add(T elem)`—Adds the specified element to this bounded set. If this addition brings the set size beyond its capacity, this method removes *and returns* the oldest element from the set (the one that was inserted first). Otherwise, it returns `null`.

The addition of an element that already belongs to the set renews it (that is, it makes the element the newest one in the set).

This method *doesn't accept* a `null` argument.

Getting a value back from `add` is a good start, but it allows you to query the state of the bounded set *only when you're modifying it*. To further improve testability, a class should give access to all the information that's relevant to its external behavior (that is, all information that affects the behavior, as perceived by the client). In this case, besides a standard `size` method, you should have a way to check the current order of the elements, because that order affects future calls to `add` and `contains`. Let's compare some ways to expose the order of the elements:

1 Give the client direct access to the internal list of objects, with the following extra method:

```
public List<T> content() {
    return data;
}
```

I probably don't need to tell you, that's very bad—you don't want the client to mess with your internal representation!

2 Give the client a *copy* of the internal list of objects:

```
public List<T> content() {
    return new ArrayList<>(data);
}
```

That's better than option 1, but it's inefficient (the copy requires linear time) and allows the caller to modify this list, which is pointless and possibly error-prone. (The caller may mistakenly believe they're modifying the bounded set itself.)

3 Give the client an *unmodifiable view* of the internal list of objects. An unmodifiable view is an object that wraps the original list while disabling all methods that can modify it (like `add` and `remove`). A couple of static methods from the class `Collections` provide unmodifiable views of standard collections. In this case, the following one-liner does the job:

```
public List<T> content() {
    return Collections.unmodifiableList(data);
}
```

Compared to the previous solutions, this one is better on all counts: it's efficient because it doesn't need to copy the list, and it doesn't pose any risks because the returned object is read-only.

The only drawback, shared by all three solutions so far, is that you're committing to a very expressive return type—a `List`. Right now, this commitment is easy to realize because your internal representation is itself a list. If in the future you change your mind about the internal representation, per-haps switching to an array, the implementation of `content` may become signif-icantly more complex. The following solution avoids this issue by exposing a more limited view of the content: an iterator instead of a list.

4 Offer to the clients a read-only iterator over the content. Recall that an iterator may change the underlying collection through its `remove` method. You have to make sure that you've disabled the `remove` method in the iterator you return. Once again, you can achieve this objective using an unmodifiable view:

```java
public class BoundedSet<T> implements Iterable<T> {
    ...
    public Iterator<T> iterator() {
        return Collections.unmodifiableList(data).iterator();
    }
```

In the next section, I'll assume you went with solution 3 (the method returning the unmodifiable list view) because that maximizes testability.

6.4.2   A test suite

Let's focus on testing the `add` method, which is the only method that modifies the bounded set. Analyzing the contract of `add`, you can identify three characteristics that are relevant to its behavior:

C1. Whether the argument of `add` is `null` or not. If it is, we expect an NPE as a penalty.

C2. The size of the bounded set before this insertion. In particular, the behavior of `add` changes if the bounded set is full—that is, its size is equal to its capacity. It's convenient to also single out the case when the bounded set is empty, because that may be error prone, like all corner cases.

C3. Whether the argument of `add` is already present in the bounded set before this insertion. This is relevant because the insertion of an already-present element doesn't evict any element, even if the set is full.

Table 6.6 summarizes these characteristics and their possible values (aka blocks).

Table 6.6   Characteristics chosen for testing the method `add` of bounded sets

Name	Characteristic	Blocks
C1	Value of argument	{null, other}
C2	Size of set before insertion	{empty, full, other}
C3	Presence of argument before insertion	{absent, present}

Two constraints between these characteristics limit the number of meaningful com-binations of blocks:

- If the element is null (C1=null), the element couldn't be present (C3≠present).

- If the bounded set is empty before this insertion (C2=empty), the element couldn't be present (C3≠present).

Because of these constraints, you're left with the following eight combinations:

1. (C1=null, C2=empty, C3=absent)   4. (other, empty, absent)   7. (other, full, present)
2. (null, full, absent)   5. (other, full, absent)   8. (other, other, present)
3. (null, other, absent)   6. (other, other, absent)

As discussed earlier in the chapter, you can collapse the first three combinations into one because those cases violate the precondition for the same reason—a `null` argument. As a result, you end up with six test cases.

To implement the test cases in JUnit, start by initializing a bounded set of capacity three as the test fixture. That's a very limited capacity but large enough to support all the interesting behaviors of bounded sets.

```
public class BoundedSetTests {
    private BoundedSet<Integer> set;   ❶ Test fixture

    @Before   ❷ Executed before each test
    public void setUp() {
        set = new BoundedSet<>(3);
    }
```

Next, I'll provide the code for the first three tests. This time, I'll use the following Hamcrest matchers to write more readable assert conditions:

- `is`—A pass-through matcher. It doesn't check anything, you just put it there to make the condition more English-friendly.
- `nullValue`—This is Hamcrest-speak for `null`.
- `contains`—Compares an `Iterable` with an explicit sequence of values. They match if they contain the same elements (according to `equals`) in the same order.

Each matcher is a static method from the class `org.hamcrest.Matchers`. You need to statically import them to use their unqualified names.

In the following tests, notice how the `content` method—added for testability—works hand in hand with the `contains` matcher. By returning a list (but an `Iterable` would have worked just as fine), it allows you to compare in a single shot the whole sequence of elements with its expected state.

```
@Test(expected = NullPointerException.class)   ❶ C1=null
public void testAddNull() {
    set.add(null);
}
@Test
public void testAddOnEmpty() {   ❷ C1=other, C2=empty
    Integer result = set.add(1);
    assertThat("Wrong return value",
               result, is(nullValue()));   ❸ Hamcrest way to check for null
    assertThat("Wrong set content",
```

```
                    set.content(), contains(1));   4  Hamcrest matcher for Iterables
    }
    @Test
    public void testAddAbsentOnNonFull() {   5  CI=other, C2=other, C3=absent
        set.add(1);
        Integer result = set.add(2);   6  Line under test
        assertThat("Wrong return value", result, is(nullValue()));
        assertThat("Wrong set content", set.content(), contains(1, 2));
    }
```

Two of the previous tests violate a commonly repeated guideline for tests: the *one assert per test* rule. The idea behind this rule is that unit tests should be focused, or, in other words, each test should have to fail for a single reason. As usual in software engineering, you should take such guidelines with a grain of salt. It's OK to split each of those tests in two: one checking the return value from add, and the other checking the state of the set after the insertion. However, the original tests are so simple that it's probably not worth the extra lines of code. The error message in the assertion clarifies the reason for the failure anyway.

6.5   *Real-world use cases*

If you've worked for a few years as a software engineer it's entirely possible that you've heard "I know unit tests are useful, but there's not enough time to write them," or, "finish writing the library first, and then if you have time go on and write unit tests." In the first scenario, it might be a matter of time before you pay the price. The second scenario reflects how things were done in the past: most tests were created after the original software was written (the so-called waterfall model). Let's examine some use cases where testing could be useful.

- You're part of a development team working on a successful middleware plat-form, and management has requested that your team expose some of the func-tionality of an application running in the financial department to calculate payroll via RESTful services. Although you trust your colleagues, you'd like to avoid giving unauthorized salary raises. To ensure the correctness of your ser-vice, you decide to create some tests. Testing RESTful services can be cumber-some, but fortunately libraries exist that can help you create clean, decoupled tests for your API.

- Putting a machine-learning (ML) model into production usually means that it becomes part of a workflow. It may be that an automated job runs early in the morning on a daily basis, querying a database and exporting data to feed the trained ML models so they can produce predictions for tomorrow's sales. An enthusiastic, newly-hired database engineer decides to take the initiative to optimize some of the queries. It turns out, though, that these changes affect the format of the query results, and the workflow breaks after data export. After that incident, the database development team decides to write some unit tests to ensure that data exported from queries conform to what the ML models expect to receive to make predictions.

- You're a computer science PhD student and have realized that it's time to turn your research into a product. You invite your most trusted fellow students, and after many rounds of conversations, you decide to establish a startup. After a couple of years, you're not Bill Gates yet, but things are looking good; your company has grown and so has your code base. You were clever enough to anticipate that this was going to happen, and the automated tests you wrote are your development team's safety net. The tests evolve in parallel with the rest of the code base. In fact, you write your tests *before* adding new functionality. This is the foundational idea of Test-Driven Development (TDD): code a scenario based on what you expect to achieve, run the tests to fail, then go back to apply the fixes to make unit tests pass.

6.6   *Applying what you learned*

EXERCISE 1
Devise and execute a testing plan for the method `getDivisors`, defined by the following contract:

- *Precondition*—The method accepts an integer n as the only parameter.
- *Postcondition*—The method returns a `List` of `Integer`s, containing all the divisors of n. For n==0, it returns the empty list. For a negative n, it returns the same list as its opposite.
  For example, for both 12 and −12, it returns $[1, 2, 3, 4, 6, 12]$.
- *Penalty*—None (All integers are valid arguments.)

EXERCISE 2
Devise and execute a testing plan for the method

```
public int indexOf(int ch, int fromIndex)
```

from the class `String`, using the input domain model approach.

EXERCISE 3
1. Using the input domain model approach, devise and execute a testing plan for the method `interleaveLists`, defined by the following contract (same as exercise 2 from chapter 5):

- *Precondition*—The method receives as arguments two `List`s of the same length.
- *Postcondition*—The method returns a new `List` containing all the elements of the two lists, in an alternating fashion.
- *Penalty*—If at least one of the lists is `null`, the method throws a `NullPointer Exception`. If the lists have different lengths, the method throws an `Illegal ArgumentException`.

2. Estimate the code coverage that your plan achieves, either manually or using a code coverage tool.

EXERCISE 4

Improve the testability of the generic interface `PopularityContest<T>`, representing a popularity contest among a (dynamically enlarging) set of objects of type `T`. The interface contains the following methods:

- `void addContestant(T contestant)`—Adds a new contestant. Addition of a duplicate contestant is ignored.
- `void voteFor(T contestant)`—Votes for the specified contestant. If that contestant doesn't belong to this contest, it throws an `IllegalArgumentException`.
- `T getMostVoted()`—Returns the contestant who has received the maximum number of votes so far. If this contest is empty (no contestants), it throws an `IllegalStateException`.

Summary

- The input domain model approach helps you identify relevant test inputs.
- You can combine input values for different parameters in different ways, leading to more or fewer tests and to different coverage levels.
- You can evaluate a test suite according to its input coverage and code coverage.
- You can enhance testability by providing more feedback from methods.
- Dependency injection helps to isolate the class under test by replacing dependencies with simpler substitutes.

Answers to quizzes and exercises

POP QUIZ 1

All parts of the contract are relevant for testing. As the postcondition describes the intended effect of the method, it dictates the assertions that the tests will be checking. Most unit tests you write send legal inputs to the method under test and check that the outputs conform to the postcondition. The precondition describes what the range of legal inputs is. Finally, as explained in the chapter, other tests will send *illegal* inputs and check that the method reacts in the way that's advertised in the penalty section of the contract.

POP QUIZ 2

Dates are a source of terrible headaches for programmers and testers alike. Even ignoring international differences and sticking to the Gregorian calendar, programs, and hence tests, need to deal with a wealth of irregularities. For starters, months are 28, 29, 30, or 31 days long, with February being particularly capricious. Table 6.7 summarizes three possible characteristics.

Table 6.7 Three possible characteristics for a "date" data type

Name	Characteristic	Blocks
C1	Leap year	{true, false}
C2	Length of month	{28, 29, 30, 31}
C3	Day of month	{first, intermediate, last}

POP QUIZ 3

- All Combinations Coverage: $n_1 * n_2 * n_3$
- Each Choice Coverage: $\max\{n_1, n_2, n_3\}$
- Base Choice Coverage: $1 + (n_1 - 1) + (n_2 - 1) + (n_3 - 1) = n_1 + n_2 + n_3 - 2$

POP QUIZ 4

Why not both? First, test with assertions off, as that's how the software will run in production. If any test fails, run it again with assertions on. They might help pinpoint the defect.

POP QUIZ 5

Adding a deserialization method would decrease testability because the new method accepts a complicated input from a file.

POP QUIZ 6

In general, read-only methods help testability because they're quite safe (hard to get wrong) and provide one more way to observe the state of the objects. As a result, adding a `groupSize` method improves testability.

EXERCISE 1

You can take the first characteristic, C1, to be the sign of the input n, as the list of standard type-based features suggests. (Refer to table 6.1.) The second characteristic, C2, may come from the postcondition and count the number of divisors that the method returns. This gives you the following four blocks:

- *No divisors*—This case applies only to $n = 0$. The contract specifies that the output must be an empty list.
- *One divisor*—This only happens for $n = 1$ and $n = -1$.
- *Two divisors*—This happens for all prime numbers and their opposites.
- *More than two divisors*—This applies to all other inputs.

Table 6.8 summarizes these characteristics.

Table 6.8 Characteristics for the input n of `getDivisors`

Name	Characteristic	Blocks
C1	Sign	{negative, zero, positive}
C2	Number of divisors	{zero, one, two, more than two }

You can see that the two characteristics are *not* independent, because C1 = zero can only be paired with C2 = zero. As a result, instead of $3*4 = 12$ combinations, we only get seven meaningful ones, and we can apply All Combinations Coverage with little effort. These are the first two tests; you can find the other five in the accompanying repository (https://bitbucket.org/mfaella/exercisesinstyle) in the class `eis.chapter6.exercises` `.DivisorTests`:

```
@Test
public void testZero() {        1  Cl = C2 = zero
   List<Integer> divisors = getDivisors(0);
   assertTrue("Divisors of zero should be the empty list",
             divisors.isEmpty());
}


@Test
public void testMinusOne() {    2  Cl = negative, C2 = one
   List<Integer> divisors = getDivisors(-1);
   List<Integer> expected = List.of(1);
   assertEquals("Wrong divisors of -1", expected, divisors);
}
```

EXERCISE 2

You can summarize the Javadoc for `indexOf` and put it into contract form as follows:

- *Precondition*—None (All invocations are legitimate.)
- *Postcondition*—Returns the index within this string of the first occurrence of the specified character, starting the search at the specified index. Returns –1 if the character doesn't occur.
  A negative `fromIndex` is treated as zero. A negative `ch` returns –1.
- *Penalty*—None

In choosing good characteristics, you have only the postcondition to guide you, in addition to the standard type-based characteristics. (You can go back to table 6.1 if you don't remember them.) You can take the first characteristic, C1, right out of the standard type-based ones: the emptiness of this string. The first parameter, `ch`, is an integer representing a (Unicode) character. You can apply the standard sign characteristic to it and baptize it C2. The second parameter, `fromIndex`, is also an integer, which should be less than the length, n, of this string. To partition its values, you need to introduce a characteristic, C3, that combines the standard sign characteristic with the relationship between `fromIndex` and n, obtaining five cases:

- `fromIndex` is negative.
- `fromIndex` is zero, and the string is empty (an invalid zero).
- `fromIndex` is zero, and the string is not empty (a valid zero).
- `fromIndex` is positive and at least as large as n (an invalid positive).
- `fromIndex` is positive and smaller than n (a valid positive).

Finally, characteristic C4 encodes the presence of the character in the specified substring. Table 6.9 summarizes these characteristics.

Table 6.9   Characteristics chosen for testing `indexOf`

Name	Characteristic	Blocks
C1	Emptiness of this string	{empty, nonempty}
C2	Sign of `ch`	{negative, zero, positive}
C3	Sign of `fromIndex` and relation with the length of this string	{negative, valid zero, invalid zero, valid positive, invalid positive}
C4	Presence of character in the substring	{present, absent}

Of the 60 possible combinations, the following 27 are consistent (I'm using "*" as a wildcard):

- (empty, *, {negative, invalid zero, invalid positive}, absent) (9 combinations)
- (nonempty, *, {negative, valid zero, invalid positive, valid positive}, absent) (12 combinations)
- (nonempty, {zero, positive}, {negative, valid zero, valid positive}, present) (6 combinations)

Assuming you don't want to write 27 tests, you can switch from All Combinations Coverage to one of the more restricted strategies I presented in the chapter. Here, I'll go with Each Choice Coverage and look for a small selection of combinations featuring each block from each characteristic at least once. Note that any solution includes at least five combinations because C3 supports five blocks. This is a possible solution:

1. (nonempty, positive, valid positive, present)
2. (nonempty, positive, negative, present)
3. (nonempty, zero, invalid positive, absent)
4. (nonempty, negative, valid zero, absent)
5. (empty, positive, invalid zero, absent)

Here's the JUnit implementation of the first test:

```
public class IndexOfTests {
    private final static String TESTME = "test me";

    @Test
    public void testNominal() {
        int result = TESTME.indexOf((int)'t', 2);
        assertEquals("test with nominal arguments", 3, result);
    }
}
```

You can find the others in the accompanying repository (https://bitbucket.org/mfaella /exercisesinstyle).

EXERCISE 3

1. The precondition suggests two properties you can include in the characteristics: the lists being non-null and having the same length. In addition, a special case for any

collection is being empty. You can fit these observations into the three characteristics in table 6.10.

Table 6.10   Characteristics chosen for testing `interleaveLists`

Name	Characteristic	Blocks
C1	Type of the first list	{null, empty, non-empty}
C2	Type of the second list	{null, empty, non-empty}
C3	Lists have the same length	{true, false}

C3 is not independent from C1 and C2; some combinations don't make sense. I'll list the combinations that do make sense:

1. (null, nonempty, false)
2. (nonempty, null, false)
3. (empty, empty, true)
4. (empty, nonempty, false)
5. (nonempty, empty, false)
6. (nonempty, nonempty, false)
7. (nonempty, nonempty, true)

If you're wondering why I skipped "(null, null, false)," it's because when a characteristic violates the precondition, it's sufficient to combine it with nominal (that is, normal) values of the others. By the way, including that combination is somewhat overcautious, but definitely not wrong. Note how only combinations 3 and 7 satisfy the precondition.

Because we have only seven combinations, we can test all of them with little effort. Here's the code for the first three.

```java
public class InterleaveTests {
    private List<Integer> a, b, result;   ❶ Fixtures

    @Before
    public void setUp() {   ❷ Initializing fixtures
        a = List.of(1, 2, 3);
        b = List.of(4, 5, 6);
        result = List.of(1, 4, 2, 5, 3, 6);
    }

    @Test(expected = NullPointerException.class)
    public void testFirstNull() {   ❸ Test l: (null, nonempty, false)
        InterleaveLists.interleaveLists(null, b);
    }

    @Test(expected = NullPointerException.class)
    public void testSecondNull() {   ❹ Test 2: (nonempty, null, false)
        InterleaveLists.interleaveLists(a, null);
    }
```

```
@Test
public void testBothEmpty() {         ⑤ Test 3: (empty, empty, true)
   a = List.of();
   b = List.of();
   List<Integer> c = InterleaveLists.interleaveLists(a, b);
   assertTrue("should be empty", c.isEmpty());
}
```

You can find the rest in the accompanying repository (https://bitbucket.org/mfaella
/exercisesinstyle).

2. First, notice that it doesn't make much sense to measure coverage of the support
method that checks the postcondition. It's not a useful objective to execute every line
in that method because we hope the postcondition will hold, which means that the
tests will always skip some lines from `interleaveCheckPost`.

Limiting our analysis to the body of `interleaveLists`, the seven tests I described
earlier achieve 100% coverage.

EXERCISE 4

The given interface is easily controllable, but you can enhance its observability. As it
stands, `getMostVoted` is the only point of access to the internal state of the object, and
a limited one. You get to know only the top voted item, and no vote count is available
for any contestant. To improve the situation, you can start by equipping the other two
methods with return values. For example:

- `boolean addContestant(T contestant)`—Adds a contestant and returns `true`
  if the contestant wasn't already a member of this contest. Otherwise, it leaves
  the contest unchanged and returns `false`.
- `int voteFor(T contestant)`—Votes for the specified contestant and returns
  the updated number of votes. If that contestant doesn't belong to this contest,
  it throws an `IllegalArgumentException`.

The new version of `voteFor` is a powerful testing tool, but it conflates voting and reading the number of votes. It may be useful for testing to also have a read-only method
for votes:

- `int getVotes(T contestant)`—Returns the current number of votes for the
  specified contestant. If the contestant doesn't belong to this contest, it throws
  an `IllegalArgumentException`.

Additionally, the method `getVotes` provides a way to check whether a contestant belongs
to the contest, without altering it.

Further reading

- G. J. Myers, C. Sandler, and T. Badgett. *The Art of Software Testing*. John Wiley
  & Sons, 2012.
  An all-around introduction to testing and other validation techniques, like
  code reviews and inspections. It combines a time-tested introduction to the

principles (the first edition was published in 1979) with an up-to-date discussion of the agile approach to testing.

- L. Koskela. *Effective Unit Testing*. Manning Publications, 2013.

  A book full of hands-on advice on designing effective tests, including a catalog of common test deficiencies (aka *test smells*).

- S. Freeman and N. Pryce. *Growing Object-Oriented Software, Guided by Tests*. Addison-Wesley, 2009.

  A process-oriented book illustrating Test-Driven Development (TDD) and mocking on a realistic example—from the creators of the popular mocking library jMock.

- P. Ammann and J. Offutt. *Introduction to Software Testing*. Cambridge University Press, 2010.

  A modern, compact treatment of testing techniques, featuring a unified view of the various flavors of coverage criteria.

Coding aloud: Readability

This chapter covers

- Writing readable code
- Documenting contracts using Javadoc comments
- Replacing implementation comments with self-documenting code

Source code serves two very different kinds of users: programmers and computers. Computers are as happy with messy code as they are with clean, well-structured systems. On the other hand, we programmers are utterly sensitive to the shape of the program. Even white space and indentation—completely irrelevant to the computer—make the difference between understandable and obscure code. (See appendix A for an extreme example.) In turn, easy-to-understand code boosts reliability, because it tends to hide fewer bugs, and maintainability, because it's easier to modify.

In this chapter, I'll show you some of the modern guidelines for writing readable code. As with the other chapters, my objective isn't to provide a comprehensive survey of readability tips and tricks. I'll focus on the main techniques that make sense on a small code unit and put them in practice on our usual running example.

7.1 *Points of view on readability*

Writing readable code is an undervalued art that schools seldom teach, but whose impact on software reliability, maintenance, and evolution is paramount. Programmers learn to express a set of desired functionalities in machine-friendly code. This encoding process takes time and inserts layer upon layer of abstraction to decompose those functionalities into smaller units. In Java parlance, these abstractions are packages, classes, and methods. If the overall system is large enough, no single programmer will dominate the entire codebase. Some developers will have a vertical view of a functionality: from its requirements to its implementation through all abstraction layers. Others may be in charge of one layer and supervise its API. From time to time, all of them will need to read and understand code their colleagues have written.

Promoting readability means minimizing the time that a reasonably knowledgable programmer needs to understand a given piece of code. A more concrete characterization would be *the time that someone who isn't familiar with the code needs to feel confident enough to modify it without breaking it*. Other names for this quality are *learnability* and *understandability*.

> **POP QUIZ 1**   Which other code quality attributes are affected by readability?

How do you write readable programs? As early as 1974, when C was two years old, this problem was deemed significant enough to deserve systematic treatment, leading to the influential book *The Elements of Programming Style*. In it, Kernighan (of C fame) and Plauger take apart a number of small programs, all drawn from published textbooks, summing up their lucid and surprisingly modern observations in a list of programming-style aphorisms. The first aphorism on expressions summarizes well the whole readability issue:

> *Say what you mean, simply and directly.*

Indeed, readability is about clearly expressing the *intent* of the code. Grady Booch, one of the architects of UML, puts forward a natural analogy:

> *Clean code reads like well-written prose.*

Now, creating well-written prose isn't something you can achieve by following a fixed set of rules. It takes years of practice, not only in writing, but also in reading well-written prose by established authors. The expressive capabilities of computer code are definitely limited compared with natural languages, so the process of creating clean code is luckily somewhat simpler, or at least more structured, than producing a beautiful essay. Still, mastering this process requires years of practice that no book (or book chapter!) can replace. In this chapter, we'll explore some basic ways to improve the readability of your code, focusing on those techniques that you can apply to our recurring example.

In the last two decades, readability has been put on the front burner by the Agile movement, thanks to the focus on *refactoring* and *clean code*. Refactoring is the idea of restructuring a working system to improve its design so that future change is easier and safer. It's one of the main ingredients in those lightweight development processes that favor fast development phases and iterative refinement of software.

Even if you or your company doesn't subscribe to the whole Agile philosophy, you can't miss the literature that comes with it, which is full of brilliant ideas about the bad (code smells), the good (clean code), and how to turn the first into the latter (refactoring). See the *Further reading* section at the end of this chapter for specific suggestions.

It would be nice to supplement the readability tips that well-known experts have developed with hard data on the effectiveness of those tips. Unfortunately, readability is inherently subjective, and it's extremely hard to come up with objective means to measure it. This hasn't stopped researchers from proposing a variety of formal models, all attempting to estimate readability with a combination of simple numerical measures, like the length of the identifiers, the number of parentheses occurring in an expression, and so on. This ongoing effort is still far from reaching a stable consensus, so I'll focus on some established industry best practices, starting with a quick look at the style policies of the biggest IT players.

7.1.1 *Corporate coding style guides*

Some of the largest software companies publish coding style guides online, including the following:

- Sun used to provide an "official" Java style guide, which hasn't been updated since 1999. A frozen archival copy is available at http://mng.bz/adVx.
- Google has a company-wide style guide: https://google.github.io/styleguide /javaguide.html.
- Twitter provides a library of common Java utilities, accompanied by a style guide: http://mng.bz/gVAZ. The guide explicitly refers to Google's and Oracle's guides as inspirations.
- Facebook also provides a style guide with its library of Java utility classes: http:// mng.bz/eDyw.

These guides mostly agree on the general principles I set forth in this chapter and only differ on the level of detail they reach and on small cosmetic issues. For example, consider the sequence of `import` statements at the beginning of a source file. Here's one such sequence in Google's format:

```
import static com.google.common.base.Strings.isNullOrEmpty;
import static java.lang.Math.PI;

import java.util.LinkedList;
import javax.crypto.Cypher;
import javax.crypto.SealedObject;
```

Here's Twitter's recommended style for the same `imports`:

```
import java.util.LinkedList;

import javax.crypto.Cypher;
import javax.crypto.SealedObject;

import static com.google.common.base.Strings.isNullOrEmpty;

import static java.lang.Math.PI;
```

Both the order and the use of empty lines are different. Oracle and Facebook, on the other hand, are fine with any layout of `imports`.

Style guides ensure some uniformity across a company's code base and are a nice addition to the welcome package for new employees, giving them something easy to sink their teeth into, before the real troubles begin. (Besides, when those troubles start biting back, they can say, "At least I'm following the style guide!") For your long-term professional growth, though, it'll be much more useful for you to peruse this chapter and then spend some time with the articulated style books I've listed at the end of the chapter, particularly *Clean Code* and *Code Complete*.

7.1.2   *Readability ingredients*

You can distinguish the ingredients contributing to readability into two categories:

-   *Structural*—Features that may affect the execution of the program; for example, its architecture, the choice of the API, the choice of control flow statements, and so on. You can further distinguish these features into three levels:

    -   *Architecture-level*—Features involving more than one class
    -   *Class-level*—Features involving a single class but transcending the boundaries of a single method
    -   *Method-level*—Features that involve a single method

-   *Exterior*—Features that don't affect execution; for example, comments, white space, and choice of variables names

In the following sections, I'll briefly recall the main guidelines regarding each category. Then, I'll guide you through applying those guidelines to the water container running example.

7.2   *Structural readability features*

Architectural-level features refer to the high-level structure of the program: how it's split into classes and the relationships occurring between them. Generally speaking, an architecture that's easy to understand should be composed of small classes with coherent responsibilities (aka *high cohesion*), tied together by an uncomplicated network of dependencies (aka *low coupling*). Another readability-enhancing technique is to use standard design patterns whenever possible. Because most developers know them, they spark familiarity and convey a complement of contextual information to the reader.

Table 7.1 Summary of structural code features affecting readability

Structural Understandability		
Level	Features	Ways to improve
Architectural	Class responsibilities Relationships between classes	Decrease coupling
		Increase cohesion
		Arch. patterns (MVC, MVP, etc.)
		Design patterns
		Refactorings (Extract Class, etc.)
Class	Control-flow	Use the most specific loop type
	Expressions	Show order of evaluation
	Local variables	Split complex expressions
	Method length	Refactorings (Extract Method, etc.)

Each of these quick tips is tied to a large body of commentary and caveats. In the spirit of this book, which focuses on small-scale properties, I won't delve into these architectural features, but you can find more information in the *Further reading* section at the end of this chapter. Table 7.1 summarizes the most relevant structural features and the corresponding best practices.

Class-level features pertain to the API of a given class and its organization in methods. For example, a golden rule is that long methods are harder to understand. At some point, certainly higher than 200 lines, you lose track of what was at the beginning of the method and end up going back and forth in your editor, trying to keep in your head what doesn't fit on a single screen. I'm listing this principle among the class-level features because, even though the problem lies in a single method, its *solution* affects more than one method: you shorten a long method by splitting it into multiple methods, and the suggested way to do this is through the *Extract Method* refactoring rule, which I'll present later in this chapter.

Now, let's zoom in on some *method-level features* that affect readability. They include the choice of control flow statements, the way you write expressions, and the use of local variables.

7.2.1 *Control flow statements*

An interesting small-scale readability issue is the choice of the most appropriate loop construct for a given scenario. Java offers four basic types of loops: standard `for`, `while`, `do-while`, and enhanced `for`. It's easy to see that the first three are equivalent, in the sense that you can convert any of them into any of the others with little effort. For example, you can convert the exit-checked loop

```
do {
    body
} while (condition);
```

into the following falsely entry-checked loop:

```
while (true) {
   body
   if (!condition) break;
}
```

Which of these two snippets is more readable? I'm sure you'll agree the first is definitely better. The second is an ugly gimmick that will only puzzle the reader, because they'll be acutely aware that there was a *more natural* way to accomplish that task. Your job when optimizing readability is to avoid that feeling and make the reading experience as smooth and uneventful as possible. That's the meaning of *clearly expressing intent.*

If you must implement a loop whose condition must be checked after each iteration as a do-while loop, what about an entry-checked loop? Because there are three options, let's compare their expressivity:

- A while loop is like a for loop whose initialization and update bits have been chopped off. If your loop needs those features, and they're reasonably compact, use a for loop—it'll help the reader recognize the role of each component. For example, the familiar

  ```
  for (int i=0; i<n; i++) {
      ...
  }
  ```

  is more readable than the equivalent

  ```
  int i=0;
  while (i<n) {
      ...
      i++;
  }
  ```

- An enhanced-for is a more specific form of a standard for loop because it applies to only arrays and objects implementing the Iterable interface. Moreover, it doesn't provide the loop body with an index or an iterator object.

To decide on a loop construct, you should apply a general rule known as the *principle of least privilege* and choose the *most specific* statement that fits your purposes. Is your loop over an array or a collection implementing Iterable? Use the enhanced for. Besides its readability value, it'll guarantee that the iteration won't go out of bounds.

Does your loop feature a compact initialization step and a similarly compact update step? Use a standard for loop. Otherwise, use a while loop.

Speaking of loops, starting from Java 8, you also have the option of using the stream library to produce functional-style looping constructs. For example, here's how you print every object in a set:

```
Set<T> set = ...
set.stream().forEach(obj -> System.out.println(obj));
```

Is it more readable than the following old-fashioned enhanced for?

```
for (T obj: set) {
   System.out.println(obj);
}
```

Probably not. A good rule of thumb is to use the functional-style API when you have some *other* reason besides just looping, such as filtering or transforming the content of the stream in some way. One particularly good reason to use data streams is when you want to split the job among multiple threads. In that case, the library will take care of a lot of nasty details for you.

READABILITY TIP Choose the most natural and specific type of loop for the job.

POP QUIZ 2 What kind of loop would you use to initialize an array of n integers with the integers from 0 to $n - 1$?

7.2.2 *Expressions and local variables*

Expressions are the basic building blocks of any programming language and can grow extremely complicated, essentially without limits. To improve readability, you should consider splitting complex expressions into simpler subexpressions and assigning their values to extra local variables that you introduce for this purpose. Naturally, you should give those new local variables descriptive names illustrating the meaning of the corresponding subexpression. (I'll return to variable names shortly.)

Reference already employs this readability-enhancing strategy when the method `connectTo` computes the amount of water that should be present in each container after the new connection is made. The shortest way to describe this calculation would be something like the following:

```
public void connectTo(Container other) {
    ...
    double newAmount = (amount * group.size() +
                        other.amount * other.group.size()) /
                       (group.size() + other.group.size());
    ...
}
```

As you can see, even split among three lines and aligned, the resulting expression is long and somewhat hard to parse. The reader is likely to struggle, or at least pause, to find the matching parentheses, because the closing parenthesis is far away from its opening. The clumsy repetitions of `group.size()` and `other.group.size()` don't help either.

That's why *Reference* introduces as many as four extra variables, just to improve readability:

```
public void connectTo(Container other) {
    ...
    int size1 = group.size(),
        size2 = other.group.size();
    double tot1 = amount * size1,
           tot2 = other.amount * size2,
```

Table 7.2 Summary of exterior code features affecting readability

Exterior Understandability	
Features	Ways to improve
Comments	Detailed documentation comments,scarce implementation comments
Names	Descriptive names
White space	White space as punctuation
Indentation	Consistent indentation

```
            newAmount = (tot1 + tot2) / (size1 + size2);
    . . .
    }
```

You shouldn't worry about the second, more readable version being less efficient. In general, the performance cost of using a few extra local variables is negligible, especially if you compare it with the readability benefit. In this particular case, the extra variables save two method invocations and may even lead to faster execution.[1]

Martin Fowler has formalized this idea as one of the *refactoring rules* he has assembled. (See the *Further reading* section for more information.) Similar to how design patterns work, each refactoring rule is given a standard name to ease communication. The name of this rule is *Extract Variable*.

> **READABILITY TIP** Refactoring rule Extract Variable: Replace a subexpression with a new local variable with a descriptive name.

7.3   *Exterior readability features*

You can use three exterior traits to improve readability: comments, names, and white space. Table 7.2 summarizes the corresponding best practices, presented in the following subsections.

7.3.1   *Comments*

Code alone can't satisfactorily document itself. Sometimes you have to use natural language to provide further insight or convey a more global perspective on some functionality. It's useful to distinguish two kinds of comments:

- *Documentation* or *specification* comments describe the contract of a method or of an entire class. They're meant to explain the rules of a class to its potential clients. You can think of them as the *public* comments. You usually extract these comments from the class and put them into a convenient form (like HTML) for easy consultation. The Java tool that performs such extraction is Javadoc (explained later in this chapter).

---

[1] As a matter of fact, the bytecode for the readable version is three bytes shorter than the other version.

▪ *Implementation* comments provide insight about the internals of a class. They may explain the role of a field or the intent of a code fragment belonging to a tricky algorithm. You can think of them as the *private* comments.

To a certain extent, when and how often to insert comments is open for debate, but the modern trend is to be generous with documentation comments and stingy with implementation ones.

The motivations stem from the following reasoning: the API precedes the implementation, is generally more stable than it, and is the only part of a class that clients should know so they can correctly employ its services. Therefore, it's particularly important for the health of the overall system that the responsibilities and contracts of each class and method be perfectly clear to its clients. As you saw in chapter 5, you can express contracts in code only up to a certain point, whose exact extent depends on the programming language of choice. Beyond that, natural language comments and other forms of documentation take over.

> **POP QUIZ 3** Is a comment describing the behavior of a private method a specification comment or an implementation comment?

Conversely, method bodies change often and are hidden from the clients. Because they change often, you need to update any comment inside them equally often, and programmers are known to forget to update a comment (or any other action having no immediate repercussions on the program behavior). You've probably been there: tasked with updating a piece of code, for a bug fix or a new feature, probably under a tight deadline. You're likely to focus on functionality, on writing code that works and passes the tests. Unless your company adopts serious forms of code inspection, no downstream filter on the quality of the comments is in place. As such, it's just natural to ignore the comments and deal with the active code lines.

If word spreads that *some* comments in a given codebase are unreliable because they may be stale, *all* of the comments immediately become pure noise, even if most of them are in fact good and up-to-date.

> **READABILITY TIP** Cut back implementation comments in favor of documentation comments, and make sure that all comments are up-to-date. (Code reviews can help.)

7.3.2   *Naming things*

According to a well-known quote by Phil Karlton, there are only two hard things in computer science: cache invalidation and naming things. Having touched on cache-related issues in chapter 4, it's time to face the second hard problem. High-level programming allows you to assign arbitrary names to program elements. In Java, these are packages, classes, methods, and all kind of variables, including fields. The language imposes some restrictions on these names (like no spaces), and practicality suggests that they should be relatively short.

I assume you're already familiar with the basic lexical convention of Java (shared by many languages, including C# and C++) based on so-called *camel case.* Here are some general guidelines about the types of names suggested for different circumstances:

- Names should be descriptive so that a reader unfamiliar with your code can surmise at least a general idea of the role of the element named. This doesn't necessarily mean that names must be *long.* For instance, in several cases single-letter names are fine:

  - i is a good name for an array index because it's a customary, and therefore clear, choice.
  - For the same reason, x is a good name for the horizontal coordinate in a Cartesian plane.
  - a and b are good names for the two parameters of a simple comparator:

    ```
    Comparator<String> stringComparatorByLength =
        (a,b) -> Integer.compare(a.length(), b.length());
    ```

    In this context, the reader doesn't need more descriptive names to figure out your intent. (On the other hand, notice the long name for the comparator itself.)
  - T is a good name for a type parameter (as in class LinkedList<T>) because of conventions, and because most type parameters would be called "type-OfElements" anyway.

- Class names should be nouns, and method names should be verbs.
- Names shouldn't use nonstandard abbreviations.

READABILITY TIP   Use descriptive names, avoid abbreviations, and follow established conventions.

POP QUIZ 4   What name is the most appropriate for the field holding the monthly salary in an Employee class: salary, s, monthlySalary, or employeeMonthlySalary?

7.3.3   *White space and indentation*

Finally, most languages, including Java, allow ample freedom regarding the visual layout of code. You can split lines at (almost) every point, freely insert white space around symbols, and insert empty lines everywhere. You should use this freedom not to express your artistic creativity (there's ASCII art for that), but to lessen the cognitive burden on the fellow programmer who's going to read your code later on.

Correct indentation is absolutely essential, but I trust you already know and practice it. One step beyond basic indentation, you can use white space to align two parts of a split line. A common case is methods with many parameters, like this String instance method:

```
public boolean regionMatches(int toffset,
                             String other,
                             int ooffset,
                             int len)
```

Regarding empty lines in code, think of them as punctuation. If a method is akin to a paragraph of text, both in length and in internal coherence, an empty code line is comparable to a period. Don't use it when a simple comma would do. You should use empty lines to visually separate code sections that are conceptually diverse, including separating different methods or disparate parts of the same method. You can see an example of the latter in the `connectTo` method, in both *Reference* (listing 7.3) and *Readable* (listing 7.4).

> **READABILITY TIP**   Use an empty line like a sentence-ending period in a paragraph of text.

In the next section, we'll develop a readability-optimized version of the container class, nicknamed *Readable*.

7.4   *Readable containers*   *[Readable]*

Let's start from *Reference* and use the following techniques to improve its readability:

- Add comments to the class as a whole and to its public methods, in a standard format that can be easily converted into HTML documentation. This step will be the only change we make to `addWater` and `getAmount` because their body is simple enough to be straightforward.
- Apply refactoring rules to the body of `connectTo` to improve its structural features.

First, it's important to familiarize yourself with the standard format for Java documentation comments: Javadoc.

7.4.1   *Documenting the class header with Javadoc*

Javadoc is the Java tool that extracts specially composed comments (using the sort of tags shown in tables 7.3 and 7.4) from source files and lays them out in nicely formatted HTML, thus producing easily navigable documentation. Javadoc originally generates the familiar online documentation for the Java API, as well as the documentation snippets that common IDEs provide on request.

Comments intended for Javadoc consumption must start with `/**`. Most HTML tags are allowed, such as

- `<p>`, to start a new paragraph
- `<i>...</i>`, to typeset text in *italics*
- `<code>...</code>`, to typeset code snippets

Table 7.3   Summary of common Javadoc tags

Tag	Meaning
`@author`	Class author (mandatory)
`@version`	Class version (mandatory)
`@return`	Description of a method return value
`@param`	Description of a method parameter
`@throws` or `@exception`	Description of the conditions for a given exception to be thrown
`{@link ...}`	Generates a link to another program element (class, method, etc.)
`{@code ...}`	Typesets a code snippet

Table 7.4   Summary of common Javadoc-compatible HTML tags

Tag	Meaning
`<code>...</code>`	Typesets a code snippet
`<p>`	Starts a new paragraph
`<i>...</i>`	Italics
`<b>...</b>`	Bold

Moreover, Javadoc recognizes various additional tags, all starting with the "@" symbol (not to be confused with Java annotations). For example, in the comment describing the whole class, you're supposed to insert the self-explanatory tags `@author` and `@version`. Both tags are supposedly mandatory for the class description, but Javadoc won't complain if they're missing.

C# documentation comments

In C#, documentation comments should start with "///" (a triple slash) and can include a variety of XML tags. The compiler itself lifts those comments from the source files and stores them in a separate XML file. Visual Studio then uses the information in that file to enrich its contextual help functionalities, and the programmer can summon an external tool to arrange the comments into a readable layout, such as HTML. A popular open-source solution is the DocFX tool, which supports multiple languages besides C#, including Java.

Rather than presenting each Javadoc tag individually, let's apply them right away to obtain a readability-optimized version of `Container`. At the very top of the `Container` source file, add the introductory comment shown in listing 7.1, providing a general description for the class. Such a comment is also the right place to introduce class-specific terminology, such as the word *group* to indicate the set of containers connected to this one.

By using the `<code>` HTML tag or the Javadoc `{@code ...}` tag, you can typeset code snippets. Tables 7.3 and 7.4 summarize the Javadoc and HTML tags you're most likely to use in a comment.

Listing 7.1 *Readable*: **The class header**

```
/**     ❶ Beginning of a Javadoc comment
 *  A <code>Container</code> represents a water container
 *  with virtually unlimited capacity.
 *  <p>        ❷ Most HTML tags are allowed.
 *  Water can be added or removed.
 *  Two containers can be connected with a permanent pipe.
 *  When two containers are connected, directly or indirectly,
 *  they become communicating vessels, and water will distribute
 *  equally among all of them.
 *  <p>
 *  The set of all containers connected to this one is called the
 *  <i>group</i> of this container.
 *
 *  @author Marco Faella     ❸ Javadoc tag
 *  @version 1.0             ❹ Another Javadoc tag
 */
public class Container {
   private Set<Container> group;
   private double amount;
```

Figure 7.1 shows the HTML page that Javadoc generates from the comment in listing 7.1.

Next, the constructor and the `getAmount` method are so simple that they need no readability enhancements, except for short documentation comments. Use the `@return` tag to describe the return value for a method.

Listing 7.2 *Readable*: **Constructor and `getAmount`**

```
/** Creates an empty container. */
public Container() {
   group = new HashSet<Container>();
   group.add(this);
}

/** Returns the amount of water currently held in this container.
  *
  * @return the amount of water currently held in this container
  */
public double getAmount() {
   return amount;
}
```

The redundancy in the comment for `getAmount` is justified by the way Javadoc displays the information. Every method is presented twice in the HTML page for the class: first, in a brief summary of all methods (see figure 7.2); then, in a more extensive section, describing each method in detail (see figure 7.3). The first sentence of the comment is included in the summary of all methods, so you can't omit it. The `@return` line is only included in the detailed description of the method.

Package eis.chapter7.readable

Class Container

java.lang.Object
    eis.chapter7.readable.Container

```
public class Container
extends java.lang.Object
```

A Container represents a water container with virtually unlimited capacity.

Water can be added or removed. Two containers can be connected with a permanent pipe. When two containers are connected, directly or indirectly, they become communicating vessels, and water will **distribute equally** among all of them.

The set of all containers connected to this one is called the *group* of this container.

Constructor Summary

Constructors	
Constructor	Description
Container()	Creates an empty container.

Figure 7.1 A snapshot of Javadoc-generated HTML documentation for *Readable*, including a class description and a list of constructors

Method Summary

All Methods	Instance Methods	Concrete Methods

Modifier and Type	Method	Description
void	addWater(double amount)	Adds water to this container.
void	connectTo(Container other)	Connects this container with another.
double	getAmount()	Returns the amount of water currently held in this container.
double	groupAmount()	Returns the total amount of water in the group of this container.
int	groupSize()	Returns the number of containers in the group of this container.
boolean	isConnectedTo(Container other)	Checks whether this container is connected to another one.

Methods inherited from class java.lang.Object

clone, equals, finalize, getClass, hashCode, notify, notifyAll, toString, wait, wait, wait

Figure 7.2 A snapshot of Javadoc-generated HTML documentation: the summary of the public methods of *Readable*

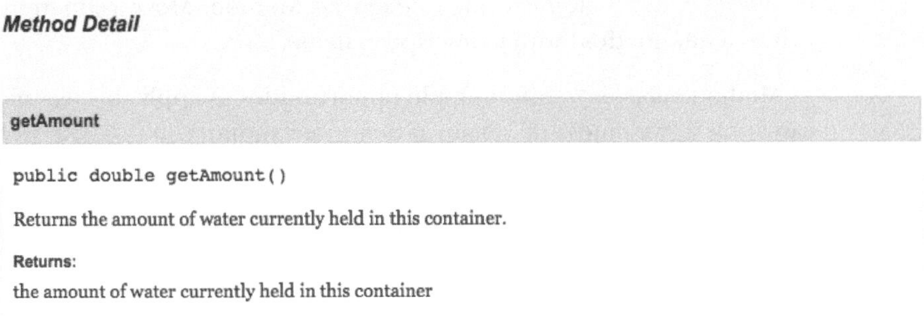

Method Detail

---

getAmount

```
public double getAmount()
```

Returns the amount of water currently held in this container.

Returns:

the amount of water currently held in this container

Figure 7.3 A snapshot of Javadoc-generated HTML documentation: a detailed description of the `getAmount` method

7.4.2 Cleaning connectTo

We now turn our attention to the `connectTo` method, which can use some refactoring to improve its readability. First, recall the implementation of this method in *Reference*, reproduced here for convenience:

Listing 7.3 *Reference*: The `connectTo` method

```
public void connectTo(Container other) {

    // If they are already connected, do nothing
    if (group==other.group) return;

    int size1 = group.size(),
        size2 = other.group.size();
    double tot1 = amount * size1,
           tot2 = other.amount * size2,
           newAmount = (tot1 + tot2) / (size1 + size2);

    // Merge the two groups
    group.addAll(other.group);
    // Update group of containers connected with other
    ❶ You can replace comments like this with a properly named support method

    for (Container c: other.group) { c.group = group; }
    // Update amount of all newly connected containers
    for (Container c: group) { c.amount = newAmount; }
}
```

I already pointed out one of the defects of the reference implementation in chapter 3: an abundance of in-method comments, trying to explain every single line. Adding such comments is the natural course of action for programmers who care about making their code understandable by fellow humans. However, it's not the most efficient way to achieve this excellent objective. A better alternative is the *Extract Method* refactoring technique.

READABILITY TIP Refactoring rule Extract Method: Move a coherent block of code into a new method with a descriptive name.

Method `connectTo` offers ample opportunities to apply this technique. In fact, you can apply it five times and obtain as many new support methods, as well as a new, much more readable version of `connectTo`, as shown in the following listing.

Listing 7.4 *Readable*: The `connectTo` method

```
/** Connects this container with another.
  *
  *  @param other The container that will be connected to this one
  */
public void connectTo(Container other) {
   if (this.isConnectedTo(other))
      return;

   double newAmount = (groupAmount() + other.groupAmount()) /
                     (groupSize() + other.groupSize());
   mergeGroupWith(other.group);
   setAllAmountsTo(newAmount);
}
```

The `@param` Javadoc tag documents a method parameter. It's followed by the parameter name and by its description. Compared to *Reference*, the method is much shorter and more readable. If you're not convinced, try reading the body aloud and notice how it almost makes sense as a short paragraph of text.

You achieve this effect by introducing five aptly named support methods. Indeed, *long method* is one of the code smells that Fowler identifies, and *extract method* is the refactoring technique aimed at getting rid of that smell. In agile parlance, the new version of `connectTo` in listing 7.4 is five extract-methods away from its old version in *Reference*.

Whereas adding a comment only explains some code, Extract Method both explains and *hides* the code, pushing it away in a separate method. In this way, it keeps the abstraction level in the original method at a higher and more uniform height, avoiding the cumbersome swing between high-level explanations and low-level implementations in listing 7.3.

Replace Temp with Query is another refactoring technique that you can use on `connectTo`.

READABILITY TIP Refactoring rule Replace Temp with Query: Replace a local variable with the invocation to a new method that computes its value.

You could apply this technique to the local variable `newAmount`, which is assigned only once and then used as the argument of `setAllAmountsTo`. A straightforward application of the technique would lead to removing the variable `newAmount` and replacing the last two lines of `connectTo` with the following:

```
mergeGroupWith(other.group);
setAllAmountsTo(amountAfterMerge(other));
```

Here, `amountAfterMerge` is a new method responsible for computing the correct amount of water in each container after the merge. However, a little thought reveals that `amountAfterMerge` needs to jump through hoops to fulfill its task because the groups *already have been merged* when the method is invoked. In particular, the set that `this` `.group` already points to contains all the elements from `other.group`.

A good compromise would be to encapsulate the expression for the new amount into a new method, but keep the local variable as well, so that we can compute the new amount *before* merging the groups:

```
final double newAmount = amountAfterMerge(other);
mergeGroupWith(other.group);
setAllAmountsTo(newAmount);
```

All in all, I wouldn't recommend this refactoring because the expression assigned to `newAmount` in listing 7.4 is quite readable and doesn't need to be hidden away in a separate method. The Replace Temp with Query rule tends to be more useful when the expression it replaces is more complicated or occurs multiple times throughout the class.

Now, let's have a look at the five new methods that support the readable version of `connectTo`. Of these five, two are better declared private because they may leave the object in an inconsistent state, so you shouldn't call them from outside the class. They are `mergeGroupWith` and `setAllAmountsTo`.

Method `mergeGroupWith` merges two groups of containers without updating their water amount. If someone were to invoke it in isolation, it would most likely leave a wrong amount of water in some or all containers. This method only makes sense in the exact context where it's used: at the end of `connectTo`, immediately followed by a call to `setAllAmountsTo`. In fact, it's debatable whether it should really be a separate method. On the one hand, having it separate allows us to document its intent with its name, instead of using a comment like we did in *Reference*. On the other hand, a separate method runs the risk of being called in the wrong context. Because we're optimizing for clarity in this chapter, we'll leave it separate. A similar argument holds for `setAllAmountsTo`.

The code for these two methods is shown in the following listing.

Listing 7.5   *Readable*: Two new private methods supporting `connectTo`

```
private void mergeGroupWith(Set<Container> otherGroup) {
    group.addAll(otherGroup);
    for (Container x: otherGroup) {
        x.group = group;
    }
}

private void setAllAmountsTo(double amount) {
    for (Container x: group) {
```

```
            x.amount = amount;
        }
    }
```

Private methods aren't deemed worthy of Javadoc comments. They're only used inside the class, so few people should ever feel the need to understand them in detail. Hence, the potential benefit of a comment doesn't repay its cost.

The cost of a comment isn't limited to the time spent writing it. Just like any other source line, it needs to be maintained, or it may become stale—that is to say, out of sync with the code it's supposed to clarify. Remember: a stale comment is worse than no comment!

Replacing comments with descriptive names doesn't rule out this particular risk. Without the proper coding discipline and processes, you may still end up with stale names, which are just as bad as stale comments.

The other three new support methods are innocuous read-only functionalities that may as well be declared public. This is not to say that you should take lightly the decision to make them public. The future maintainability cost of adding any public member to a class is much greater than the cost of adding the same member with private visibility. Additional costs for a public method include

- appropriate documentation describing its contract
- precondition checks to withstand interactions with possibly incorrect clients
- a set of tests providing confidence in its correctness

In this particular case, these costs are arguably quite limited because the three methods under consideration are simple read-only functionalities with no preconditions to speak of.[2] Besides, these three methods provide information to the clients that isn't otherwise available. As such, they significantly improve the class *testability*, as discussed in chapter 5.

Listing 7.6 *Readable*: Three new public methods supporting `connectTo`

```
/** Checks whether this container is connected to another one.
 *
 *  @param other the container whose connection with this will be checked
 *  @return <code>true</code> if this container is connected
 *                           to <code>other</code>
 */
public boolean isConnectedTo(Container other) {
    return group == other.group;
}

/** Returns the number of containers in the group of this container.
 *
 *  @return the size of the group
 */
```

---

[2] To be precise, `isConnectedTo` requires its argument to be non-null. This is such a trivial precondition that you don't need to document or actively check it. Violating it will raise an NPE just as expected.

```
public int groupSize() {
   return group.size();
}


/** Returns the total amount of water in the group of this container.
 *
 *  @return the amount of water in the group
 */
public double groupAmount() {
   return amount * group.size();
}
```

Incidentally, the `isConnectedTo` method also improves the testability of our class by making directly observable something that we could only surmise in all previous implementations.

All six methods that make up the `connectTo` functionality are very short, the longest being `connectTo` itself, at six lines. Brevity is one of the main tenets of clean code.

7.4.3 Cleaning addWater

Finally, there's `addWater`. Its body doesn't change compared to *Reference*. We just improve its documentation to better reflect its contract, using Javadoc syntax.

Listing 7.7 *Readable*: The `addWater` method

```
/** Adds water to this container.
 *  A negative <code>amount</code> indicates removal of water.
 *  In that case, there should be enough water in the group
 *  to satisfy the request.
 *
 *  @param amount the amount of water to be added
 */
public void addWater(double amount) {
   double amountPerContainer = amount / group.size();
   for (Container c: group) {
      c.amount += amountPerContainer;
   }
}
```

Compare this Javadoc method description with the contract for `addWater` I presented in chapter 5:

- *Precondition*—If the argument is negative, there's enough water in the group.
- *Postcondition*—Distributes water equally to all containers in the group.
- *Penalty*—Throws `IllegalArgumentException`.

Notice how the comments in the listing don't mention the reaction to the client violating the precondition by removing more water than is actually present. That's because this implementation (just like *Reference*) doesn't check that condition and allows containers to hold a negative amount of water. Looking back at figure 7.2, you can witness the HTML page that Javadoc generates from those comments.

What if the implementation checked that condition and actually implemented the penalty that the contract established by throwing `IllegalArgumentException`? Both the Javadoc style guide and the *Effective Java* book suggest to document unchecked exceptions using the `@throws` or `@exception` tags (which are equivalent).[3] A line like the following, added inside the method comment, would work:

```
@throws IllegalArgumentException
        if an attempt is made to remove more water than actually present
```

A quick look at the official Java API documentation shows that this is indeed standard practice. As an example, the documentation for the `get(int index)` method from `ArrayList`, returning the element at position `index` in the list, reports that the method will throw the unchecked exception `IndexOutOfBoundsException` if the index is out of the proper range.

> **POP QUIZ 5**   Suppose a public method may throw an `AssertionError` if it detects a violation of a class invariant. Would you document this circumstance in the Javadoc for this method?

7.5   *Final thoughts on readability*

This chapter is somewhat different from the previous ones in that you can readily apply its advice to most, if not all practical scenarios. Even though I said in chapter 1 that readability may contrast with other quality objectives, such as time or space efficiency, in most of these conflicts it's readability that should prevail. Human readability is a huge benefit when a given piece of sofware will inevitably need to evolve, because of bugs being found or new features being requested.

Still, we shouldn't confuse code clarity with algorithmic simplicity. I'm not suggesting to shun an efficient algorithm in favor of a naive one in the name of readability. Rather, you should pick the best algorithm for the job and then strive to code it in the cleanest possible way. Clarity rightfully defies performance hacks, not proper engineering.

For the sake of completeness, I should mention a couple of scenarios in which readability is either a luxury or something to be actively avoided. Examples of the first are tightly timed programming challenges like hackathons or coding competitions. Those scenarios require contestants to quickly write throwaway code that just works. Any delay is a cost, and style considerations go out the window.

Another special scenario arises when companies don't want their source code to be analyzed by others, including the legitimate users of their software. By hiding or obfuscating their source code, such companies hope to hide their algorithms or data. In such cases, it may seem natural to abandon code readability and go for the most cryptic lines that get the job done. In fact, there's a specific type of software, called an *obfuscator*, whose job is precisely to translate a program into another program that is functionally

---

[3]   See Item 74 in *Effective Java*, 3rd ed.

equivalent to the first, but extremely hard to understand for a human reader. You can obfuscate all programming languages,[4] from machine code to Java bytecode or source code. Just googling "Java obfuscator" provides a rich selection of open source and commercial tools for this task. Given the availability of such tools, even the most secretive company can benefit from internally handling clean, self-explanatory code, which is then rendered obscure before being publicly released.

7.6 *And now for something completely different*

In this section, you'll apply the guidelines for readable code to a different example. It's a single method that accepts a two-dimensional array of doubles and . . . does something to it. I've written the method's body in an intentionally sloppy style; not exactly obscure, but not very readable either. As an exercise, try to understand what it does before reading ahead.

```
public static void f(double[][] a) {
    int i = 0, j = 0;
    while (i<a.length) {
        if (a[i].length != a.length)
            throw new IllegalArgumentException();
        i++;
    }
    i = 0;
    while (i<a.length) {
        j = 0;
        while (j<i) {
            double temp = a[i][j];
            a[i][j] = a[j][i];
            a[j][i] = temp;
            j++;
        }
        i++;
    }
}
```

Did you feel the pain? Those `while` loops and meaningless variable names really put a strain on your brain. Imagine a whole program written in the same style!

As you might have guessed, the mystery method *transposes* a square matrix, a standard operation that swaps rows with columns. The first `while` loop checks whether the provided matrix is square-shaped—has as many rows as columns. Since Java matrices can be irregular, this entails checking that *each* row has the same length as the number of rows. Here's an annotated version of the same method, to help you recognize the various parts:

```
public static void f(double[][] a) {
    int i = 0, j = 0;
    while (i<a.length) {      ❶ For each row
        if (a[i].length != a.length)   ❷ If the row length is "wrong"
```

---

[4] Some languages are designed to be unreadable and hardly need any obfuscation. Do you know any? Hint: Bⁱ⁵ʲⁱᵘ

```
            throw new IllegalArgumentException();
        i++;
    }
    i = 0;
    while (i<a.length) {      ③ For each row
        j = 0;
        while (j<i) {         ④ For each column less than i
            double temp = a[i][j];   ⑤ Swap a[i][j] and a[j][i]
            a[i][j] = a[j][i];
            a[j][i] = temp;
            j++;
        }
        i++;
    }
}
```

It's time to improve the readability of this method using this chapter's guidelines. First, the initial squareness check is the ideal occasion for the Extract Method refactoring rule: it's a coherent operation with a clearly specified contract. Once you put it in a separate method, it might also be useful in other contexts. That's why I'm declaring it `public` and equipping it with a full Javadoc comment.

Since the squareness check doesn't modify the matrix, you can use an enhanced `for` as its main loop:

```
/** Checks whether a matrix is square-shaped
 *
 * @param matrix a matrix
 * @return {@code true} if the given matrix is square
 */
public static boolean isSquare(double[][] matrix) {
    for (double[] row: matrix) {
        if (row.length != matrix.length) {
            return false;
        }
    }
    return true;
}
```

Then, the transpose method itself invokes `isSquare` and then performs its job with two straightforward `for` loops. An enhanced `for` would be useless here, because you need row and column indices to perform the swap.

Along the way, improve the names of the variables, and of the method itself, by making them more descriptive. You can keep names `i` and `j` for the row and column indices because those are standard names for array indices.

```
/** Transposes a square matrix
 *
 * @param matrix a matrix
 * @throws IllegalArgumentException if the given matrix is not square
 */
public static void transpose(double[][] matrix) {
    if (!isSquare(matrix)) {
        throw new IllegalArgumentException(
```

```
                         "Can't transpose a nonsquare matrix.");
    }
    for (int i=0; i<matrix.length; i++) {      ❶ For each row
        for (int j=0; j<i; j++) {              ❷ For each column less than i
            double temp = matrix[i][j];        ❸ Swap a[i][j] and a[j][i]
            matrix[i][j] = matrix[j][i];
            matrix[j][i] = temp;
        }
    }
}
```

7.7 Real-world use cases

You've seen and applied some very important principles to improve the readability of this code. Here are a couple use cases to help you understand the practical importance of this trait.

- Imagine being one of the cofounders of a small startup and having managed to win a bid to develop software for the company that manages gas infrastructure, and the objective of the project is to implement regulatory law. Things look good: you've been assigned a prestigious project and, because legislation doesn't change easily, you realize that after delivering you'll be able to enjoy the fruit of your labor for the duration of the maintenance contract. You and your colleagues make a strategic decision to deliver your solution as fast as possible to impress your client. To achieve that, you decide to cut back on luxuries such as readability, documentation, unit tests, and so on. After a couple of years, your company has grown, but half of the original team has left the company, and you still have the contract with the gas operator. Then one day, the impossible happens: legislation changes, and you're asked to modify your software to implement the new requirements. You learn the hard way that figuring out how your existing code works is harder than implementing new requirements. Code readability is so important that it's a determining factor for how teams operate in software companies (http://mng.bz/pyKE).
- You're an enthusiastic, talented developer eager to contribute to the open source community. You have a great idea (or at least, so you think), and your goal is to share your code on github, hoping that it will attract contributors and eventually be used by people for real projects. You realize that readability is the key to attracting contributors, who will initially be unfamiliar with your code base and probably reluctant to ask questions about it.

The following examples show how seriously the programming world has taken the idea of readability.

- Working hard to make your code readable is something you have to do regardless of the programming language you're using. However, for some programming languages, readability is a design characteristic. Python is among the most popular languages, and one of the reasons for this popularity is arguably its inherent readability. In fact, readability is considered so important that the language designer introduced the famous PEP8 (Python Enhancement Proposal), a coding style guide whose basic goal is (surprise!) to improve readability.

- Let's talk about Python again. (Yes, this book features Java, but these principles are universal.) Python is a dynamically typed language, so you don't have to specify the type of function parameters and return values. However, PEP 484 introduced optional *type hints* in Python 3.5, providing a standard way to declare those types. These hints have absolutely no effect on performance, nor do they provide runtime type inference. Their purpose is to enhance readability and support more static type checks, thus also improving reliability.

7.8   *Applying what you learned*

EXERCISE 1

Given the following data:

```
List<String> names;
double[] lengths;
```

What kind of loop would you use to accomplish the following tasks?

   1 Print all names in the list.

   2 Remove from the list all names longer than 20 characters.

   3 Compute the sum of all lengths.

   4 Set a Boolean flag to `true` if the array contains a zero length.

EXERCISE 2

As you might know, the method `charAt` from the class `String` returns the character of this string at a given index:

```
public char charAt(int index)
```

Write a Javadoc comment describing the contract of this method and *then* compare it to the official documentation.

EXERCISE 3

Examine the following method. Guess what it does and make it more readable. (Don't forget to add a Javadoc method comment.) You can find the source code for this exercise and the next one in the online repository (https://bitbucket.org/mfaella /exercisesinstyle).

```
public static int f(String s, char c) {
    int i = 0, n = 0;
    boolean flag = true;
    while (flag) {
        if (s.charAt(i) == c)
            n++;
```

```
            if (i == s.length() -1)
                flag = false;
            else
                i++;
        }
        return n;
    }
```

EXERCISE 4

The following method comes from a collection of algorithms hosted in a github repository (starred by 10k people and forked 4k times). The method performs a *breadth-first visit* of a graph, represented as an adjacency matrix of type `byte`. You don't have to know this algorithm to complete this exercise. Just know that the `a[i][j]` cell contains 1 if there's an edge from node `i` to node `j`, and 0 otherwise.

Improve the method readability in two steps. First, make only exterior changes to variable names and comments. Then, make structural changes. All changes must preserve both the API (types of parameters) and the visible behavior (the on-screen output).

```java
/**
 * The BFS implemented in code to use.
 *
 * @param a Structure to perform the search on a graph, adjacency matrix etc.
 * @param vertices The vertices to use
 * @param source The Source
 */
public static void bfsImplement(byte [][] a,int vertices,int source){
                           //passing adjacency matrix and number of vertices
    byte []b=new byte[vertices];      //flag container containing status
                                      //of each vertices
    Arrays.fill(b,(byte)-1);   //status initialization
    /*      code    status
             -1  =   ready
              0  =   waiting
              1  =   processed       */

    Stack<Integer> st = new Stack<>();      //operational stack
    st.push(source);                                  //assigning source
    while(!st.isEmpty()){
        b[st.peek()]=(byte)0;                         //assigning waiting status
        System.out.println(st.peek());
        int pop=st.peek();
        b[pop]=(byte)1;                      //assigning processed status
        st.pop();                         //removing head of the queue
        for(int i=0;i<vertices;i++){
            if(a[pop][i]!=0 && b[i]!=(byte)0 && b[i]!=(byte)1 ){
                st.push(i);
                b[i]=(byte)0;                         //assigning waiting status
        }}}
}
```

Summary

- Readability is a major factor contributing toward reliability and maintainability.
- You can promote readability through both structural and exterior means.
- One of the objectives of common refactorings is to improve readability.
- Self-documenting code is preferable to implementation comments.
- You should detail and format documentation comments in standard ways to make them easily browsable.

Answers to quizzes and exercises

POP QUIZ 1

Readability positively affects maintainability and reliability because readable code is easier to understand and modify in a safe manner.

POP QUIZ 2

You can't use an enhanced `for` because you need to modify the array's entries, and you need an index for that. The best choice for iterating over a whole array using an explicit index is a standard `for` loop.

POP QUIZ 3

You should consider a comment describing the behavior of a private method an implementation comment. Private methods are not exposed to the clients.

POP QUIZ 4

The most appropriate name is probably `monthlySalary`. Alternatives `s` and `salary` contain too little information, whereas `employeeMonthlySalary` needlessly repeats the class name.

POP QUIZ 5

You shouldn't document an `AssertionError` because that kind of exception is only thrown if an internal error occurs.

EXERCISE 1

1 An enhanced `for` is the ideal loop for the first task:

```
for (String name: names) {
    System.out.println(name);
}
```

2 This is the job for an iterator:

```
Iterator<String> iterator = names.iterator();
while (iterator.hasNext()) {
    if (iterator.next().length() > 20) {
        iterator.remove();
    }
}
```

3 Once again, use an enhanced `for`:

```
double totalLength = 0;
for (double length: lengths) {
   totalLength += length;
}
```

or the following stream-based one-liner:

```
double totalLength = Arrays.stream(lengths).sum();
```

4 Common wisdom suggests using a `while` loop when the data (the content of the array) determines the exit condition. I think an enhanced `for` plus a `break` statement is at least as appropriate, as it automatically takes care of the case when the whole array needs to be scanned.

```
boolean containsZero = false;
for (double length: lengths) {
   if (length == 0) {
      containsZero = true;
      break;
   }
}
```

The stream library provides a handy alternative:

```
boolean containsZero = Arrays.stream(lengths).anyMatch(
                       length -> length == 0);
```

EXERCISE 2

Here's a slightly simplified version of the Javadoc from OpenJDK 12:

```
/**
 * Returns the {@code char} value at the
 * specified index. An index ranges from {@code 0} to
 * {@code length() - 1}. The first {@code char} value of the sequence
 * is at index {@code 0}, the next at index {@code 1},
 * and so on, as for array indexing.
 *
 * @param      index   the index of the {@code char} value.
 * @return     the {@code char} value at the specified index of this string.
 *             The first {@code char} value is at index {@code 0}.
 * @exception  IndexOutOfBoundsException  if the {@code index}
 *             argument is negative or not less than the length of this
 *             string.
 */
```

EXERCISE 3

It's easy to see that the method simply counts the occurrences of a character inside a string. The `while` loop and the flag are useless detours, replaced by a simple `for` loop in the following solution:

```
/** Counts the number of occurrences of a character in a string.
 *
 * @param s a string
 * @param c a character
 * @return The number of occurrences of {@code c} in {@code s}
 */
```

```
public static int countOccurrences(String s, char c) {
    int count = 0;
    for (int i=0; i<s.length(); i++) {
        if (s.charAt(i) == c) {
            count++;
        }
    }
    return count;
}
```

The stream library also allows an alternative implementation, where the method body consists of the following one liner:

```
return (int) s.chars().filter(character -> character == c).count();
```

The cast to `int` is due to the fact that the terminal operation `count` returns a value of type `long`. A more robust implementation would take precautions against overflow.

EXERCISE 4

Let's jump to the final version, including both exterior and structural improvements. First, notice that the algorithm maintains a *status* for each node, which can take one of three values: fresh (not encountered yet), enqueued (put in the stack but not visited yet), and processed (visited). In the original implementation, this information is encoded in the array of bytes b. The first structural improvement is to use an enumeration for this purpose. Unfortunately, enumerations can't be local to a method, so you have to put the following declaration in class scope (outside the method):

```
private enum Status { FRESH, ENQUEUED, PROCESSED };
```

Now you can refactor the main method, taking advantage of this enumeration, improving variable names, removing implementation comments, and fixing white space and indentation. You should end up with something like this:

```
/** Visits the node in a directed graph in breadth first order,
  * printing the index of each visited node.
  *
  * @param adjacent      the adjacency matrix
  * @param vertexCount   the number of vertices
  * @param sourceVertex the source vertex
  */
public static void breadthFirst(
                    byte[][] adjacent, int vertexCount, int sourceVertex) {
    Status[] status = new Status[vertexCount];
    Arrays.fill(status, Status.FRESH);

    Stack<Integer> stack = new Stack<>();
    stack.push(sourceVertex);

    while (!stack.isEmpty()) {
        int currentVertex = stack.pop();
        System.out.println(currentVertex);
        status[currentVertex] = Status.PROCESSED;
        for (int i=0; i<vertexCount; i++) {
            if (adjacent[currentVertex][i] != 0 && status[i] == Status.FRESH)
```

```
                {
                    stack.push(i);
                    status[i] = Status.ENQUEUED;
                }
            }
        }
    }
```

In the previous method, I left the use of the `Stack` class because it doesn't affect readability, but you should know that the `Stack` class has been superseded by `LinkedList` and `ArrayDeque`.

Further reading

- R. C. Martin. *Clean Code.* Prentice Hall, 2009.
  A detailed and comprehensive style guide written by one of the authors of the "Manifesto for Agile Software Development." You can find related higher level design recommendations in the follow-up book, *Clean Architecture* (Prentice Hall, 2017).
- S. McConnell. *Code Complete.* Microsoft Press, 2004.
  A wide-ranging, well-researched, nicely typeset handbook on coding practices, from the fine points of proper variable naming all the way to project scheduling and team management.
- Brian W. Kernighan and P. J. Plauger. *The Elements of Programming Style.* McGraw-Hill, Inc., 1974.
  Arguably the first book to systematically tackle the code readability problem. Examples are in Fortran and PL/I. An updated second edition followed in 1978. Kernighan returned to the same topic 20 years later with R. Pike in the first chapter of *The Practice of Programming* (Addison-Wesley, 1999).
- Martin Fowler. *Refactoring: Improving the Design of Existing Code.* Addison-Wesley, 2018.
  The second edition of the classic book that popularized and standardized the notion of refactoring. You can take a look at the catalogue of refactoring rules from the book on the author's website at https://martinfowler.com. The most popular IDEs let you apply many of these rules with a simple click or two.
- Donald E. Knuth. *Literate Programming.* Center for the Study of Language and Information, 1995.
  A collection of essays promoting programming as an art form akin to literature.
- *How to Write Doc Comments for the Javadoc Tool.*
  The official Javadoc style guide, as of this writing, available at http://mng.bz /YeDe.

Many cooks in the kitchen:
Thread safety

The plan for this chapter is to make your implementation *thread-safe*. For a class to be thread-safe, multiple threads should be able to interact with the objects of that class with no explicit synchronization. In other words, a thread-safe class takes care of the synchronization issues. The clients can just freely invoke any class method, even simultaneously on the same object, with no adverse effects. The design-by-contract methodology I presented in chapter 5 allows you to precisely characterize what an adverse effect would be: the violation of a postcondition or an invariant.

Admittedly, thread safety is not as general a property as efficiency or readability. However, its importance is on the rise because of the ubiquity of parallel hardware. Compared with other functional defects, lack of thread safety can go unnoticed for much longer. Some synchronization defects become apparent only in special circumstances, when the timing and the scheduling are just right (or wrong) for a race condition to mess up the state of an object or for a deadlock to freeze your program. That's one more reason to read this chapter carefully!

This chapter assumes you're familiar with basic multithreading in Java, such as creating threads and using `synchronized` blocks to achieve mutual exclusion. As a self-test, consider working through exercise 1 at the end of this chapter. It'll remind you of the main properties of the `synchronized` keyword.

8.1   Challenges to thread safety

The two main enemies of thread safety are *race conditions* and *deadlocks*. Generally speaking, the first arises from too little synchronization and the latter from too much of it. A race condition occurs when two operations requested concurrently by different threads may lead to at least one operation violating its postcondition. It's easy to obtain a race condition by manipulating shared objects with no synchronization.

Say that multiple threads share an instance of the following class:

```
public class Counter {
    private int n;
    public void increment() { n++; }
    ...
}
```

If two threads invoke `increment` at about the same time, it's possible for the counter to be incremented once, instead of twice.[1] That's because n++ is not an *atomic* operation. It's roughly equivalent to the following sequence of *three* atomic operations:

1 Copy the current value of n on a register (for a register machine) or on the stack (for the JVM).
2 Increment it by one.
3 Store the updated value of n back into the `Counter` object to which it belongs.

If two threads execute the first step at the same time (or, in any case, before either of them has had the opportunity to store the updated value in the third step), both threads will read the same old value for n, increment it, and then store the same n+1 value. That is, the same value n+1 will be stored twice.

You can check this by yourself if you run the class `eis.chapter8.threads.Counter` from the online repository (https://bitbucket.org/mfaella/exercisesinstyle). It launches five threads that call the `increment` method on the same object 1,000 times each. At the end, the program prints the value of the counter. On my laptop, on three executions I got the following outputs:

```
4831
4933
3699
```

As you can see, race conditions are extremely common under these conditions. In the last execution, over 26% of the increments were lost due to a race condition. As you

---

[1]   It's also possible that the two threads will see different values for the counter because of *visibility* issues that are unrelated to the race condition.

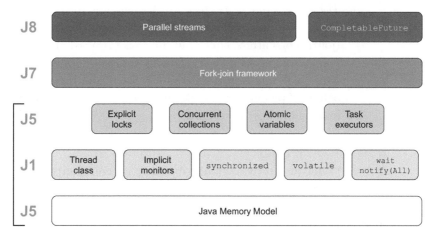

Figure 8.1 **The main layers of multithreading support in Java, labeled with the Java version in which they were initially introduced (or fixed, in the case of the JMM). This chapter only deals with the three lowest levels.**

might know, you solve race conditions by introducing synchronization primitives, such as *mutexes* or *monitors,* that render all calls to increment *mutually exclusive*: if one such call is executing on a given Counter object, any other call to the same object must wait for the current one to finish before it can enter the method. In Java, the synchronized keyword constitutes the basic form of synchronization.

At the other extreme, unregulated synchronization may lead to a deadlock, a situation when two or more threads become permanently stuck, waiting for each other in a cyclic fashion. An example of this phenomenon arises in section 8.2.

In the rest of this chapter, you'll learn how to recognize and avoid both race conditions and deadlocks, using low-level synchronization primitives like synchronized blocks and explicit locks. In the spirit of this book, I'll stick to a practical and to-the-point presentation tailored to the water container running example, which turns out to require an interesting and nonstandard form of synchronization.

To get a more comprehensive understanding of multithreading issues and solutions, you should review the fundamental *memory model* rules of your language of choice. In Java, the best reference is still the book *Java Concurrency in Practice,* mentioned in the *Further reading* section. Moreover, you should become familiar with the higher level concurrency facilities that your language offers.

Since the beginning, Java has been at the forefront of multithreading support, thanks to its native support for threads. In recent years, such support has been steadily increasing, with three progressively higher levels of abstraction, illustrated in figure 8.1:

- *Executor services (Java 5).* A small set of classes and interfaces that take care of creating the appropriate number of threads to perform user-defined tasks. Check out the interface ExecutorService and the class Executors from the package java.util.concurrent.

- *The fork-join framework (Java 7)*. A smart way to split a complex computation among multiple threads (fork) and merge their results into a single value (join). For starters, check out the `ForkJoinPool` class.
- *Parallel streams (Java 8)*. A powerful library for applying uniform operations to sequential data providers. You can start from the `Stream` class, but you'd be better off picking up a book from the *Further reading* section to appreciate the many subtleties of this library.

8.1.1   *Levels of concurrency*

If thread safety was truly our only objective, we could apply a simple technique that works in all circumstances and with all self-contained classes: use a global lock to synchronize all methods. In Java, locks are implicitly provided with each object, so as a global lock for all containers, we can use the one attached to the object `Container.class`.[2] Then, we can wrap the body of all methods in the `Container` class in a synchronized block, like this:

```
synchronized (Container.class) {
    ...  ❶ Method body
}
```

In this way, all access to the class is fully *serialized*. That is, even if method calls arrive from different threads to different objects, only one method at a time can enter its body. This coarse-grained approach is extremely harsh and voids any performance gain that might have come from concurrency. Worse, the lock acquire and release operations may actually slow down even a single-threaded program.[3] We can call this technique *class-level concurrency* and put it at one end of a spectrum, whose notable cases are summarized in table 8.1.

Table 8.1   Common concurrency policies for a class, ordered by increasing amount of concurrency allowed. The second column describes the operations that are allowed to proceed simultaneously. The third column identifies the locks that are needed to implement that policy.

Name	What is concurrent?	How many locks?
Class-level	Access to different classes	One lock per class
Object-level	Access to different objects	One lock per object
Method-level	Access to different methods	One lock per method of each object
Anarchy	Everything	No locks

Ideally, we'd like to ensure thread safety while maintaining as much concurrency as possible. To this aim, proceed in two steps:

---

[2] That's the same lock that any synchronized static method of the class would use.

[3] Optimized runtime environments may employ techniques to avoid those overheads. For example, HotSpot's *biased locking* recognizes when a single thread mostly owns a lock and optimizes that case.

1 *Specification step*—Figure out how much concurrency your class(es) can support, that is, what methods or code fragments can run simultaneously with no race conditions arising. In practice, those are the code fragments that operate on different data.

2 *Implementation step*—Add synchronization primitives that allow the legal cases of concurrency while serializing the illegal ones.

Whenever the objects of a class are isolated (that is, they don't contain references to each other or to shared objects of other types), multiple methods can run in parallel, as long as they operate on different objects, and the proper thread-safe implementation involves simply slapping `synchronized` on all instance methods. This is the common case of *object-level concurrency*, illustrated by plain old classes like the following:

```
public class Employee {
    private String name;
    private Date hireDate;
    private int monthlySalary;
    ...
    public synchronized increaseSalary(int bonus) {
        monthlySalary += bonus;
    }
}
```

By the way, you can improve even such a simple case: best practices dictate *not* declaring entire methods synchronized because that may come into conflict with an `Employee` being used as a monitor by a client. It's more robust, but slightly more cumbersome and space-inefficient, to use a private field as the monitor. In this way, being synchronized becomes a private implementation matter, as it should be:

```
public class Employee {
    private String name;
    private Date hireDate;
    private int monthlySalary;
    private Object monitor = new Object();
    ...
    public increaseSalary(int bonus) {
        synchronized (monitor) {
            monthlySalary += bonus;
        }
    }
}
```

Moving on to the third row of table 8.1, *method-level concurrency* is quite uncommon, and for good reasons. It makes sense only when all methods are independent of one another. For two methods of the same object to be independent, they need to operate on different parts of the object state. If *all* methods in a class are mutually independent, that's a sign of poor cohesion; you've put together information that belongs to different classes. Before mulling over the concurrency policy, you'd better split that class into multiple classes.

C# monitors

Just like in Java, C# objects have associated monitors that you can acquire and release using the following syntax:

```
lock (object) {
   ...
}
```

You can declare an entire method synchronized by tagging it with the following *method attribute*, analogous to a Java annotation:

```
[MethodImpl(
 MethodImplOptions.Synchronized)]
```

Differently from Java, you also can manually lock and unlock the implicit monitor of an object using calls `Monitor.Enter(object)` and `Monitor.Exit(object)`.

POP QUIZ 1   Who cares about the concurrency policy of a class—its users or its implementors?

Finally, the *anarchy* level generally applies to classes that are either stateless or immutable. In both cases, concurrent usage by multiple threads is innocuous. For example, comparators (that is, objects implementing the `Comparator` interface) are usually stateless. They can be freely shared among threads with no special precautions. I'll talk about immutability in section 8.4.

Our water containers sport a custom concurrency level, halfway between class-level and object-level, requiring a little more effort for us to both describe and implement them, as demonstrated in the following sections.

8.1.2   A concurrency policy for water containers

No matter the implementation, containers need to reference each other in some way; otherwise, they can't fulfill their contractual obligations. Specifically, the methods `connectTo` and `addWater` must be able to change the state of multiple containers. As a result, it's not enough to lock the current object to obtain thread safety.

The `connectTo` method is the trickiest because it modifies two groups of containers, eventually merging them into a single one. To avoid race conditions, no other thread should access any container that belongs to either of the two groups being merged. More precisely, reading the state of such a container with `getAmount` may be allowed, but changing it with `addWater` or `connectTo` should definitely be forbidden, that is, delayed until the first `connectTo` terminates.

Summarizing, we obtain the following concurrency policy for the `Container` class:

1 The class must be thread-safe.
2 If containers a and b don't belong to the same group, any method invocation on a can run concurrently with any method invocation on b.
3 All other pairs of invocations require synchronization.

Only property 1 is intended for the users of the `Container` class. It tells clients that they can use the class from different threads simultaneously, without worrying about synchronization issues.

Properties 2 and 3, instead, are destined for the `Container` class developers and set out the target level of supported concurrency. Relative to table 8.1, this level lies between class-level and object-level concurrency because it allows concurrency between different groups of objects. In the rest of this chapter, we'll examine different ways to achieve this objective using Java synchronization primitives, namely `synchronized`, `volatile`, and the `ReentrantLock` class.

8.2 Dealing with deadlocks

Rather than modifying *Reference*, we'll work with *Speed1* from chapter 3, which is more efficient and more suited to thread safety. Recall the basic structure of *Speed1*: each container holds a reference to a *group* object, which in turn knows the amount of water in each container and the set of all members of that group, as shown in the following snippet:

```
public class Container {
    private Group group = new Group(this);

    private static class Group {
        double amountPerContainer;
        Set<Container> members;

        Group(Container c) {
            members = new HashSet<>();
            members.add(c);
        }
    }
}
```

It's quite clear from the policy specification that groups are the synchronization units of our class. In practice, `connectTo` should acquire the monitors of the two groups being merged. Anytime a method needs more than one monitor, the risk of a deadlock arises. A deadlock is a condition where two or more threads are stuck, each one waiting for a monitor that another one holds. They're waiting for each other in a cyclic pattern, forever.

The simplest deadlock scenario occurs when thread 1 attempts to acquire monitor A and then monitor B, whereas thread 2 requests them in the opposite order. An unlucky scheduling may cause thread 1 to successfully acquire A and then thread 2 to successfully acquire B before thread 1 does. At that point, the threads are stuck in a deadlock. This scenario can easily play out with the following natural but faulty implementation of `connectTo`:

```
public void connectTo(Container other) {
    synchronized (group) {
        synchronized (other.group) {
            ...   ❶ The actual operation here
        }
```

```
      }
   }
```

If one thread invokes a.connectTo(b) and another thread simultaneously invokes b.connectTo(a), they risk the textbook case of deadlock. Generally speaking, you have two ways to avoid such deadlocks without restricting the class clients in any way: *atomic lock sequences* or *ordered lock sequences*.

POP QUIZ 2   Can you get into a deadlock if each thread is guaranteed to hold one lock at a time?

8.2.1   *Atomic lock sequences*

First, you can render atomic the sequence of lock acquisitions that generates that dead-lock risk. This entails using an extra lock—let's call it globalLock—to make sure that no two such sequences can run concurrently. In this way, a sequence of lock requests can start only when no other sequence is in progress. If a sequence blocks because one of the required locks is busy, it'll block while holding the global lock, so no other sequence can start and risk going into a deadlock. Notice that even sequences that require a completely different set of locks must stall until the current sequence completes. This is a very cautious approach that avoids deadlocks by limiting the amount of concurrency allowed.

In Java, the global lock can't be an implicit lock because by design implicit locks must be released in the opposite order in which they were acquired. So, if globalLock is acquired before monitor A, it can't be released before the latter. In other words, the following fragment is faulty:

```
synchronized (globalLock) {
   synchronized (group) {
      synchronized (other.group) {
}  ❶ We'd like to release globalLock here.
         ...  ❷ The actual operation here
      }
   }
}
```

Despite the misleading indentation, the first right brace is releasing other.group, not globalLock as intended. *Explicit* locks provided in the Java API by the ReentrantLock class overcome this limitation. A ReentrantLock is more flexible than an implicit lock: in particular, it can be freely acquired and released at any time using its lock and unlock methods. In this approach, we'd add an explicit lock to the class:

```
private static final ReentrantLock globalLock = new ReentrantLock();
```

Then, we'd use that global lock to guard the beginning of connectTo, until the two implicit locks are acquired, as you can see in the following listing.

> **Listing 8.1   *AtomicSequence*: Preventing deadlocks by an atomic lock sequence**

```
public void connectTo(Container other) {
   globalLock.lock();
```

```
synchronized (group) {
   synchronized (other.group) {
      globalLock.unlock();
      ...   ❶ Compute new amount
      group.members.addAll(other.group.members);
      group.amountPerContainer = newAmount;
      for (Container x: other.group.members)
         x.group = group;
   }
}
}
```

Because only one thread can hold `globalLock` at any given time, only one thread can be in the middle of the sequence of two `synchronized` lines, and no deadlock can arise.

POP QUIZ 3 What happens if an exception is thrown from inside a `synchronized` block? What if instead the thread throwing the exception owns a `ReentrantLock`?

8.2.2 *Ordered lock sequences*

The second and more efficient way to avoid deadlocks is to order monitors in a global sequence known to all threads, and make sure that all threads request them in that order. You can establish such a global sequence by assigning a unique integral ID to each group. In turn, you obtain unique IDs by introducing a global (that is, static) counter that's incremented for each new instance and provides the ID for every new object.

You need to properly synchronize access to such a shared counter; otherwise, a race condition affecting two simultaneous increments may result in two groups having the same ID. The easiest solution is to employ the class `AtomicInteger`, one of the atomic variable types in figure 8.1. Objects of that class are thread-safe mutable integers. As its name suggests, the instance method `incrementAndGet` is perfect for generating unique sequential IDs in a thread-safe manner.

The following listing shows the beginning of the `Container` class, including its fields and the nested class. It's very similar to *Speed1*, except for the addition of unique group IDs.

Listing 8.2 *OrderedSequence*: Preventing deadlocks by ordered locking

```
public class Container {
   private Group group = new Group(this);

   private static class Group {
      static final AtomicInteger nGroups =
         new AtomicInteger();   ❶ Total number of groups so far
      double amount;
      Set<Container> elems = new HashSet<>();
      int id = nGroups.incrementAndGet();   ❷ Automatically assigned progressive ID

      Group(Container c) {
```

```
        elems.add(c);
    }
}
```

Each new `Group` object now receives a unique progressive ID, starting from 1, just like an auto-increment field in a database. As you can see in listing 8.3, the method `connectTo` will request the two monitors in the order of their IDs, thus avoiding deadlocks.

Identity hash code

A similar technique involves ordering lock acquisitions based on the identity hash-code of the corresponding object (in our case, group), that is, the hashcode that the `hashCode` method in `Object` returns. If that method has been overridden, you can still recover the original hash code for an object by invoking the static method `System.identityHashCode()`.

That approach saves some memory and a few lines of code because the identity hash-code is a built-in identifier for any object. On the other hand, it isn't a *unique* identifier, as it's possible—though unlikely—for two objects to have the same hashcode. Progressive IDs, instead, are unique by design, as long as the number of objects of that type is less than 2^{32}. Even then, you may switch to a `AtomicLong` id.

Listing 8.3   *OrderedSequence:* Method `connectTo`.

```
public void connectTo(Container other) {
    if (group == other.group) return;
    Object firstMonitor, secondMonitor;
    if (group.id < other.group.id) {
        firstMonitor  = group;
        secondMonitor = other.group;
    } else {
        firstMonitor  = other.group;
        secondMonitor = group;
    }
    synchronized (firstMonitor) {
        synchronized (secondMonitor) {
            ...  ❶ Computes new amount
            group.members.addAll(other.group.members);
            group.amountPerContainer = newAmount;
            for (Container x: other.group.members)
                x.group = group;
        }
    }
}
```

If you have some way to assign unique IDs to the objects that you need to lock, this is the way to go to avoid deadlocks. If instead those objects don't come with unique IDs and you can't modify their class, the global locking technique from the previous section may be your only option.

POP QUIZ 4 Why does the ordered locking technique prevent deadlocks?

8.2.3 A hidden race condition

The two techniques from sections 8.2.1 and 8.2.2 are general ways to avoid deadlocks, but in the case of water containers, they're affected by subtle race conditions. The problem is that the group objects that double as monitors *can be replaced* by a simultaneous connection operation. As a result, an invocation to `connectTo` may end up acquiring the lock of an obsolete group that's no longer associated with any container. In that case, the operations that `connectTo` performs won't be mutually exclusive with other operations on the new group of this container.

It's quite straightforward to recognize this problem in the ordered lock technique from section 8.2.2. The first lines of `connectTo`, comparing group IDs and establishing the order between monitors, aren't guarded by any synchronization. Hence, it may happen that either of the two groups changes before the current thread has a chance to acquire the corresponding monitor. The natural solution is to add a global lock that protects that first phase, from the beginning of the method to just after the two monitors have been acquired. This would bring the code close to our other solution, the atomic lock sequence. But globally locking the first phase renders useless the whole lock ordering machinery because the global lock is enough to prevent deadlocks! At the end of the day, you'd end up with *exactly* the atomic lock sequence version. But is the latter free from race conditions?

Close scrutiny or focused testing reveal that it's not. It's still possible for `connectTo` to acquire the wrong monitor and break the stated concurrency policy, as shown in figure 8.2. Indeed, suppose thread 1 starts `a.connectTo(b)` but is preempted[4] before updating the group of b, that is, before the assignment `b.group = a.group`. This may happen for a number of reasons, the simplest being that some other thread is scheduled to run on the same hardware core. After all, your JVM doesn't run in isolation. It shares your hardware with an OS and plenty of other processes.

At this point, suppose that thread 2 runs `b.connectTo(c)`. The second thread gets stuck on `synchronized (b.group)`, because the first thread holds that monitor. When the first thread releases it, the second thread will acquire it, even though that monitor doesn't correspond to any group anymore because it's the monitor of an obsolete group object that's ready for GC. The second thread is under the "illusion" that it's holding the monitor for the group of b, whereas it's actually holding a stale monitor. Its subsequent operations *won't* be mutually exclusive with other operations on the *current* group of b.

This scenario is depicted in figure 8.2, and solved in the next section, which finally presents a truly thread-safe water container implementation.

---

[4] That is, its execution is suspended by the OS scheduler.

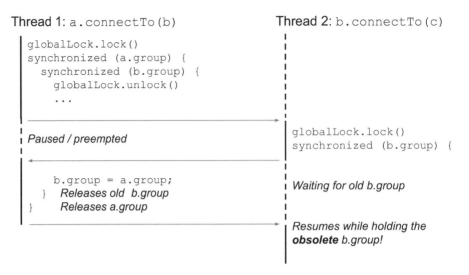

Thread 1: `a.connectTo(b)`   Thread 2: `b.connectTo(c)`

```
globalLock.lock()
synchronized (a.group) {
  synchronized (b.group) {
    globalLock.unlock()
    ...
```

| *Paused / preempted* |

```
globalLock.lock()
synchronized (b.group) {
```

Waiting for old b.group

```
    b.group = a.group;
  }   Releases old  b.group
}     Releases a.group
```

Resumes while holding the **obsolete** *b.group!*

Figure 8.2   A race condition affecting the atomic lock sequence `connectTo` implementation

8.3   *Thread-safe containers*   *[ThreadSafe]*

To get a truly thread-safe implementation, we start with *OrderedSequence* (listings 8.2 and 8.3), which is free from deadlocks and allows full parallelism between method calls involving different groups of containers, and we set out to solve the race conditions described in the previous section. The new implementation, denoted by *ThreadSafe*, has the same fields and the same nested `Group` class as *OrderedSequence*, and, like *OrderedSequence*, it doesn't need any global locking when connecting two containers. However, it may try to acquire the right monitors multiple times, as explained in the following section.

8.3.1   *Synchronizing connectTo*

To remove the race condition, you must make sure that `connectTo` acquires the monitors of the *current* groups of the two containers being connected. To do this without sacrificing too much concurrency, you need to shift your mindset from classic lock-based synchronization to a form of *lock-free synchronization*. Unless you use a global lock and lose all parallelism, you can never be sure to acquire the right monitors on your first attempt. You need to try multiple times, as shown in the following listing, until you recognize that the acquired monitors are the current ones. That's why you should wrap the ordered lock sequence code borrowed from *OrderedSequence* into a potentially infinite loop.

Listing 8.4   *ThreadSafe*: Method `connectTo`

```
public void connectTo(Container other) {
  while (true) {
```

```
if (group == other.group) return;
Object firstMonitor, secondMonitor;
if (group.id < other.group.id) {
    firstMonitor  = group;
    secondMonitor = other.group;
} else {
    firstMonitor  = other.group;
    secondMonitor = group;
}
synchronized (firstMonitor) {    ❶ Tentatively acquires monitors
    synchronized (secondMonitor) {
        if ((firstMonitor == group && secondMonitor == other.group) ||
            (secondMonitor == group && firstMonitor == other.group)) {
            ...  ❷ The actual operation here
            return;
        }
    }
}
    ❸ At least one of the two monitors was stale—retry.
}
}
```

In every iteration, you tentatively acquire the two chosen monitors, only to immediately check whether they're current, that is, whether their respective containers still point to them as their groups. If the check is positive, you perform the usual group merging operations (omitted in the listing). Otherwise, you release the two monitors and try again by rereading the group fields of the two containers being merged. You can call this an *optimistic* approach to synchronization: you assume that no other thread is messing with these two containers. If your assumption is violated, you try again.

Lock-free synchronization

The pattern of repeatedly attempting an operation on a shared object until no contention is detected is reminiscent of the common compare-and-swap (CAS) loop in lock-free synchronization. CAS is a CPU instruction with three arguments—src, dst, and old—whose effect is to swap the content of memory locations src and dst, only if the current content of dst is equal to old. You can use it to safely update a shared variable without using a mutex.

Toward this end, you first read the shared variable (dst) and put its value in a local variable (old). Then, you compute the new value for the shared variable, usually based on its old value, and store it in another local variable (src). Finally, you call CAS with the above arguments to update the shared variable only if another thread hasn't modified it in the meantime. If CAS reports failure, the whole operation is restarted, ad infinitum, as you can see in the following pseudo-code:

```
do {
    old = dst
    src = some new value, usually based on old
} while (cas(src, dst, old) == failed)
```

Ours is a hybrid scenario where we ensure that we get the right monitors using a lock-free technique, whereas the remaining merging operations are performed under classic lock protection.

8.3.2 *Synchronizing addWater and getAmount*

Let's move on to the remaining two methods: `addWater` and `getAmount`. `addWater` exhibits a structure similar to the one of `connectTo`. Indeed, even when acquiring the monitor of a *single* group, it's possible that another thread will replace the group of this container in the meantime.

The reason is that entering even the simplest synchronized block isn't an atomic operation. For a detailed analysis we need to go behind the scenes of the Java code and take a look at the corresponding bytecode.

The JVM architecture

Contrary to most actual microprocessors, which are based on registers, the JVM is an abstract machine providing each method invocation (that is, each call frame) with an operand stack and a sequence of local variables. When entering a method, the operand stack is empty and the local variables contain the arguments of the current method. When executing an instance method, the first local variable contains `this`. Arithmetic and logical operations take their arguments from and return their result to the operand stack. Moreover, the JVM is object-aware, in the sense that field access, method invocations, and other OO operations correspond directly to specific bytecode instructions.

You can use the `javap` command-line tool included in the JDK to visualize the content of a class file in human-readable form. You can view the bytecode of all methods in a class by running `javap -c classname`.

For example, suppose `addWater` started as follows:

```
public void addWater(double amount) {
    synchronized (group) {   ❶
        ...
    }
}
```

The second line translates to the following bytecode:

1:	aload_0	Push the first local variable (`this`) on the stack
2:	getfield #5	Pop top of stack and push its `group` field
3:	dup	Duplicate top of stack
4:	astore_2	Store top of stack into local variable #2
5:	monitorenter	Pop top of stack and acquire its monitor

As you can see, what appears like an atomic lock acquisition is in fact translated into a short sequence of bytecode instructions whose last instruction actually requests the monitor. If another thread changes the group of this container between bytecode lines 2 and 5, the current thread will acquire the monitor of an obsolete group, and its subsequent operations won't be mutually exclusive with other operations on the new group of this container. In that case, the culprit must be a concurrent invocation to connectTo because that's the only method modifying the group references.

We must try multiple times, as shown in the following listing, until we're certain that the acquired monitor is current.

Listing 8.5 *ThreadSafe*: Method addWater

```
public void addWater(double amount) {
    while (true) {
        Object monitor = group;
        synchronized (monitor) {          ❶ Tentatively acquires the monitor
            if (monitor == group) {       ❷ The monitor is up-to-date.
                double amountPerContainer = amount / group.elems.size();
                group.amount += amountPerContainer;
                return;
            }
        }
                ❸ The monitor was stale—retry.
    }
}
```

Finally, as you can see in listing 8.6, getAmount is a simple getter, so you may be wondering whether it's really necessary to apply any synchronization to it. After all, it only reads a primitive value. In the worst case, it may read a slightly stale value that's just being modified. Right? Wrong. The Java memory model specifies that even a single read of a double value isn't an atomic operation. That is to say that the 64-bit read operation may be divided into two 32-bit reads, and those two reads may be interleaved with a write operation by another thread. Without the synchronized block, you might end up reading an absurd value, whose higher 32 bits are new and whose lower 32 bits are stale, or vice versa. By the way, adding the volatile modifier to the amount field also would solve this problem by rendering the read operation atomic.

Listing 8.6 *ThreadSafe*: Method getAmount

```
public double getAmount() {
    synchronized (group) {
        return group.amount;
    }
}
```

For getAmount, you don't need to worry about the accessed group being stale because that would only give us a slightly out-of-date value, but not a wrong one. In a multi-threaded environment, even the now-current value can be updated and become stale at any time. Given that fact, it's pointless to spend extra effort to ensure that we're reading the amount from the current group.

Compare this situation with addWater. If you update a stale group with addWater, you get an inconsistency because you'd be adding water to a group that that no container points to. The added water would vanish, and the method would have violated its postcondition.

8.4   *Immutability*   *[Immutable]*

Thread unsafety ultimately arises from one thread writing to shared memory while other threads are reading from or writing to the same memory location. An entirely diffent approach to obtaining thread safety is to ensure that all the shared objects are immutable, so the previous situation can't occur, because no thread can modify an object after it has been initialized and shared. Unfortunately, this approach doesn't play well with the API we established in chapter 1. The simple fact that you can invoke getA mount twice on the same container and get two different values back implies that

Immutability in C#

In C#, you create an immutable class by declaring all of its fields as `read only` and making sure that all referenced objects also belong to immutable classes.

C# strings are immutable just like Java's, except that C# offers the option to bypass immutability by using the `unsafe` keyword. Another example of an immutable class is `System.DateTime`.

containers have mutable state. Mutable objects are the default in Java, even though the language features a couple of immutable classes in pretty prominent places, like `String` and `Integer`. In fact, those standard classes make sure that all Java programmers have some experience with immutable objects and know that it's possible to base their programs on them.

As a refresher, a class is immutable if all its fields are final, and all the references it holds point to other immutable classes.[5] Whereas a method of a mutable class can change the state of the current object, the analogous method of an immutable class creates and returns a *new* object of the same type, with the desired content.

Let's quickly review this principle in action in the standard `String` and `Integer` classes. Those classes offer no method that modifies their content. To aid the programmer, however, this immutability is cleverly disguised by compile-time mechanisms that allow you to write, for a `String` s and an `Integer` n:

```
s += " and others";
n++;
```

As you probably know, despite appearances, the previous two lines don't modify the objects that s and n point to, but rather create new objects that replace the old ones. For example, the compiler turns the innocent-looking string concatenation into the following eyesore, which even involves an entirely different class:

```
StringBuilder temp = StringBuilder();
temp.append(s);
temp.append(" and others");
s = temp.toString();
```

---

[5] To be precise, a class can be immutable even if no field is final, but the final keyword ensures that it's so. This is the same distinction between a final and an *effectively* final variable, the latter property being relevant to inner class visibility issues.

Similarly, for an `Integer` increment, the compiler generates bytecode that unboxes the value, increments it, and then wraps it again via a static factory method.[6] That process looks similar to the following Java snippet:

```
int value = n.intValue();          ❶ Unwrapping
n = Integer.valueOf(value + 1);    ❷ Rewrapping
```

Back to our actual purposes, we're discussing immutable classes in this chapter because they're automatically thread-safe. Multiple threads can invoke methods on the same object, and those invocations can't step on each other's toes, simply because they can't write to the same memory. In particular, if one of those methods is supposed to return a complex value, it'll do so by creating a new object that other threads can't possibly see until the method actually returns it.

POP QUIZ 5 Why are immutable classes automatically thread-safe?

Immutability and functional languages

In other programming paradigms, such as the functional paradigm, immutability is the default and sometimes the only option. For example, in OCaml, all variables are immutable, except when specified by the `mutable` modifier. That works because the program is one huge (or small) expression, and iteration is replaced by recursion. Notice that recursion provides an *appearance* of mutability, in the sense that the parameters of a recursive function are bound to different values in different steps of the recursion.

JVM languages Scala and Kotlin also favor functional-style programming and immutability: variables are immutable by default, but you can create mutable ones using the `var` keyword.

8.4.1 The API

Let's break the confines of the API I established in chapter 1 and sketch the public interface for an immutable version of our containers, offering the same services as the mutable one. Assuming that containers are immutable, the `addWater` method must return a new container with the updated water amount, but this isn't enough. If the current container is connected to other ones, new objects with an updated water amount must replace all those other containers. Imagine how cumbersome it would be to invoke `addWater` and receive as a result the set of all updated containers that are connected to the current one. We need to put the API through a more extensive refactoring.

The idea is to base the API design on a larger perspective, in which the main object we manipulate is a *system* of containers. Each system is created with a fixed number n of containers, indexed from 0 to $n-1$, and is itself immutable. Operations that change the state of even a single container must *appear* to return a new system of containers.

---

[6] Compared to a constructor, a factory method is not forced to return a new object. In fact, `valueOf` caches all integers in the range –128 to 127.

Whether the new object internally shares data with the old one is an implementation issue that I'll discuss later.

As a first attempt, let's draft an API supporting a `ContainerSystem` class and a `Container` class. The following snippet shows how you might go about creating a system of 10 containers and then adding 42 units of water to the sixth one. Since these objects are immutable, adding water returns a new system of containers.

```
ContainerSystem s1 = new ContainerSystem(10);    ❶ A new system of 10 containers
Container c = s1.getContainer(5);    ❷ The sixth container
ContainerSystem s2 = s1.addWater(c, 42);    ❸ A new system where c holds 42 units of water
```

This type of behavior, when a mutating operation returns a new object, is called a *persistent* data structure. The name expresses the fact that such data structures make available to the clients their entire history. For example, in the previous snippet, system `s1` is still available after you've obtained system `s2` from it. The opposite situation, when a data structure is modified in-place and doesn't keep its past state, is called *ephemeral*, and it's the default behavior of classical imperative data structures. Because persistent data structures offer more functionality, it's not surprising that they're generally less efficient, in terms of time and space, than ephemeral ones.

Going back to the new API, notice that the container `c` is immutable and belongs to system `s1`. This raises an important design choice: is `c` also a valid container for `s2`? That is, can we invoke something like `s2.addWater(c, 7)`? If we can't, the API is very cumbersome to use. Every modification to any container generates a new system and invalidates all current container objects. If we can, then we can expect `c` to represent the "container of index 5" in *any* system of containers. In other words, `c` becomes a thinly disguised alias for the index 5. Neither scenario is particularly satisfying. Instead, let's get rid of `Container` altogether (as in *Memory3* and *Memory4* from chapter 4) and identify containers using bare integer IDs.

The first snippet, which creates a 10-container system and adds water to the sixth container, becomes the following:

```
ContainerSystem s1 = new ContainerSystem(10);
ContainerSystem s2 = s1.addWater(5, 42);    ❶ Adds 42 liters to container 5
```

What if we realize we need an eleventh container, but we don't want to start a new system from scratch? An instance method of `ContainerSystem` can return a new system with an extra container:

```
ContainerSystem s3 = s2.addContainer();    ❷ Adds 11th container
```

Naturally, the `connectTo` method (renamed `connect` for the occasion) must accept two container IDs and return an entirely new system of containers:

```
s3 = s3.connect(5, 6);    ❸ Connects containers 5 and 6
double amount = s3.getAmount(5);    ❹ Holds the value 21.0
```

Summarizing, you end up with the following methods:

```
public class ContainerSystem {
    public ContainerSystem(int containerCount)
    public ContainerSystem addContainer()
    public int containerCount()    ❺ The number of containers in this system

    public ContainerSystem connect(int containerID1, int containerID2)
    public double getAmount(int containerID)
    public ContainerSystem addWater(int containerID, double amount)
}
```

8.4.2 *The implementation*

To convert a given mutable implementation to immutability, you can apply the following *copy-on-write* technique:

1. A system of containers holds the same data that was spread among all containers in the mutable implementation.
2. Each mutating operation (`addWater` and `connectTo`) creates and returns a new system holding a modified copy of the entire data structure.

This is the simplest way to turn a mutable class into an immutable one, but generally not the most efficient. A more sophisticated approach would try to reuse as much as possible of the old object, when you apply a mutating operation to it, instead of making a full duplicate. In the case of water containers, you can imagine a smart immutable implementation duplicating containers on-demand, that is, copying only the group of containers that a given mutating operation (say, a call to `addWater`) affects, and reusing all other containers until they also become involved in a call to `addWater` or `connectTo`.

Persistent data structures

Designing efficient immutable data structures is an active area of research. The objective is to approach the efficiency of mutable data structures while enjoying the benefits of immutability, especially in conjunction with functional languages.

Several third-party libraries provide "smart" Java persistent collections, where the modified copy shares some data with the original one, saving both time and space compared to a plain copy-on-write approach. Examples include PCollections (https://github.com/hrldcpr/pcollections) and Cyclops (https://github.com/aol/cyclops).

In principle, you could apply the simple copy-on-write approach to *any* of the solutions we explored in the previous chapters, producing as many different implementations of the immutable API as we developed in the previous section. In practice, most of the mutable implementations you've seen so far make little sense once they become immutable copy-on-write classes. Consider the most efficient mutable implementation from chapter 3: the parent-pointer trees from *Speed3*. The value of that implementation is tied to its mutability: it's efficient to update and to query. If every `connectTo` operation were to copy the entire forest of trees (yes, that's what a set of trees is called), you'd completely lose the update efficiency because each `connectTo` takes linear time. At that point, you might as well use a simpler data structure to begin with.

Indeed, let's sketch an immutable version of *Memory3* instead. That implementation is based on two arrays, which are easy and efficient to copy. The method `connectTo` will still require linear time, but at least you'll be able to copy all of the data with two simple lines. Also, copying two chunks of contiguous memory is faster than copying a linked forest of trees, despite having the same asymptotic complexity.

First, recall the data structures that *Memory3* uses:

- The `group` array maps a container ID to its group ID.
- The `amount` array maps a group ID to the amount of water found in each container of that group.

Each instance of `ContainerSystem` will hold these two arrays. It may be a good idea to declare them as `final`, as a hint to their immutability. Of course, a final array reference doesn't prevent the content of the array from being modified. That's why the final modifier in this case is just a reminder that you're aiming at a much stronger form of immutability.

In *Memory3*, you keep the `amount` array as short as possible: when two containers are connected and their groups are merged, one cell is removed from `amount` because there's one less group around. Here, we're not particularly concerned with memory occupancy, so you can take the simpler approach and keep the two arrays at the same length, equal to the total number of containers.

The only public constructor for `ContainerSystem` creates a system with a given number of empty and isolated containers. To accomplish this aim, the constructor gives each container its own group, and the ID of the i-th group is just i.

Given a container ID, the `getAmount` method will access the `group` array to obtain the group ID for that container, then the `amount` array to obtain the water amount in that group, as you can see in the following listing:

> **Listing 8.7   *Immutable*: Fields, constructor, and method `getAmount`**

```
public class ContainerSystem {
    private final int group[];          ❶ From containerID to its groupID
    private final double amount[];      ❷ From groupID to
                                          the per-container amount
    public ContainerSystem(int containerCount) {
        group = new int[containerCount];
        amount = new double[containerCount];
        for (int i=0; i<containerCount; i++) {
            group[i] = i;      ❸ The groupID of the i-th container is i.
        }
    }

    public double getAmount(int containerID) {
        final int groupID = group[containerID];
        return amount[groupID];
    }
```

The `getAmount` method is straightforward (and very similar to the one in *Memory3*) because it provides a read-only functionality. Next, let's consider the first mutating method: `addContainer`, the method that returns a new system with one extra container. Because the two arrays are declared final, you must initialize them in a constructor. Later, you'll use the same constructor for the other mutating methods, `addWater` and `connect`, so it's convenient to pass two parameters to it:

- The existing system to be copied.
- The new number of containers. Method `addContainer` uses this parameter to increase the number of containers by one, whereas the other mutating methods leave this number unchanged.

Listing 8.8 shows both `addContainer` and its support constructor.

Listing 8.8 *Immutable*: Method `addContainer` and support constructor

```
public ContainerSystem addContainer() {
    final int containerCount = group.length;
    ContainerSystem result =
        new ContainerSystem(this, containerCount + 1);   ❶ Call to private constructor
    result.group[containerCount] = containerCount;
    return result;
}
private ContainerSystem(ContainerSystem old, int length) {
    group = Arrays.copyOf(old.group, length);    ❷ An efficient way to copy an array
    amount = Arrays.copyOf(old.amount, length);
}
```

Next, `addWater` also needs to create an entirely new system of containers, with updated water amounts. Unless there's no water to be added, it invokes the private constructor from the previous listing and then updates the amount in the appropriate group, as shown in the following listing.

Listing 8.9 *Immutable*: Method `addWater`

```
public ContainerSystem addWater(int containerID, double amount) {
    if (amount == 0)     ❶ No need for a new system!
        return this;

    ContainerSystem result =
        new ContainerSystem(this, group.length);   ❷ Call to private constructor
    int groupID = group[containerID],
        groupSize = groupSize(groupID);
    result.amount[groupID] += amount / groupSize;
    return result;
}
```

Finally, the `connect` method also creates a new system of containers using the private constructor and then connects two containers by merging their groups. You can find its source code in the accompanying repository(https://bitbucket.org/mfaella /exercisesinstyle).

8.5   *And now for something completely different*

In this section, you'll face a different application requiring the same techniques I introduced earlier in the chapter in the context of water containers. You'll design a class `Repository<T>`, representing a fixed-size container that stores its elements in indexed cells, like an array. Repositories come with a built-in operation that switches the content of two cells. Naturally for this chapter, your users want this class to be thread-safe so that multiple threads can easily share and manipulate repositories.

In detail, the class must offer the following constructor and methods:

- `public Repository(int n)`—Creates a repository with n cells, initially holding `null`
- `public T set(int i, T elem)`—Inserts object `elem` into the i-th cell and returns the object previously located there (or `null`)
- `public void swap(int i, int j)`—Swaps the contents of cells i and j

As discussed earlier, before implementing the class itself, you need to clarify its concurrency policy. Recall that such a policy specifies which operations will be able to proceed in parallel and which need to be mutually exclusive instead.

Because different repositories don't share any data, the simplest concurrency policy that guarantees thread safety is the *object-level* policy: one lock per repository and all methods synchronized on that lock. If many threads use a repository concurrently, this policy may give bad performance because all operations on the same repository—even those involving different indices—must acquire the same lock.

A more permissive and efficient concurrency policy forbids concurrent access to the same index and allows all other operations to proceed concurrently. You can state it as follows:

- Two calls to `set` on the same index must be serialized.
- Two calls to `swap` that share at least an index must be serialized.
- A call to `swap(i, j)` and a call to `set` on index `i` or `j` must be serialized.
- All other operations are allowed to proceed concurrently.

This policy requires a lock for each cell in the repository, including empty cells (those holding `null`). Hence, the class needs one extra object for each cell, used as a monitor for that cell. You can store the elements and the monitors in two `ArrayList`s:

```
public class Repository<T> {
   private final List<T> elements;
   private final List<Object> monitors;

   public Repository(int size) {
      elements = new ArrayList<>(size);
      monitors = new ArrayList<>(size);
      for (int i=0; i<size; i++) {
         elements.add(null);        ❶ Lists must be filled before you can call get and set.
         monitors.add(new Object());
      }
   }
}
```

The `set` method simply acquires the monitor of the cell being written:

```
public T set(int i, T elem) {
   synchronized (monitors.get(i)) {
      return elements.set(i, elem);
   }
}
```

The `swap` method acquires the monitors of the two cells being swapped, in increasing index order, to avoid deadlocks:

```
public void swap(int i, int j) {
   if (i == j) return;
   if (i > j) {      ❷ Makes sure that i is the smaller index
      int temp = i;
      i = j;
      j = temp;
   }
   synchronized (monitors.get(i)) { {      ❸ Acquires monitors in index order
      synchronized (monitors.get(j)) {
         elements.set(i, elements.set(j, elements.get(i)));
         ❹ This one-liner uses the fact that List.set
      }          returns the value previously at that position.
   }
}
```

Notice that in this way you're allowing different threads to read and even modify an `ArrayList` at the same time, provided they use different indices. However, `ArrayList` is *not* a thread-safe class. Is this code wrong? If you read the `ArrayList` documentation carefully, you'll realize that the caller only needs to serialize *structural modifications* (such as calling `add`); concurrent calls to `get` and `set` on different indices are fine.

8.6   *Real-world use cases*

In this chapter, we've discussed how to make water containers thread-safe so that multiple threads can interact with them without requiring the client code to handle synchronization explicitly. But why did we decide to get into trouble refactoring the code to make it thread-safe? The single-threaded version works just fine. To answer this question, let's look at some use cases where concurrency is not only beneficial but crucial.

- You love chess, and at the same time you're a gifted programmer. For fun and practice, you decide to create a chess program in Java to play against your computer. After a few games of chess, you realize that your program is great (modesty is not one of your traits), and you want to share it with the world. You decide to turn your program into a service, where the computer will be able to compete against multiple users. You can handle multiple games in two ways: either you put users in a queue and handle them serially, or you can exploit concurrency and handle many players simultaneously. The second approach can take advantage of parallel hardware, such as a multi-core machine.

- Applications, operating systems, network devices, databases—in other words, virtually all ongoing services in a computational system—create logs. They don't generate such log files for fun: well-managed organizations analyze their contents in batches or in real time to mitigate risks. A basic analysis workflow involves parsing log files; identifying important patterns or anomalies; and generating aggregate statistics, reports, and alerts. A common pattern for dealing efficiently with large log files is the *Map-Reduce* paradigm. As you might have guessed, this pattern consists of two steps: map and reduce. The map step enables the log analysis system to process independent chunks of log data concurrently, often on a distributed network of machines, and generate intermediate results. The reduce step collects the results and computes the final aggregates. The fork-join framework I mentioned at the beginning of this chapter is a variant of this idea, tailored to single multicore architectures.

- If you've ever lived in the United Kingdom, you've probably realized that football is extremely popular. In fact, during a Sunday afternoon, you can categorize people into those who drink beer and those who don't. Football players and minors are those who don't (hopefully). Having noticed this passion for sports, you decide to create a platform that will send live sports news feeds and distribute them to your subscribers. The live feeds will produce streams of data and put them in a container data structure, and subscriber clients will request data from the container to inform your subscribers. A thread-safe news container will enable data producers and consumers to run in multiple threads, giving your clients the satisfaction of raising a pint to their team before their neighbors.

- A program isolated from the rest of the world is rarely very useful. On the contrary, real programs will frequently wait for some input/output operation from an external resource, such as a file or a network connection. Multithreading allows a user-facing program to remain responsive while waiting on such slow peripherals. For example, think of a single-threaded web browser that stops being interactive while downloading a file from the network. Can you guess how many users this web browser would have? At most one: its creator.

8.7 *Applying what you learned*

EXERCISE 1
The following subclass of `Thread` increments all elements of an array of integers by one. As you can see, all instances of this class share the array.

```
class MyThread extends Thread {
    private static int[] array = ...   ❶ Some initial value

    public void run() {
        _____1_____     ❷ A placeholder
        for (int i=0; i<array.length; i++) {
```

```
            _____2_____
            array[i]++;
            _____3_____
        }
        _____4_____
    }
}
```

A program creates *two* instances of `MyThread` and launches them as two concurrent threads, with the intention of incrementing each array element by two. Which of the following insertions make the program correct by removing all race conditions? (Multiple options may be correct.)

(a)   1 = "synchronized (this) {"   4 = "}"

(b)   1 = "synchronized {"   4 = "}"

(c)   1 = "synchronized (array) {"   4 = "}"

(d)   2 = "synchronized (this) {"   3 = "}"

(e)   2 = "synchronized (array) {"   3 = "}"

(f)   2 = "synchronized (array[i]) {"   3 = "}"

EXERCISE 2

Design the thread-safe class `AtomicPair`, which holds two objects and offers the following methods:

```java
public class AtomicPair<S,T> {
    public void setBoth(S first, T second);
    public S getFirst();
    public T getSecond();
}
```

Respect the following concurrency policy: Calling `setBoth` is an atomic operation. That is, if a thread calls `setBoth(a,b)`, any subsequent call to `getFirst` and `getSecond` will view both updated values.

EXERCISE 3

In a simple social network, each user holds a set of friends, and friendship is symmetrical. The implementation is based on the following class:

```java
public class SocialUser {
    private final String name;
    private final Set<SocialUser> friends = new HashSet<>();

    public SocialUser(String name) {
        this.name = name;
    }
    public synchronized void befriend(SocialUser other) {
        friends.add(other);
        synchronized (other) {
            other.friends.add(this);
        }
    }
    public synchronized boolean isFriend(SocialUser other) {
```

```
        return friends.contains(other);
    }
}
```

Unfortunately, when multiple threads establish friendships at the same time, sometimes the system hangs and needs to be restarted. Do you know why? Can you fix the problem by refactoring `SocialUser`?

EXERCISE 4
Consider the following mutable class, `Time`, representing a time of the day in hours, minutes, and seconds:

- `public void addNoWrapping(Time delta)`—Adds a delay to this time, maxing out at one second before midnight (23:59:59)
- `public void addAndWrapAround(Time delta)`—Adds a delay to this time, wrapping around at midnight
- `public void subtractNoWrapping(Time delta)`—Subtracts a delay from this time, stopping at 00:00:00
- `public void subtractAndWrapAround(Time delta)`—Subtracts a delay from this time, wrapping around if needed

Convert this API into an *immutable* version and implement it.

Summary

- A reasoned *concurrency policy* is a crucial prerequisite for thread safety.
- The main enemies of thread safety are race conditions and deadlocks.
- You can avoid deadlocks by using a global lock or an ordered lock policy.
- Differently from implicit locks, you can acquire and release explicit locks in any order.
- Immutability is an alternative path to thread safety.

Answers to quizzes and exercises

POP QUIZ 1
Users of a class should know only that the class is thread-safe. The rest of the concurrency policy is intended for the class implementors. In practice, however, users may be interested in the concurrency policy for appraising the class performance.

POP QUIZ 2
You can't get into a deadlock if the locks are *reentrant*, that is, if a thread can reacquire a lock that it already owns. In Java, both implicit and explicit locks are reentrant. In other frameworks, such as Posix mutexes, locks can be non-reentrant, and a single thread can deadlock if it tries to reacquire a lock it already owns.

POP QUIZ 3

If an exception is thrown from inside a `synchronized` block, the monitor is automatically released. On the other hand, you need to explicitly release a `ReentrantLock`. That's why its `unlock` operation is usually put in the `finally` part of a `try...catch` block, to make sure it's executed under all circumstances.

POP QUIZ 4

The ordered locking technique prevents deadlocks because requesting locks in a fixed global order prevents cycles from being formed.

POP QUIZ 5

Immutable classes are automatically thread-safe because you can only read their objects, and concurrent reads by multiple threads pose no safety concerns. Methods creating new objects may employ mutable local variables because they live on the stack and aren't shared with other threads.

EXERCISE 1

The correct options are (c) and (e). Both ensure that if a thread is performing `array[i]++`, the other thread can't be performing the same instruction, even on a different `i`. What's more, (c) completely serializes the threads: one `for` loop is executed entirely before the other loop can start.

Options (a) and (d) don't provide any mutual exclusion because the two threads would be synchronizing on two different monitors. Options (b) and (f) cause compilation errors because a synchronized block needs to specify the object providing the monitor (and `array[i]` is not an object).

EXERCISE 2

To obey the concurrency policy, you just use synchronized blocks in all three methods, locking the same monitor. As explained in this chapter, it's better to synchronize on a private object rather than synchronize on `this`, even if the latter would allow you to replace the synchronized blocks with a sleeker method modifier.

```
public class AtomicPair<S,T> {
    private S first;
    private T second;
    private final Object lock = new Object();   ❶ Provides a private monitor

    public void setBoth(S first, T second) {
        synchronized (lock) {
            this.first = first;
            this.second = second;
        }
    }
    public S getFirst() {
        synchronized (lock) {
            return first;
        }
    }
    ...     ❷ getSecond is analogous.
}
```

It may look odd to put a single `return` statement in a synchronized block, but it's essential for both *mutual exclusion* and *visibility* reasons. First, you don't want `getFirst` and `getSecond` to occur when `setBoth` is halfway through its body. Second, without a synchronized block, threads calling `getFirst` would have no guarantee of seeing the updated value of `first`. By the way, declaring both `first` and `second` as `volatile` would solve the second issue (visibility) but not the first one (mutual exclusion).

EXERCISE 3

The class `SocialUser` may cause a deadlock if a thread invokes `a.befriend(b)` and another thread simultaneously invokes `b.befriend(a)`, for two `SocialUser` objects a and b. To avoid this risk, you can adopt the ordered locking technique, which starts with equipping each object with a unique `id`:

```
public class SocialUserNoDeadlock {
   private final String name;
   private final Set<SocialUserNoDeadlock> friends = new HashSet<>();
   private final int id;
   private static final AtomicInteger instanceCounter = new AtomicInteger();

   public SocialUserNoDeadlock(String name) {
      this.name = name;
      this.id = instanceCounter.incrementAndGet();
   }
}
```

The `befriend` method then avoids deadlocks by requesting the two locks in the order of increasing `id`:

```
public void befriend(SocialUserNoDeadlock other) {
   Object firstMonitor, secondMonitor;
   if (id < other.id) {
      firstMonitor = this;
      secondMonitor = other;
   } else {
      firstMonitor = other;
      secondMonitor = this;
   }
   synchronized (firstMonitor) {
      synchronized (secondMonitor) {
         friends.add(other);
         other.friends.add(this);
      }
   }
}
```

EXERCISE 4

To convert the API from mutable to immutable, you make every mutating method return a new object of the class. It's also a good idea to declare all fields `final`. The rest is simple arithmetic, needed to carry the overflows from seconds to minutes and from minutes to hours.

```
public class Time {
    private final int hours, minutes, seconds;

    public Time addNoWrapping(Time delta) {
        int s = seconds, m = minutes, h = hours;
        s += delta.seconds;
        if (s > 59) {      ❶ Second overflow: carries over to minutes
            s -= 60;
            m++;
        }
        m += delta.minutes;
        if (m > 59) {      ❷ Minute overflow: carries over to hours
            m -= 60;
            h++;
        }
        h += delta.hours;
        if (h > 23) {      ❸ Hour overflow: set to max
            h = 23;
            m = 59;
            s = 59;
        }
        return new Time(h, m, s);      ❹ Returns new object
    }
```

You can find the rest of this class in the accompanying repository (https://bitbucket
.org/mfaella/exercisesinstyle). Notice that the standard Java class `java.time.LocalTime`
provides functionality similar to that which this `Time` class provides.

Further reading

- B. Goetz, T. Peierls, Joshua Bloch, J. Bowbeer, D. Holmes, and D. Lea. *Java Concurrency in Practice.* Addison-Wesley, 2006.
  The must-read on Java concurrency. It discusses all kinds of concurrency issues in a fortunate combination of technical rigor and captivating style. Unfortunately, as of this writing it hasn't been updated with the high-level concurrency facilities added to the JDK starting from version 7. (See the next book for that.)

- R.-G. Urma, M. Fusco, and A. Mycroft. *Modern Java in Action.* Manning Publications, 2019.
  A comprehensive introduction to data streams, with a chapter dedicated to parallel computation using streams and the fork-join framework.

- Joshua Bloch. *Effective Java.* Addison-Wesley, 2017.
  As a rule, I'm trying to suggest different books for each chapter, but I'm making an exception for this book because it contains so much good advice on so many different topics. Chapter 11 is entirely devoted to concurrency, and item 17 to immutability in particular.

- R. J. Anderson and H. Woll. "Wait-Free Parallel Algorithms for the Union-Find Problem." 1991.
  The thread-safe water container class developed in this chapter is based on *Speed1*, which is not a particularly efficient representation. This research paper

shows how to create a thread-safe implementation of the much faster parent-pointer trees of *Speed3* which in addition is wait-free. It achieves thread safety using the compare-and-swap instruction instead of locks.

- Chris Okasaki. *Purely Functional Data Structures.* Cambridge University Press, 1998.

   The author of this book expanded his PhD thesis into an in-depth treatise on persistent data structures, with examples in ML and Haskell.

Please recycle: Reusability

This chapter covers

- Generalizing a piece of software to a wider context
- Using generics to write reusable classes
- Using and customizing mutable collectors on data streams

In the previous chapters, you developed concrete classes that solved a specific problem. Now, assume you need to generalize your solution to a broader variety of problems. Ideally, you should discern the essential features of the problem, separate them from what's merely incidental, and develop a solution for all the problems that share the same essential structure. Unfortunately, discerning the essential from the incidental is far from obvious. Roughly speaking, you should try to keep the key structure—that is, the part that may be useful in other contexts.

This final chapter assumes you're familiar with generics, including bounded type parameters.

9.1 Establishing boundaries

In the first decades of OOP, reusability was considered one of the selling points of the paradigm. The promise was that all you ever had to do was write small, reusable components and combine them with existing reusable components pulled off the shelf.

After some 50 years of practice (the first OO language was 1967's Simula), some of this promise has been confirmed, and some has proven to be off target.

Programmers pull reusable components off the shelf all the time: they're libraries and frameworks. A large part of today's development focuses on web applications that benefit greatly from a set of standard services packaged as a framework. On the other hand, once you cross the boundaries of your framework into application-specific code, reusability quickly fades into the background, pushed aside by more pressing functional and nonfunctional concerns, such as correctness, performance, and time to market.

In this chapter, you'll develop a library of objects that behave somewhat like water containers, with generality in mind. As is often the case with libraries, the question is: How general should it be? Should it extend from water containers to oil containers, or all the way to an intergalactic network of connectable planets with trade routes and population levels? To guide you in this choice, let's consider a couple of scenarios that you probably want to capture with the generalized framework, and another scenario that you may *not* want to capture because it would stretch the generalization too far.

SCENARIO 1 The municipal water company using your `Container` library is reporting that total water amounts show discrepancies of up to 0.0000001 liters of water a year.

You track these unfortunate inconsistencies to floating-point rounding errors. Fixing them requires representing water amounts with rational numbers with arbitrarily large numerators and denominators (say, two `BigInteger` objects).

Supporting this change is relatively straightforward: the business logic remains the same, whereas you replace the type of the amount field by a type variable `T`, and you require `T` to implement an interface providing the appropriate arithmetic operations.

SCENARIO 2 A social network wants to track the total number of likes that all sets of related posts receive. Two posts are considered related if both of them have attracted a comment coming from the same user.

At first glance, scenario 2 seems to have little to do with water containers, until you realize that you can treat each *post* as a container. When two posts receive a comment by the same person, they become connected. Instead of `addWater`, the scenario calls for a method adding one or more likes to this post. Finally, instead of `getAmount`, you need a method that returns the total number of likes that all posts connected to this one collected.

The scenario is not too different from water containers after all: in both cases, the objects can be permanently connected with each other, and what really counts is the set of directly or indirectly connected objects. Moreover, in both cases, objects have a property that you can read or update locally, but the effect of an update depends on the group of connected items.

On the other hand, the specific ways you update the local property and the ways it influences the global property are a little different. In the following sections, you'll see how you can reconcile them under a single contract. But first, here's a third extension scenario.

SCENARIO 3 A mobile phone carrier needs to manage its network of antennas. The company can permanently connect antennas to each other, and it wants to know how many direct connections you need to traverse from each given antenna to each other antenna (aka the length of the shortest path).

In this scenario, you still have items that you can permanently connect with each other. But the main property of interest—connection distance between antennas—concerns *two* given items, and its value depends on which *direct* connections exist. In particular, the value of this property is not shared among a group of connected antennas. Hence, this scenario needs radically different connection representations and management. Supporting it would make your code so generic that customizing it for a concrete scenario would require more effort than writing a specific solution from scratch.

Based on these descriptions, you'll develop a generic implementation of water containers that can accommodate scenarios 1 and 2, but not scenario 3.

9.2 The general framework

First, you'll formalize with an interface the essential features of a generic container:

1 A generic container possesses an attribute of some type V (for *value*). Clients can read the attribute or update it locally on a container, but the actual effect of an update depends on the group of connected containers. For concrete water containers, it will be V = Double.

2 Clients can permanently connect generic containers to each other.

Conceptually, these two features are independent, so you might represent them with two different interfaces (say, Attribute and Connectable). However, because you'd end up using them together all the time, let's put both features in a single interface called ContainerLike.

Having an attribute of type V (feature 1) simply translates to equipping the interface with two methods like the following:

```
public interface ContainerLike<V> {
    V get()                     ❶ Generalization of getAmount
    void update(V value)        ❷ Generalization of addWater
    ...
}
```

The fact that the effect of an update depends on the group of connected containers doesn't show in the API. As for connecting one generic container to another (feature 2), choosing the right method signature is trickier. Ideally, we'd like generic containers to be connectable to other generic containers *of the same type*, but we can't exactly ask that in a Java interface. In the theory of programming languages, this is the well-known *binary method* problem.

Binary methods

A binary method is a method of a class that accepts as an argument another object of the same class, like the `connectTo` method of water containers. Common examples include the methods for object equality and for comparing two objects for order. In Java, these correspond to the `equals` method from the class `Object` and the `com pareTo` method from the `Comparable` interface. The type system of common OO languages like Java and C# can't express the constraint that all subclasses of a given class or interface must have a binary method of a specified form. That is, you can't write something like:

```
public interface Comparable {
    int compareTo(thisType other);
}
```

where `thisType` is an imaginary keyword representing the class implementing this interface.

As a consequence, Java adopts two different solutions for the above-mentioned methods:

- The parameter of `equals` is simply declared as `Object`. Subclasses need to check at runtime whether the argument is of the appropriate type.
- The language designers solved the `Comparable` case via generics. The interface is equipped with a type parameter `T`, and the parameter of `compareTo` is declared as being of type `T`. This solution increases type safety but allows unintended uses like the proverbial

```
class Apple implements Comparable<Orange> { ... }
```

In C#, the situation is similar, and solved in a similar manner, except that equality is supported in two ways: both an `Equals` method from the class `Object` with parameter `Object` and the `IEquatable<T>` interface.

Let's examine a couple of different solutions for the signature of `connectTo`:

- `void connectTo(Object other)`—Similar to the signature of `Object::equals`. With this signature, you're just giving up on type safety, not enlisting the compiler into helping you in any way. The body of `connectTo` would need to check the dynamic type of its argument and then perform a downcast before it could do anything with it.
- `void connectTo(ContainerLike<V> other)`—You're getting some help from the compiler, but not quite enough. With this signature, `connectTo` accepts any other generic container that happens to have an attribute of the same type as this generic container. To perform its job, `connectTo` still needs to cast

its argument to something more specific that exposes its representation for container connections.

POP QUIZ 1 Is it a good idea to insert a `public boolean equals(Employee e)` method into an `Employee` class? Why or why not?

A better alternative mimics the solution that Java chose for `Comparable`: introduce an extra type parameter T, representing the type of objects that generic containers can be connected to, and hope that the parameter will be used in the proper way. We can't ask that T be the same class that's implementing the interface, but we can ask that it be *a* (possibly different) class implementing the same interface.

Listing 9.1 `ContainerLike`: The generic interface for containers

```
public interface ContainerLike<V, T extends ContainerLike<V,T>{}> {
    V get();
    void update(V val);
    void connectTo(T other);
}
```

The intended use of `ContainerLike` is to be implemented as follows:

```
class MyContainer implements ContainerLike<Something, MyContainer> { ... }
```

just like the intended use of `Comparable` is:

```
class Employee implements Comparable<Employee> { ... }
```

If a class adheres to that scheme (that is, it sets T to be itself), its `connectTo` method won't need to perform a downcast because it will receive as argument an object that's already of the same type as "this," which is exactly what the method needs to do its group-merging job.

Implementing generics in Java

In Java, generics are implemented via *erasure*, meaning that the compiler uses type parameters to perform a more expressive type checking and then throws them away. Type parameters are not included in the bytecode, nor does the JVM support them.

This implementation strategy restricts what you can do with generics. For example, you can't instantiate a type parameter with `new T()`, and you can't compare the runtime type of an expression with a type parameter using `exp instanceof T`.

Implementing generics in C# and C++

Contrary to Java, C++ and C# implement generics via *reification*, meaning that each specific version of a generic class, like `List<String>` is converted into a concrete class, either at compile time (C++) or at runtime (C#). Different versions of the same class may or may not share code, depending on the type arguments and the smartness of the compiler and runtime environment.

This implementation choice allows you to use type parameters in most places where a regular type would work, but it may introduce overhead, either in terms of (object) code duplication or in terms of the resources needed to maintain the runtime type information.

POP QUIZ 2   If T is a type parameter, can you allocate an array of type T in Java? What about C#?

9.2.1   *The attribute API*

Next, we need to introduce an interface that represents the behavior of the attribute when we update its value with update and especially when we connect generic containers with connectTo.

To delimit the level of generality that we want to support, we make the following assumptions:

1 When locally updating the property, you can compute the new group value based only on the current group value and the new local value. In other words, the group value must contain enough information to perform the required update.

2 When merging two groups, you can obtain the new group value based only on the two old group values.

Compare assumptions 1 and 2 with the two generalized scenarios presented at the beginning of the chapter. Scenario 1 poses no problem because it's a simple variation of the basic water container setting. In scenario 2, the property of interest is the total number of likes accrued by all connected posts—that's their "group value." Locally updating the property means adding likes to a particular post. As a result, the group value increases by the same amount, in accordance with assumption 1.

Let's check whether assumption 2 holds. When two groups of posts are connected (that is, when a user who commented on the first group of posts comments on a post from the second group), you can merge their group values by adding them up. You need no further information to compute the new group value, so that confirms assumption 2.

Equipped with the above assumptions, let's sketch the API defining the behavior of the attribute that all containers hold. To avoid confusion between the local value and the group value, let's call the latter the group *summary*. First of all, you should distinguish the type V of the local value from the type S of the group summary. In some cases, they will be the same; for example, in scenario 2, both types would be Integer because they represent like counts. In the case of water containers instead, they'll turn out to be different types, as I explain in section 9.5.

Now, introduce an interface Attribute<V,S> providing the operations that containers need to perform their contractual obligations, described earlier as features 1 and 2:

- A new generic container needs to initialize its group summary (method `seed`).
- The `get` method of a generic container needs a method to unwrap its summary into a local value of type `V` (method `report`).
- The `update` method of generic containers needs to update its summary (method `update`).
- The `connectTo` method needs a method that merges two summaries (method `merge`).

You end up with an interface similar to the following listing, whereas table 9.1 summarizes the dependencies between the methods of generic containers and those of the `Attribute` interface.

Listing 9.2 `Attribute`: The generic interface for the property of containers

```
public interface Attribute<V,S> {
    S seed();                           ❶ Provides the initial summary
    void update(S summary, V value);    ❷ Updates a summary with a value
    S merge(S summary1, S summary2);    ❸ Merges two summaries
    V report(S summary);                ❹ Unwraps a summary
}
```

Table 9.1 Relationships between the methods of generic containers and the methods of the `Attribute` interface

Method of generic container	Method of property
constructor	seed
get	report
update	update
connectTo	merge

Notice how an `Attribute` object itself is stateless: it doesn't contain the value of the attribute. That's for the generic container to hold in a separate object of type `S` (for a group summary) or `V` (for a cached local value).

The `Attribute` interface bears a definite resemblance to the interface introduced in Java 8 to collect the outcome of a stream operation in a single result. The next section takes the opportunity to briefly present streams and mutable collectors.

9.2.2 *Mutable collectors*

Streams complement collections by providing a handy composable framework for sequential operations. Here, I'll quickly introduce the framework and then focus on a specific feature that's relevant to the water container example: *mutable collectors.* For a more comprehensive account of the framework, check out the resources at the end of this chapter.

You can turn standard collections into streams using the `stream` method. In turn, stream objects support a variety of *intermediate* and *terminal* operations. Intermediate operations turn a stream into another stream of the same type or a different type. Terminal operations produce some output that's not a stream. One of the simplest terminal operations is `forEach`, which executes a code snippet on every element of the stream. Let `listOfStrings` be... what it says; the following fragment prints all strings in the list:

```
listOfStrings.stream().forEach(s -> System.out.println(s));
```

The argument of `forEach` is an object of type `Consumer`. Because the latter is a functional interface, you can instantiate it using the convenient Lambda-expression syntax. Let's add an intermediate operation to print only the strings that are longer than 10 characters:

```
listOfStrings.stream().filter(s -> s.length() > 10)
                .forEach(s -> System.out.println(s));
```

Sometimes you want to collect the result of a sequence of stream operations into a new collection. You can do that with the `collect` terminal operation, accepting a mutable collector as an object of type `Collector`. Static factory methods from the `Collectors` class provide common collectors. For example, the following snippet gathers the filtered strings into a list:

```
List<String> longStrings =
        listOfStrings.stream().filter(s -> s.length() > 10)
                            .collect(Collectors.toList());
```

Other standard collectors allow you to put the result into a set or a map. You can create your own collectors by implementing the `Collector` interface. To understand the various parts of the `Collector` interface, consider what you'd do with a plain old collection if you wanted to summarize it into a single mutable result. You'd have some sort of *summary* object, initialized with some default value and then updated on every element in the collection. After scanning all the elements, you might want to convert the summary into a different type—let's call it the *result* type.

```
Collection<V> collection = ...
Summary summary = new Summary();       ❶ Initial summary
for (V value: collection) {
    summary.update(value);             ❷ Updates summary with value
}
Result result = summary.toResult();    ❸ Converts summary to result
```

The `Collector` interface abstracts these three steps, plus another step you need for *parallel* collectors. If the loop over all the values is assigned to multiple threads (that is, each thread takes care of a subset of the values), each thread builds its own summary, and you eventually need to *merge* these summaries before they can produce a final result. This merge operation is the fourth and final ingredient in a collector.

Calling S the type of the summary and R the type of the final result, you might expect the `Collector` interface to contain methods like the following:

```
S supply();
void accumulate(S summary, V value);
S combine(S summary1, S summary2);
R finish(S summary);
```

1 Initial summary
2 Updates summary with value
3 Merges two summaries
4 Converts summary to result

Notice the close similarity between this imaginary collector and the `Attribute` interface introduced earlier for abstracting the water level value of containers. However, the actual `Collector` interface introduces one more level of indirection by having each method return an *object* that performs the corresponding function. This is in line with the rest of the stream framework and with the functional programming style by which it's inspired. The return types for all four methods are *functional interfaces*, that is, interfaces that each have a single abstract method. Table 9.2 outlines the characteristics of these four interfaces.

Table 9.2 Functional interfaces mutable collectors use. They're among the more than 40 functional interfaces in the `java.util.function` package.

Interface	Type of abstract method	Role
`Supplier<S>`	void → S	Provides the initial summary
`BiConsumer<S,V>`	(S, V) → void	Updates a summary with a value
`BinaryOperator<S>`	(S, S) → S	Merges two summaries
`Function<S,R>`	S → R	Converts a summary into a result

You use a fifth method to state whether this collector possesses two standard characteristics:

- *Concurrency*—Does this collector support concurrent execution by multiple threads?
- *Order*—Does this collector preserve the order of the elements?

An internal enumeration called `Characteristics` provides the flags corresponding to these features. Summarizing, you get the following methods:

```
public interface Collector<V,S,R> {
    Supplier<S> supplier();
    BiConsumer<S,V> accumulator();
    BinaryOperator<S> combiner();
    Function<S,R> finisher();
    Set<Characteristics> characteristics();
}
```

1 Initial summary
2 Updates summary with value
3 Merges two summaries
4 Converts summary to result
5 Whether it's concurrent, ordered, etc.

This use of functional interfaces makes collectors easily interoperable with Lambda expressions and method references, two handy ways to implement functional interfaces. In the next section, I'll introduce method references and guide you through the implementation of a concrete collector of strings.

POP QUIZ 3   What's the role of the `combiner` method of a collector? When will you use it?

AN EXAMPLE: STRING CONCATENATION

Let's wrap up with an example: a custom collector that concatenates a sequence of strings into a single string, using a `StringBuilder` as a temporary summary. As `String Builder` isn't thread-safe, the collector won't be concurrent.[1] On the other hand, it preserves the order of the strings because it concatenates them in order. This arrangement is convenient because those are exactly the default characteristics for a collector, so you can return an empty set from the method `characteristics`.

Now, if it wasn't for Lambda expressions and method references, you'd have to put up with a lot of anonymous classes to define your collector. In fact, you'd need *five* anonymous classes: an outer class for the collector itself and four inner classes to instantiate the corresponding functional interfaces. Just consider the first method:

```
Collector<String,StringBuilder,String> concatenator =
    new Collector<>() {        ❶ Outer anonymous class
        @Override
        public Supplier<StringBuilder> supplier() {    ❷ Provides the initial summary
            return new Supplier<>() {    ❸ First inner anonymous class
                @Override
                public StringBuilder get() {
                    return new StringBuilder();
                }
            };
        }
        ...   ❹ Overriding the other four methods of Collector
    };
```

Method references...

...were added to Java 8 as a new type of expression that turns an existing method or constructor into an instance of a functional interface, using the double colon notation "::". In its simplest form, a method reference adapts an instance method to a suitable interface. For example

```
ToIntFunction<Object> hasher = Object::hashCode;
```

where `ToIntFunction<T>` is a functional interface whose only method is

```
int applyAsInt(T item)
```

A method reference also can refer to a method of a specific object:

```
Consumer<String> printer = System.out::println;
```

You also can apply method references to static methods and constructors.

---

[1]   To make a concurrent collector, you could use `StringBuffer` instead of `StringBuilder`, or add explicit synchronization.

With method references, the previous snippet becomes much simpler. You can provide the supplier by a reference to the constructor of `StringBuilder`. The compiler takes care of wrapping the constructor into an object of type `Supplier<StringBuilder>`.

```
Collector<String,StringBuilder,String> concatenator = new Collector<>() {
    @Override
    public Supplier<StringBuilder> supplier() {
        return StringBuilder::new;   ❶ Reference to the constructor
    }
    ...   ❷ Overriding the other four methods of Collector
};
```

Even better, the class `Collector` provides a static method `of` that dispenses with even providing the outer anonymous class, leading to the following handy solution. Here, I've provided all four main methods of the interface as method references:

```
Collector<String,StringBuilder,String> concatenator =
    Collector.of(StringBuilder::new,      ❶ The supplier (reference to a constructor)

                 StringBuilder::append,   ❷ The update function
                 StringBuilder::append,   ❸ The merge function (another append method)

                 StringBuilder::toString);  ❹ The finisher
```

Method references don't allow you to specify the signature of the method you're referring to, just its name. The compiler infers the signature from the *context* where the method reference occurs. Such context must identify a specific functional interface. For example, in the previous snippet, the update function reference resolves to the following method from `StringBuilder`:

```
public StringBuilder append(String s)
```

because the context calls for a `BiConsumer<StringBuilder,String>`. You may have noticed a mismatch here: `append` returns a value, whereas a `BiConsumer` returns `void`. The compiler happily lets you get away with it, just like you're allowed to invoke a method returning a value and ignore that value. Table 9.3 summarizes this compatibility rule.

Table 9.3 Comparing the signatures and types of the method `StringBuilder::append` and the functional interface `BiConsumer`. `SB` is short for `StringBuilder`.

	Method	Target functional interface
Signature	SB append(String s)	BiConsumer<SB,String>
Type	(SB,String) → SB	(SB,String) → void

TIP You can assign a reference to a non-void method to a void functional interface.

Moving to the merge function method reference in the snippet, its context requires a `BinaryOperator<StringBuilder>`, that is, a method accepting two `StringBuilders` (including `this`) and returning another `StringBuilder`. A different `append` method from the `StringBuilder` class can fill this role:

```
public StringBuilder append(CharSequence seq)
```

This case *also* requires a conversion because the method `append` accepts a `CharSequence`, whereas the target functional interface expects a `StringBuilder`. This conversion is permitted because `CharSequence` is a super-type of `StringBuilder`. Table 9.4 summarizes the situation.

Table 9.4   Comparing the signatures and types of the method `StringBuilder::append` and the functional interface `BinaryOperator`. SB is short for `StringBuilder`.

	Method	Target functional interface
Signature	`SB append(CharSequence seq)`	`BinaryOperator<SB>`
Type	`(SB,CharSequence) → SB`	`(SB,SB) → SB`

TIP   You can assign a reference to a method accepting an argument of type `T` to a functional interface whose method expects a subtype of `T`.

By the way, a collector very similar to this `concatenator` is included in the JDK as the object returned by the static method `Collectors.joining()`.

POP QUIZ 4   Can you assign a method reference to a variable of type `Object`?

9.2.3   *Adapting Attribute to functional interfaces*

You can equip `Attribute` with the same type of adapter that you find in `Collector`: a static method that takes four functional interfaces and turns them into an object of type `Attribute`. With this method, clients can create concrete implementations of `Attribute` using four Lambda expressions or method references, like you just did with the string concatenator.

This adapter method takes the following form:

```
public static <V,S> Attribute<V,S> of(Supplier<S> supplier,
                                       BiConsumer<S,V> updater,
                                       BinaryOperator<S> combiner,
                                       Function<S,V> finisher) {
    return new Attribute<>() {    ① Anonymous class
      @Override
      public S seed() {
         return supplier.get();
      }
      @Override
      public void update(S summary, V value) {
         updater.accept(summary, value);
      }
      @Override
      public S merge(S summary1, S summary2) {
         return combiner.apply(summary1, summary2);
```

```
    }
    @Override
    public V report(S summary) {
        return finisher.apply(summary);
    }
};  ❷ End anonymous class
}
```

9.3 A generic container implementation

You can now devise a generic implementation of `ContainerLike` that manages connections and groups, while delegating the behavior of the property to an object of type `Attribute`. A good choice and a nice exercise would be to base this implementation on *Speed3* from chapter 3 because it exhibits the best overall performance.

First, recall the basic structure of *Speed3*, based on parent-pointer trees. Each container is a node in a tree, and only the root containers know the amount of water and the size of their group. Containers hold three fields, two of which are relevant only to root containers:

- The amount of water that the group holds (if this container is a root)
- The size of this group (if this container is a root)
- The parent container (or a self-loop, if this container is a root)

In fact, this is the beginning of *Speed3*:

```
public class Container {
    private Container parent = this;    ❶ Initially, each container is the root of its tree.
    private double amount;
    private int size = 1;
```

The generic version, called `UnionFindNode`, replaces the `amount` field with an object of type `S`, holding the group summary, and an object of type `Attribute`, holding the methods for manipulating summaries and values. The fields and constructor of `Union FindNode` are shown in the following listing.

Listing 9.3 UnionFindNode: Fields and constructor

```
public class UnionFindNode<V,S>
    implements ContainerLike<V,UnionFindNode<V,S>{}> {

    private UnionFindNode<V,S> parent = this;    ❶ Initially, each node is a root.
    private int groupSize = 1;

    private final Attribute<V,S> attribute;    ❷ Contains the methods for
    private S summary;                             manipulating the attribute

    public UnionFindNode(Attribute<V,S> dom) {
        attribute = dom;
        summary = dom.seed();
    }
```

The methods `get` and `update` identify the root of their tree (as in *Speed3*) and then invoke the appropriate attribute method to unwrap the summary or update the summary based on a new value, as shown in listing 9.4. The private support method `find RootAndCompress` is responsible for finding the root and flattening the path leading to the root to speed up future calls.

Listing 9.4   UnionFindNode: Methods `get` and `update`

```
public V get() {    ❶ Returns current value of attribute
   UnionFindNode<V,S> root = findRootAndCompress();
   return attribute.report(root.summary);
}
public void update(V value) {    ❷ Updates attribute
   UnionFindNode<V,S> root = findRootAndCompress();
   attribute.update(root.summary, value);
}
```

Finally, the method `connectTo` enforces the link-by-size policy I explained in chapter 3 and invokes the `merge` method of the `Attribute` to merge the summaries of the two groups being connected. As promised, `connectTo` doesn't need to perform any cast on its argument, thanks to the expressive signature you chose earlier.

Listing 9.5   UnionFindNode: Method `connectTo`

```
public void connectTo(UnionFindNode<V,S> other) {
   UnionFindNode<V,S> root1 = findRootAndCompress(),
                      root2 = other.findRootAndCompress();
   if (root1 == root2) return;
   int size1 = root1.groupSize, size2 = root2.groupSize;
      ❶ Merges the two summaries
   S newSummary = attribute.merge(root1.summary, root2.summary);

   if (size1 <= size2) {    ❷ The link-by-size policy
      root1.parent    = root2;
      root2.summary   = newSummary;
      root2.groupSize += size1;
   } else {
      root2.parent    = root1;
      root1.summary   = newSummary;
      root1.groupSize += size2;
   }
}
```

Figure 9.1 summarizes the three classes I've presented so far. Together, they form a generic framework to generate container-like behaviors.

9.4   *General considerations*

Let's stop this flurry of code for a second and think about the general process of *generalizing* a given set of functionalities to a wider context. Before this process starts, you need a clear motivation to generalize your code or specifications. It may be tempting to generalize a solution just because you envision it becoming an elegant framework,

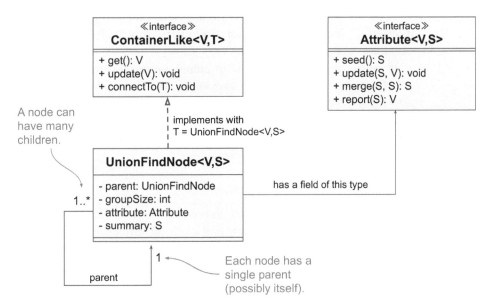

Figure 9.1 A UML class diagram for the generic water container framework

or perhaps just for the challenge! If you're programming for fun or to learn a new language, those reasons are good enough. On the job, though, you better have a business-related motivation to turn a fine yet specific solution into a general framework that's likely to be slower, more complicated, and harder to maintain. Good business-oriented motivations boil down to one of the following:

- The general solution can be a product in itself. You and your colleagues/ managers deem that your organization can release the general solution independently as a library or framework that other organizations can use.
- The general solution can cater to different functions in your product. Perhaps the general solution can replace and unify separate specific solutions that are part of your product.
- The general solution can support *future* evolutions of your product. You should handle this motivation with care. As I mentioned before, programmers and designers are inclined to overengineer and overgeneralize software. The extreme-programming YAGNI motto—*You aren't gonna need it*—recognizes and challenges this tendency.

Once you identify a clear motivation, it's time to establish one or more extra application scenarios (aka use cases) that the current implementation or specification doesn't cover but should cover, according to your motivation. That's what I did at the beginning of this chapter, presenting two target scenarios and one scenario that's beyond the scope of the generalization.

These use cases guide you toward a general API, often in the form of one or more interfaces. In the case of water containers, this analysis led to the two interfaces `ContainerLike` and `Attribute`.

If you started with a concrete implementation, it's time to adapt it to the general interfaces you designed in the previous step. That's what you did when you started with the concrete `Container` class from version *Speed3* (from chapter 3) and converted it to the generic class `UnionFindNode`. Now you'll need some extra code—hopefully not too much—to recover the original functionality using the new generic framework. That's the aim of the next section.

9.5   *Recovering water containers*   [Generic]

In this section, I'll show you how to recover a concrete implementation of water containers, with their concrete water-level attribute, using the generic implementation you developed in the previous section. The result is a class that behaves pretty much like *Speed3*, except with a couple of abstraction levels added. That's the cost for a generic implementation that you can easily adapt to a range of conditions.

9.5.1   *Updated use case*

The use case for the concrete implementation will be similar, but not identical, to the one I've been using in the rest of the book. The only difference is in the names of two methods: instead of the specific `getAmount` and `addWater`, you get the generic names `get` and `update` that the `ContainerLike` interface provides. As a result, the first lines of the standard use case become the following:

```
Container a = new Container();
Container b = new Container();
Container c = new Container();
Container d = new Container();

a.update(12.0);      ❶ update is analogous to addWater.
d.update(8.0);
a.connectTo(b);
   ❷ get is analogous to getAmount.
System.out.println(a.get()+" "+b.get()+" "+c.get()+" "+d.get());
```

The desired output from the previous fragment is the same as in the original use case:

```
6.0 6.0 0.0 8.0
```

9.5.2   *Designing the concrete attribute*

Every concrete class based on `UnionFindNode` needs to fix types `V` and `S` and supply an object of type `Attribute<V,S>`. For water containers, `V = Double` because that's the natural type for water amounts. At first glance, it may seem that a summary of type `S = Double` also would work. After all, shouldn't the group summary just be the total amount of water in the group? You might argue that you can then compute the amount per container by dividing the group amount by the size of the group, and the latter would be stored in the `groupSize` field of the root node. However, the `Attribute` object doesn't have access to the `UnionFindNode` object it belongs to! As a result, it can't access its `groupSize` field. You're forced to replicate the group size information and store a separate copy inside the summary. That's another cost due to the generality of the solution.

Instead of a simple `S = Double`, you need a custom class to play the role of the group summary. Let's call it `ContainerSummary`. Every summary holds the total group amount and the size of the group. Besides a natural two-parameter constructor, I'll add a default constructor, as shown in listing 9.6. In that way, I can later refer to it with a method reference (OK, "constructor reference" would be more precise) and fill in the "seed" operation of the `Attribute` interface.

Listing 9.6 `ContainerSummary`: **Fields and constructors**

```
class ContainerSummary {
   private double amount;
   private int groupSize;

   public ContainerSummary(double amount, int groupSize) {
      this.amount = amount;
      this.groupSize = groupSize;
   }
   public ContainerSummary() {    ❶ Default constructor
      this(0, 1);    ❷ Calls the other constructor with 0 water and 1 container in the group
   }
```

Next, the following listing contains the three methods that provide the remaining attribute operations.

Listing 9.7 `ContainerSummary`: **Summary manipulation methods**

```
   ❶ Analogous to addWater
public void update(double increment) {
   this.amount += increment;
}
   ❷ Used when connecting two containers

public ContainerSummary merge(ContainerSummary other) {
   return new ContainerSummary(amount + other.amount,
                               groupSize + other.groupSize);
}
   ❸ Returns amount per container
public double getAmount() {
   return amount / groupSize;
}
```

Finally, you can use the static method `of` from the `Attribute` interface and four method references to instantiate the `Attribute` object that `UnionFindNode` needs. There's a slight mismatch between the primitive type `double` that the methods in `Container Summary` use and the wrapper type `Double` that `Attribute` expects. But not to worry:

auto(un)boxing makes sure that you can use method references involving primitive types even when the context calls for wrapper types.

You can then expose this `Attribute` object to the clients as a class constant, that is, a final static field, as in the following listing.

Listing 9.8   `ContainerSummary`: The `Attribute` field

```
public static final Attribute<Double,ContainerSummary> ops =
    Attribute.of(ContainerSummary::new,    ❶ Reference to default constructor
                 ContainerSummary::update,
                 ContainerSummary::merge,
                 ContainerSummary::getAmount);
```

Figure 9.2 features a UML class diagram for `ContainerSummary` and its relationship to `Attribute`. Notice how the constructor and the three methods of `ContainerSummary` correspond to the four methods of the interface.

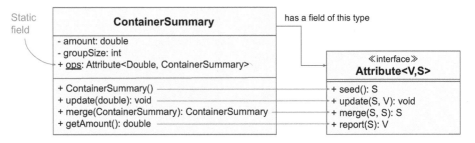

Figure 9.2   A UML class diagram for `ContainerSummary` and its relationship to `Attribute`. The first parameter of methods `update`, `merge`, and `report` is bound to `this` in the corresponding methods of `ContainerSummary`.

9.5.3   *Defining the concrete water container class*

Once you've defined the concrete summary and its support methods, you can recover the usual behavior of water containers with just three lines, by extending `UnionFind Node` and passing the appropriate `Attribute` object to its constructor, as shown in the following listing.

Listing 9.9   `Generic`: Water containers in three lines

```
public class Container extends UnionFindNode<Double,ContainerSummary> {
    public Container() {
        super(ContainerSummary.ops);
    }
}
```

That was pretty neat, but we did run into some limitations of Java generics. If you think about it, it's a waste of space that all `UnionFindNodes` must carry a reference to the same `Attribute` object. If generics were reified instead of erased, that reference could have been a *static* field of `UnionFindNode<Double,ContainerSummary>`. In that way, all nodes of that type would have shared a single reference to the object responsible for manipulating summaries.

Incidentally, listing 9.9 is the shortest definition of a functioning water container class in the book. It's even shorter than the one in the appendix, which is explicitly optimized for brevity! Of course, the version in this section is cheating; we've moved all the functionality to the generic framework. If you count all that code (classes `Union` `FindNode` and `ContainerSummary`, and interfaces `ContainerLike` and `Attribute`) the generic version is actually the *longest* in the book!

9.6 Social network posts

To witness the generality of your solution, let's design another concrete container version, this time addressing the second scenario I presented at the beginning of this chapter: posts in a social network, connected by common commenters and counting total likes. In fact, this scenario turns out to be simpler than water containers. This time, it's enough for the group summary to hold the total number of likes that the posts in the group accrue; there's no need to know the size of the group. As a result, the summary is just a wrapper around an integer.

Listing 9.10 `PostSummary`: **Field and constructors**

```
class PostSummary {
    private int likeCount;

    public PostSummary(int likeCount) {
        this.likeCount = likeCount;
    }
    public PostSummary() {}    ❶ Allows for a method reference later
```

The default constructor fulfills the "seed" operation of `Attribute`. The methods shown in the following listing provide the other three operations. Once again, you can use the static method `of` to pack those four operations into an object of type `Attribute`.

Listing 9.11 `PostSummary`: **Methods and static field**

```
    public void update(int likes) {
        likeCount += likes;
    }
    public PostSummary merge(PostSummary summary) {
        return new PostSummary(likeCount + summary.likeCount);
    }
    public int getCount() {
        return likeCount;
    }
    public static final Attribute<Integer,PostSummary> ops =
        Attribute.of(PostSummary::new,    ❶ Reference to default constructor
                    PostSummary::update,
                    PostSummary::merge,
                    PostSummary::getCount);
}
```

Just like you did with water containers in the previous section, you can instantiate the class representing social network posts with the three lines in the following listing:

Listing 9.12   Post: Counting likes with the generic framework

```
public class Post extends UnionFindNode<Integer,PostSummary> {
    public Post() {
        super(PostSummary.ops);
    }
}
```

9.7   And now for something completely different

Rather than a single class, this last example features a stand-alone application with a GUI. It's an opportunity to apply the principles outlined in this book on a larger scale. In the online repository,[2] you can find a simple GUI application that plots a *parabola*, that is, a curve whose equation is in the form

$$y = ax^2 + bx + c.$$

You can see a screenshot in figure 9.3. The top panel plots the function for a fixed range of x values. The middle panel lists the value of the function for five fixed values of x. The bottom panel allows the user to interactively change the value of the three parameters, a, b, and c.

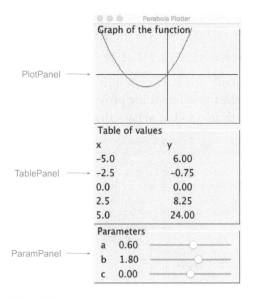

Figure 9.3   A screenshot of the plotting program

---

[2]   The baseline version of the plotting app is in the package `eis.chapter9.plot`, whereas the generalized version sits in `eis.chapter9.generic.plot`.

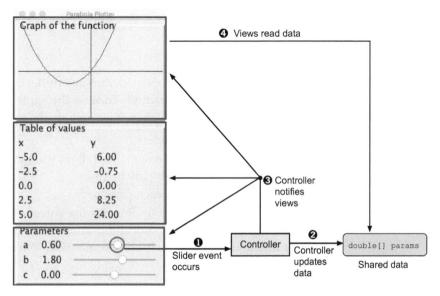

Figure 9.4 The communication scheme for the baseline plotting program. Parameters are stored in a plain array of doubles, shared among all components. In this scheme, each controller must know all views.

The baseline implementation is composed of four classes—one for each panel and one Main class that ties them together. It can plot only parabolas, and it contains a couple of defects:

- *Code duplication*—Both TablePanel and PlotPanel contain code that evaluates a parabola at a given point. It would be better to have that code in a single place.
- *An ad-hoc communication scheme*—When you change a parameter by moving a slider, the code responding to the event (aka the *controller*) asks all panels to repaint. This is not so bad, but imagine a full-blown version of this application, with tons of widgets that can change the visualization in different ways. If you keep this communication scheme, you need to make all widgets aware of all panels that visualize the function (aka *views*). Figure 9.4 depicts a typical flow of events in this architecture.

Let's generalize this app so that it can plot arbitrary parametric functions with any number of parameters, that is, curves of equation

$$y = f(a_1, \ldots, a_n, x),$$

where $a_1, \ldots, a_n$ are parameters. To be clear, I'm not talking about accepting the function definition from text, which would require a parser. The generalized app should just be able to switch to a different type of function with as little programmer effort as possible. The program should automatically adapt the GUI to the type of function that it's displaying. For example, the number of sliders in the bottom panel must equal the number of parameters. Along the way, we'll also address the two design shortcomings I listed earlier.

9.7.1   An interface for parametric functions

The first step in the generalization process is to identify an interface—call it `Parametric Function`—representing a parametric function. To allow the application to fully adapt to a specific parametric function, the interface must include the following services:

- Providing the number of parameters.
- Providing the names of each parameter. This allows you to customize the labels "a," "b," and "c" in the parameter panel.
- Getting and setting the value of each parameter.
- Evaluating the function on a given value, for the current value of its parameters. This functionality solves the code duplication issue discussed earlier. The parametric function will be the only place responsible for computing the value of the function.

To translate these functionalities into Java, you have to index parameters from 0 to $n - 1$, and obtain an interface like the following:

```
public interface ParametricFunction {
    int getNParams();      ❶ Returns the number of parameters

    String getParamName(int i);   ❷ Returns the name of parameter i

    double getParam(int i);   ❸ Returns the value of parameter i

    void setParam(int i, double val);   ❹ Sets the value of parameter i

    double eval(double x);   ❺ Returns the value of this function at x
}
```

At this point, you recover the old concrete behavior with a `Parabola` class that implements this interface. (I'm skipping precondition checks for simplicity.)

```
public class Parabola implements ParametricFunction {
    private final static int N = 3;   ❶ Three parameters
    private final static String[] name = { "a", "b", "c" };
    private double[] a = new double[N];

    public int getNParams()          { return N; }
    public String getParamName(int i) { return name[i]; }
    public double getParam(int i)     { return a[i]; }
    public void setParam(int i, double val) { a[i] = val; }
    public double eval(double x)      { return a[0]*x*x + a[1]*x + a[2]; }
}
```

You can imagine how easy it is to define a different parametric function. For example, suppose you want to plot the hyperbola with equation

$$y = \frac{a}{x} = f(a, x).$$

The following class does the trick:

```
public class Hyperbola implements ParametricFunction {
    private final static int N = 1;    ❶ One parameter
    private final static String[] name = { "a" };
    private double[] a = new double[1];

    public int getNParams()            { return N; }
    public String getParamName(int i) { return name[i]; }
    public double getParam(int i)      { return a[i]; }
    public void setParam(int i, double val) { a[i] = val; }
    public double eval(double x)       { return a[0] / x; }
}
```

If you compare `Parabola` and `Hyperbola`, you'll notice immediately that they share a lot of code. The only substantial difference lies in their implementation of `eval`, which is where the specific function is actually defined. This suggests that an abstract class, inserted between the interface and the concrete classes, might carry most of the weight of these classes.

The abstract class—call it `AbstractFunction`—can be responsible for storing and managing parameters, and even for providing standard parameter names (the letters "a", "b", and so on). Basically, the abstract class takes care of everything, except computing the value of the function with `eval`, which is left abstract. Here's a possible implementation for the abstract class (once again, omitting some checks for simplicity):

```
public abstract class AbstractFunction implements ParametricFunction {
    private final int n;
    protected final double[] a;    ❶ Accessible to subclasses for efficiency

    public AbstractFunction(int n) {    ❷ Constructor for the subclasses
        this.n = n;
        this.a = new double[n];
    }

    public int getNParams()        { return n; }
    public String getParamName(int i) {
        final int firstLetter = 97;    ❸ ASCII code for 'a'
        return Character.toString(firstLetter + i);
    }
    public double getParam(int i) { return a[i]; }
    public void setParam(int i, double val) { a[i] = val; }
}
```

The abstract class streamlines the definition of concrete functions. For example, here's what `Hyperbola` looks like when taking advantage of `AbstractFunction`:

```
public class Hyperbola extends AbstractFunction {
    public Hyperbola() { super(1); }
    public double eval(double x) { return a[0] / x; }
}
```

9.7.2   *A communication discipline*

You can take the opportunity of this refactoring to also improve the communication scheme of the program. Now you have a central object, the parametric function, which holds the relevant data (the parameters) and provides the information to be displayed (the function values). It's the ideal situation for applying the well-known model-view-controller (MVC) architectural pattern.

Model-View-Controller...

...is an architectural pattern proposed in the 1970s for desktop programs with GUIs. It suggests to assign software components to three categories:

- *Models*—Components holding the data relevant to the application
- *Views*—Components presenting the data to the user
- *Controllers*—Components responding to user inputs

In the original pattern, controllers aren't supposed to interact directly with views. Upon receiving a user command—such as a button click—the controller informs or modifies the model. In turn, the model is reponsible for notifying those views that need to be updated.

Since its inception, the MVC pattern has been adopted by and adapted to different scenarios, particularly web application frameworks. It also has given rise to variants such as model-view-adapter and model-view-presenter.

In the context of the plotting app, the parametric function is the model class, the three panels are views, and the event handlers responding to the sliders are controllers. Design the refactored app to adhere to the communication scheme that MVC originally intended:

- When the program starts, the three views register themselves as *observers* of the model. The model (the parametric function) holds references to them.

  To avoid cluttering the `ParametricFunction` interface with unrelated features, you can assign the responsibility for holding these references and sending notifications to a separate class—`ObservableFunction` in the repository—that wraps a parametric function and adds these functionalities.[3]
- When the user moves a slider in the parameter panel of the GUI, the controller updates the value of the corresponding parameter in the model. The controller *doesn't* take any other action.
- Whenever the model receives a call to `setParam` to update the value of a parameter, it notifies all registered views that something in the model has changed.

Here are the main bits of the `ObservableFunction` class. First, it wraps a `Parametric Function` object, and at the same time it implements that interface. It also keeps track

---

[3] This mechanism is an example of the Decorator design pattern.

of its observers as a list of `ActionListener`s. The latter is a standard interface from the Java AWT windowing kit, whose only method is `void actionPerformed(ActionEvent e)`. The `ActionEvent` parameter is meant to carry information about the event that's being notified. You'll support a single type of event: the user changing the value of one of the function's parameters. That's why you can use a single dummy event object for all notifications. Here's the beginning of the `ObservableFunction` class:

```
public class ObservableFunction implements ParametricFunction {
    private final ParametricFunction f;    ❶ Inner parametric function
    private final List<ActionListener> listeners = new ArrayList<>();
    private final ActionEvent dummyEvent =
        new ActionEvent(this, ActionEvent.ACTION_FIRST, "update");

    public ObservableFunction(ParametricFunction f) { this.f = f; }
```

The core responsibility of `ObservableFunction` is to notify all observers when a call to `setParam` is made:

```
public void setParam(int i, double val) {
    f.setParam(i, val);
    for (ActionListener listener: listeners) {    ❶ Notifies observers
        listener.actionPerformed(dummyEvent);     ❷ A dummy event carrying no actual info
    }
}
```

All other methods are passed through to the inner `ParametricFunction` object. For example, here's the implementation of `getParam`:

```
public double getParam(int i) {    ❶ Passed through to inner function
    return f.getParam(i);
}
```

Figure 9.5 depicts the new communication scheme. Because a single object—the model—is responsible for notifying all views, you can afford to split the three views of the previous version into a higher number of views. For example, instead of considering the whole `TablePanel` as a view, you can treat as views the five labels in the "y" column. After all, they're the only part of that panel that the program needs to redraw when the user updates one of the parameters.

This communication scheme is more robust than the custom solution that the baseline plotting app used. It's easier to add new views or controllers. To activate a new view, it's sufficient to pass the model to it and register it as another model observer. You don't need to modify any controllers. Symmetrically, it's possible to add new controllers to the GUI (that is, new interactive widgets) without changing the view components.

9.8 Real-world use cases

As you've seen in this chapter, generics are a very powerful feature that enables defining type-safe data structures that can work with different data types. Types become parameters (generics are also known as *parametric polymorphism*) whose specification

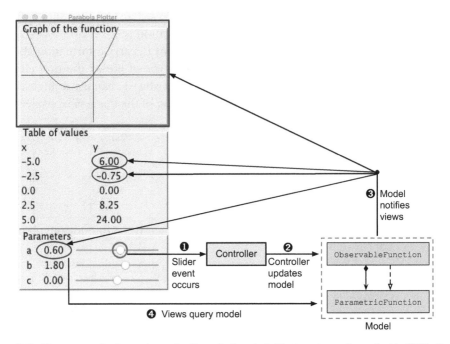

Figure 9.5   The communication scheme for the refactored plotting program. According to MVC, the controller interacts with the views only through the model. The arrows between `ObservableFunction` and `ParametricFunction` indicate that the former implements the latter, and in addition contains a reference to an inner `ParametricFunction`.

you defer until the time of declaration. Type parameterization promotes code reusability because it's possible to avoid repeating the same algorithm over and over for different data types. To make this more concrete, I'll present some further use cases:

- Probably one of the most important use cases of generics is a data container: vectors, lists, sets, trees, queues, stacks, and so on. Can you identify an important principle all these containers have in common? They're agnostic to the type of the object they're handling. They only take care of the organization of the objects: if you pop an item off the stack, the container doesn't care about the type of the object that you popped.
- As you've seen in the previous chapter, multithreading has always been one of the major features of the Java language, and one that has evolved with new releases. What stands out in this evolution, though, is the concurrency utilities that the language designers added in Java 1.5, when they introduced generics to the language. Since the early days, it was possible to represent a threaded task by implementing the `Runnable` interface. That interface has a single `run` method that doesn't accept any parameter or return any value. Hence, it's limited to those cases where no result value is expected from the thread. On the other hand, the newer `Callable` interface is a generic interface that returns a

parameterized type. To execute a task, you must submit an object implementing `Callable` to an `ExecutorService` to launch it. Can you guess what type the executor service returns? Another parameterized type: `Future`. The type `Future<T>` bears the semantics of an expectation, that you're expecting some result of type `T` once the computation is complete.

- In the first use case I discussed how data structures use generics to organize data. It's often the case, however, that you use generics for containers holding a *single* element of a parametric type. `AtomicReference<T>` is an example of a single-element container that you can use in a setting where it's required to perform an atomic, thread-safe operation. Thus it's possible to share the object among different threads without having to use synchronization. Another example is the recent `Optional<T>` class, which replaces the need to return `null` values and is featured in exercise 3 in this chapter.

- In a production codebase, it's common to use a data access object (DAO) that provides an interface for accessing a persistence mechanism (such as a relational database). The purpose of the DAO is to provide operations on the persistence mechanism without exposing its internals to the client. Imagine writing a DAO to perform some CRUD operations on a database: create, delete, update, findAll, and so on. You might want to use this DAO to persist different entity types defined in your domain model. Using generics, it's possible to parameterize the DAO and use these common operations for different entity types.

9.9 Applying what you learned

EXERCISE 1
Recall that Java generics are implemented via *erasure* and C# generics via *reification*. As a consequence, table 9.5 shows three instructions involving a type parameter `T` that are valid in C# but invalid in Java. What's a Java workaround in each of those three cases? In other words, what's an alternative way to obtain a similar effect?

Table 9.5 Some limitations of Java generics, compared to C#, of what you can do with a type parameter `T`. Note that the first example requires the type constraint "`where T: new()`" to be correct C#.

Instruction type	Incorrect in Java	Correct in C#
New object	`new T()`	`new T()`
New array	`new T[10]`	`new T[10]`
Runtime type checking	`exp instanceof T`	`exp is T`

EXERCISE 2

Using the generic `UnionFindNode` infrastructure, design a solution to the first scenario discussed at the beginning of this chapter: water containers with arbitrary precision rational water levels (in the mathematical sense of rational numbers).

Hint: Don't reinvent the wheel. Start from an existing class for arbitrary precision rational numbers. There are a couple online.

EXERCISE 3

Design a `Schedule<E>` class handling generic events of type `E`, where `E` must be a subtype of the following interface:

```
public interface Event {
    void start();
    void stop();
}
```

The class `Schedule<E>` must provide the following methods:

- `public void addEvent(E event, LocalTime startTime, LocalTime stopTime)`—Adds an event to this schedule, with specified start and stop times. If the event overlaps with another event from this schedule, this method throws an `IllegalArgumentException`. If this schedule has already been launched (method `launch`), this method throws an `IllegalStateException`.
- `public void launch()`—From the moment you call this method, this schedule is responsible for invoking the `start` and `stop` methods of its events at the right time. You can't add any more events to the schedule after launch.
- `public Optional<E> currentEvent()`—Returns the currently active event, if any. In case you missed it, `Optional` is the modern alternative to returning a `null` value. An `Optional<E>` can contain an object of type `E` or be empty. If the client has already launched this schedule, but there's no active event at this time, this method returns an empty `Optional`. If the client hasn't launched this schedule, this method throws an `IllegalStateException`.

In addition, implement a concrete class of events—say, `HTTPEvent`—whose start and stop actions spawn HTTP GET messags to specified URLs.

EXERCISE 4

Write a method that accepts a collection of objects and partitions them according to an equivalence predicate.

```
public static <T> Set<Set<T>{}> partition(
    Collection<? extends T> c,
    BiPredicate<? super T, ? super T> equivalence)
```

`BiPredicate<U,V>` is a standard functional interface whose only method is `boolean test(U u, V v)`. You can assume that the equivalence predicate satisfies the rules of an equivalence relation—reflexivity, symmetry, and transitivity—just like the `equals` method from `Object`.

For example, say you want to group strings according to their length. You can define the corresponding equivalence as the following `BiPredicate`:

```
BiPredicate<String,String> sameLength = (a, b) -> a.length() == b.length();
```

You may then call the `partition` method on a set of strings:

```
Set<String> names = Set.of("Walter", "Skyler", "Hank", "Mike", "Saul");
Set<Set<String>{}> groups = partition(names, sameLength);
System.out.println(groups);
```

As a result, you should get those five strings gathered in two groups according to their length:

```
[[Walter, Skyler], [Saul, Mike, Hank]]
```

Hint: This exercise is closer to water containers than you may think.

Summary

- Modern programming combines powerful reusable frameworks with application-specific code.
- Generics help write reusable components.
- Reusable components may incur extra costs compared to an *ad-hoc* solution.
- Java 8 streams make heavy use of generics to offer a highly configurable data-processing framework.
- Generalizing a piece of software starts by defining a set of target scenarios.
- Reusable software components often revolve around a set of key interfaces.
- The original model-view-controller architecture prescribes responsibilities and communication protocols for desktop applications with GUIs.

Answers to quizzes and exercises

POP QUIZ 1

It's not a good idea to insert a `public boolean equals(Employee e)` method into an `Employee` class. First, note that you're overloading and not overriding the `equals` method from `Object`. As a consequence, employees end up with two different equality methods: an identity-based one inherited from `Object`, and a presumably content-based one with a more specific parameter type. When comparing two employees, you might end up calling either method, depending on the static type of the second employee:

```
Employee alex = ..., beth = ...;
alex.equals(beth);              ❶ Content-based comparison
alex.equals((Object) beth);    ❷ Identity-based comparison
```

This situation is prone to errors and likely not what the programmer intended.

POP QUIZ 2

No, in Java you can't allocate an array of type T (new T[...]), where T is a type parameter. That's because arrays store their type and use that information to check at runtime that every write or cast operation is legal. Due to erasure, the bytecode doesn't store the actual value of T at runtime, so that mechanism can't work. You shouldn't confuse this limitation with the ability to declare a variable of type T[], which is perfectly legal.

In C#, you can allocate an array of type T because the type parameters are reified—their actual value is known at runtime.

POP QUIZ 3

Only parallel collectors use the combiner method of a collector. It returns an object that you can use to merge the partial results that different threads obtain as they're cooperating to execute a stream operation.

POP QUIZ 4

You can't directly assign a method reference to a variable of type Object, as in:

```
Object x = String::length;   ① Compile-time error
```

because the context doesn't contain enough information to identify a specific functional interface. If you must do something like that, a cast might come in handy:

```
Object x = (ToIntFunction<String>) String::length;   ② Valid Java
```

EXERCISE 1

When you need runtime type information, and generics aren't enough, reflection is usually the solution. For example, instead of "new T()," you can carry around an object t of type Class<T> and then dynamically invoke a constructor using the following fragment:

```
Constructor<T> constructor = t.getConstructor();   ① Returns the default constructor
T object = constructor.newInstance();
```

Depending on the context, an alternative solution is to have the client provide a Supplier<T>, a functional interface that can wrap a constructor or any other way to produce objects of type T.

The recommended workaround to "new T[10]" involves using a collection instead of an array:

```
List<T> list = new ArrayList<T>();
```

As you saw in chapter 4, with a List you get a variety of extra services, and you pay very little overhead (but you can't write list[i]; life's hard).

Finally, you can again emulate a runtime check similar to "exp instanceof T" via reflection. If you have an object t of type Class, you can check whether a given expression is a subtype of t via

```
t.isInstance(exp);
```

EXERCISE 2

As the class for arbitrary precision rational numbers, I picked `BigRational` by Robert Sedgewick and Kevin Wayne.[4] It's an intuitive implementation of immutable rationals that you can use like this:

```
BigRational a = new BigRational(1, 3);    ❶ One-third
BigRational b = new BigRational(1, 2);    ❷ One-half
BigRational c = a.plus(b);
System.out.println(c);    ❸ Prints 5/6
```

You can equip water containers with amounts of type `BigRational` by modifying the `Container` class presented in section 9.5. First, you redefine the group summary class, with an amount field of type `BigRational` and the same integral group size field. Whenever you need to perform arithmetics on water amounts, you need to use the methods of `BigRational`, like `plus` or `divides`. I'll provide here a fragment of the group summary class, called `RationalSummary`. You can find the rest in the online repository.

```
class RationalSummary {
   private BigRational amount;
   private int groupSize;
   ...
   public void update(BigRational increment) {
      amount = amount.plus(increment);    ❶ BigRationals are immutable
   }
   ...
   public static final Attribute<BigRational,RationalSummary> ops =
      Attribute.of(RationalSummary::new,
                   RationalSummary::update,
                   RationalSummary::merge,
                   RationalSummary::getAmount);
}
```

Once you have the group summary class, you get the container class by extending `UnionFindNode` and passing the `Attribute` object to its constructor:

```
public class Container extends UnionFindNode<BigRational,RationalSummary> {
   public Container() {
      super(RationalSummary.ops);
   }
}
```

EXERCISE 3

The class `Schedule` must store a sorted sequence of non-overlapping events. To allow it to do so, define a support class—say `TimedEvent`—to keep together the event and its start and stop times. This can be a private internal class of `Schedule`.

A `TreeSet<TimedEvent>` with a custom order between elements can efficiently keep timed events sorted and detect overlaps at the same time. Recall that all implementations of the `Set` interface reject duplicate elements. `TreeSet` implements `Set` and bases all its operations on the order between its elements, including detecting duplicates (that is, it doesn't invoke `equals`). To reject a timed event that overlaps with

---

[4] You can find a copy in the online repository at https://bitbucket.org/mfaella/exercisesinstyle.

a previously inserted one, define the order so that overlapping events are equivalent (compareTo returns zero). In other words, use the following order:

- If event a comes *entirely before* event b, a is "smaller" than b, and vice versa.
- If two events overlap, they're "equivalent" (compareTo returns zero).

Here is the gist of the TimedEvent class:

```
public class Schedule<E> {

    private class TimedEvent implements Comparable<TimedEvent> {
        E event;                                ❶ This class is private—no need to hide its fields.
        LocalTime startTime, stopTime;
        @Override
        public int compareTo(TimedEvent other) {
            if (stopTime.isBefore(other.startTime)) return -1;
            if (other.stopTime.isBefore(startTime)) return 1;
            return 0;   ❷ Overlapping events appear "equivalent."
        }
        ...    ❸ Trivial constructor omitted
    }
}
```

Each Schedule object holds the following fields:

- private volatile boolean active;—Set by launch and reset at the end of the helper thread that executes the schedule. The volatile modifier ensures visibility across threads.
- private volatile Optional<E> currentEvent = Optional.empty();— Maintained by the helper thread that executes the schedule. The currentEvent method returns its value.
- private final SortedSet<TimedEvent> events = new TreeSet<>();— The sequence of timed events.

Method addEvent adds a new timed event to the TreeSet and checks three illegal cases.

```
public void addEvent(E event, LocalTime startTime, LocalTime stopTime)
{
    if (active)
        throw new IllegalStateException(
            "Cannot add event while active.");
    if (startTime.isAfter(stopTime))
        throw new IllegalArgumentException(
            "Stop time is earlier than start time.");
    TimedEvent timedEvent = new TimedEvent(event, startTime, stopTime);
    if (!events.add(timedEvent))    ❶ Insertion fails in case of overlap
        throw new IllegalArgumentException("Overlapping event.");
}
```

The actual execution of the schedule is forked out to another thread, so as not to block the launch method. You can find the code for launch and two examples of concrete event classes (PrintEvent and HTTPEvent) in the online repository.

EXERCISE 4

You can solve this exercise using an implementation of the generic container framework, such as `UnionFindNode`. The idea is to create a node for each element of the given collection and connect two nodes whenever their elements are equivalent according to the given predicate. After you've laid out all the connections, the groups of connected nodes form the desired output.

To eventually get the desired output, each node must know the set of nodes connected to it. Let's put that information into the group summary. You need an implementation of `Attribute<V,S>` with both `V` and `S` equal to `Set<T>`. Once again, the adapter method `Attribute.of` comes in handy:

```
public static <T> Set<Set<T>{}>
    partition(Collection<? extends T> collection,
              BiPredicate<? super T, ? super T> equivalent) {

    Attribute<Set<T>,Set<T>{}> groupProperty = Attribute.of(
            HashSet::new,      ❶ Reference to constructor
            Set::addAll,       ❷ Reference to method of interface

            (set1, set2) -> {  ❸ Merges two sets
                Set<T> union = new HashSet<>(set1);
                union.addAll(set2);
                return union;
            },
            set -> set);       ❹ No need to unwrap anything
```

The first actual operation involves creating a node for each element in the collection. You also need to keep track of which node belongs to which element. You can use a map for that:

```
Map<T,UnionFindNode<Set<T>,Set<T>{}>{}> nodeMap = new HashMap<>();
for (T item: collection) {
    UnionFindNode<Set<T>,Set<T>{}> node =
        new UnionFindNode<>(groupProperty);
    node.update(Set.of(item));    ❶ Initializes the group
    nodeMap.put(item, node);      ❷ Assigns the node to the current item
}
```

Then, you turn each equivalence into a connection between two nodes:

```
for (T item1: collection) {
    for (T item2: collection) {
        if (equivalent.test(item1, item2))
            nodeMap.get(item1).connectTo(nodeMap.get(item2));
    }
}
```

Finally, you collect all groups into a set, which is the desired partition of elements:

```
Set<Set<T>{}> result = new HashSet<>();
for (T item: collection) {
    result.add(nodeMap.get(item).get());
}
return result;
}
```

Further reading

- M. Naftalin, P. Wadler. *Java Generics and Collections.* O'Reilly, 2006.
  You won't find the latest gimmicks in this Java 5 book, but a solid coverage of generics and their subtleties.
- J. Tulach. *Practical API Design: Confessions of a Java Framework Architect.* Apress, 2008.
  Writing effectively reusable code is closely tied to defining proper APIs. This is one of the few books devoted entirely to that topic.
- R.-G. Urma, M. Fusco, and A. Mycroft. *Modern Java in Action.* Manning Publications, 2019.
  As mentioned in chapter 8, this book includes one of the best accounts of the stream library.
- J. Skeet. *C# in Depth.* Manning Publications, 2019.
  An up-to-date presentation of the evolution of C# across versions, including a reasoned comparison between the implementation of generics in C#, C++, and Java.

appendix A
Code golf:
Succinctness

Just like the objective of golf is to complete the course in the fewest number of strokes, code golf is a game that involves writing the shortest possible program to accomplish a given task. Several websites host code-golf tournaments, propose new tasks, and maintain player rankings. When the deadline for a given challenge expires, all submissions become public, and you can peek at the tricks that the best golfers used.

This appendix is almost the opposite of chapter 7 in that it will present the most obscure code in the book while breaking all style rules ever conceived. You've been warned.

Besides the fun factor, code golf can be a way to explore the dark corners of a language and learn a few tricks that may come in handy in normal programming circumstances.

A.1   The shortest I came up with   *[Golfing]*

When code golfing, it's important to establish the constraints you're supposed to respect. A looser interpretation of the rules may lead to a shorter solution, but you don't want to end up with a class that works only with a specific use case. Let's establish the boundaries of this exercise:

- We want a `Container` class that fulfills the standard use case established in chapter 1 and repeated throughout the book.
- This class must also respect the functional specifications laid out in chapter 1.
- We *don't* require anything else: no robustness, no performance constraints, and especially no readability.

In my solution, I represent a group of connected containers using a circular list, just like *Speed2*. Instance field n (for *next*) is a pointer to the next container in the group.

281

Also like *Speed2*, when you add water with `addWater`, the amount is stored locally in the instance field, a, and is never actually distributed among the other connected containers. As a consequence, every call to `getAmount` needs to scan the whole group, sum up the amounts that every container holds, and finally return the total amount divided by the size of the group.

Before I present the actual code, here's a legend for the five instance fields:

- a—Total amount ever added to this container.
- s, t—Temporary variables that `getAmount` needs; under normal circumstances, they'd be local variables of that method; moreover, s should really be an integer. I'm declaring them as fields because doing so saves a few characters.
- n—Pointer to the *next* container within the list representing the group of this container.
- c—Temporary variable that both `connectTo` and `getAmount` use; when not executing those methods, c equals n.

Take a look at the following code for the compact `Container` implementation. I left some basic white space and indentation for readability. If I remove all unnecessary white space, the class measures 223 bytes and still works as intended. For a comparison, *Reference* takes 1322 bytes, including white space.

Listing A.1   *Golfing*: Water containers in 223 bytes

```
public class Container {
    float a,s,t;     ❶ s,t are used like local variables
    Container n=this,c=n;
    public float getAmount() {
        for(s=t=0;s<1||c!=n;c=c.n,s++)     ❷ Notice the comma
            t+=c.a;
        return t/s;
    }
    public void connectTo(Container o) {
        c=o.n; o.n=o.c=n; n=c;     ❸ Swaps next pointers
    }
    public void addWater(float w) {
        a+=w;     ❹ Just accumulates locally
    }
}
```

To understand this obscure implementation, start by reading the `addWater` method, which is the easiest. The newly added water is summed to the a (for *amount*) field, and no other line modifies that field. Hence, the a field of a given container indicates the amount of water ever added to that container.

Then, move to the method `connectTo`. Recall from chapter 3 that merging two circular lists starting from arbitrary nodes is particularly easy: it suffices to swap their "next" pointers. The method `connectTo` does exactly that. Moreover, it updates the value of the support variables c and o.c to be equal to the new (that is, swapped) value of n and o.n, respectively.

NESTED ASSIGNMENTS As in C, you can concatenate multiple assignments in Java. Such a sequence is evaluated right to left, so all variables in the sequence are assigned the value of the rightmost expression.

Finally, there's the rather daunting loop in `getAmount`. Its purpose is to compute the total amount in all containers in this group, while at the same time measuring the size of the group. After the loop, you can find the total amount in the variable `t` and the size of the group in `s`, which explains why the method returns `t/s`.

COMMAS IN FOR LOOPS In C, the expression `exp1, exp2` evaluates both expressions in order and then returns the value of the second one. In Java, a similar syntax is allowed only inside the first and third clause of a `for` loop. It's meant to gracefully support loops with multiple indices:

```
for (i=0, j=n; i<n; i++, j-{}-) ...
```

With this in mind, the loop initialization and update parts should be quite clear. Both the size and the total amount start at zero. For each iteration, the size is incremented by one, and the container pointer `c` moves to the next container in the group.

The staying condition requires some explanation. The loop must stop when it has visited the whole circular list, that is, when the container pointer goes back to its original value. In our case, the container pointer `c` starts with the value of the next pointer `n`. As a result, the loop must continue as long as `c!=n`. But there's a catch: the `for` loop checks its staying condition *before* each iteration. To force the loop to perform at least one iteration, I had to add the staying condition `s<1`.

It's very likely that shorter solutions exist. Can you find one? If you do, drop me a line, I'd be glad to hear about it!

Further reading

Code golf is not a topic that has attracted a lot of literature. Until the International Olympic Committee accepts it as a proper sport, the best way to learn more about it is to browse the websites dedicated to it:

- *Anarchy Golf,* http://golf.shinh.org—On this website, you can witness the author's modest achievements in the AWK language; search for `marcof`.
- *Code Golf on StackExchange,* https://codegolf.stackexchange.com—Another website hosting code golf contests.
- *The International Obfuscated C Code Contest,* http://www.de.ioccc.org/—This is a competition about writing the most obscure and surprising C code. It shares with code golf the tendency to explore the dark corners of programming languages in a fun way.

A nice example of large-scale code golf and extreme encodings is the 2004 game *.kkrieger.* It's a *Doom*-quality 3D first-person shooter packed in a 96KB executable file—you read that right.

appendix B
The ultimate water container class

After enduring 17 different versions of water containers, you may be wondering what's the best one, what's the ultimate water container class? The answer is not simple. In some sense, any of those versions (except *Novice*) can be the best one, given the right circumstances. For example, *Speed1* is the best if you absolutely need constant-time `addWater` and `getAmount`. Similarly, *Memory4* is the best if you absolutely need to squeeze as many containers as possible in a given amount of memory. In both cases, those versions are optimal only if you don't care about any other software quality, which is admittedly a very unrealistic assumption.

In fact, treating software qualities separately, as I've done in this book, is purely a pedagogic device. In practice, you may want to think about those different properties separately, but you need to deliver code that fulfills all of them simultaneously. When two qualities contrast with each other, the context (aka your boss) will tell you which quality should prevail in your specific business situation.

Generally speaking, most projects call for the following software qualities: readability, reliability, and time efficiency. Only a relatively small subset care about memory efficiency, reusability, or thread safety. Given that situation, let's sketch a version of `Container` that optimizes the first three qualities. It'll be a blend of the fastest implementation (*Speed3* from chapter 3) and the most readable implementation (*Readable* from chapter 7), with reliability enhancements I presented in chapters 5 and 6.

More precisely, you can start with *Speed3* and perform the following improvements:

- (Readability) Add Javadoc comments to all public methods
- (Readability) Apply readability best practices, such as the Extract Method refactoring rule

- (Reliability) Add precondition checks to all public methods
- (Reliability) Include the test suite developed in chapter 6 (section 6.2)

I'll present the main parts of the resulting class in the following sections, whereas you can find the full source code in the online repository (https://bitbucket.org/mfaella /exercisesinstyle)

B.1 Readability enhancements

Recall that *Speed3* achieves its performance by representing groups of connected containers as parent-pointer trees. The root of each tree knows the size of its group and the per-container amount of water. Connecting two containers entails attaching the smaller of the two trees to the larger one—the so-called link-by-size policy.

Let's focus on the `connectTo` operation because it benefits the most from a readability overhaul. Besides adding a proper documentation comment in Javadoc format, you can apply Extract Method and delegate the actual tree merging operation to a new support method, `linkTo`. In this way, `connectTo` becomes extremely simple: it finds the two group roots, checks whether they're the same (in that case, no operation is performed), and finally merges the two trees according to the link-by-size policy.

This method also gets a small reliability enhancement: if you call it with a `null` argument, it throws an NPE with a custom error message, as shown in the following listing.

Listing B.1   *Ultimate*: Ultimate `connectTo`

```
/** Connects this container with another.   ❶ Javadoc comment
 *
 *  @param other the container that will be connected to this one
 */
public void connectTo(Container other) {
  Objects.requireNonNull(other,
      "Cannot connect to a null container.");   ❷ Precondition check
  Container root1 = findRootAndCompress(),      ❸ This support method is the same
          root2 = other.findRootAndCompress();     as in chapter 3.
  if (root1==root2) return;   ❹ Checks if they're already connected

  if (root1.size <= root2.size) {   ❺ Link-by-size policy
      root1.linkTo(root2);
  } else {
      root2.linkTo(root1);
  }
}
```

The support method `linkTo` performs the rest of the job. In turn, `linkTo` gives rise to another extracted support method called `combinedAmount`, which computes the per-container amount after merging two groups.

Listing B.2 *Ultimate*: Private methods supporting `connectTo`

```
private void linkTo(Container otherRoot) {
    parent = otherRoot;
    otherRoot.amount = combinedAmount(otherRoot);
    otherRoot.size += size;
}
private double combinedAmount(Container otherRoot) {
    return ((amount * size) + (otherRoot.amount * otherRoot.size)) /
           (size + otherRoot.size);
}
```

B.2 Reliability enhancements

Adding water to a container is the only operation with a nontrivial precondition: you can't remove more water than is available. The following listing shows the revised version of `addWater`, checking its precondition and documenting its behavior with Javadoc.

Listing B.3 *Ultimate*: Ultimate `addWater`

```
/** Adds water to this container.    ❶ Javadoc comment
 *  A negative <code>amount</code> indicates removal of water.
 *  In that case, there should be enough water in the group
 *  to satisfy the request.
 *
 *  @param amount the amount of water to be added
 *  @throws IllegalArgumentException if <code>amount</code>
 *  is negative and there's not enough water to satisfy the request
 */
public void addWater(double amount) {
    Container root = findRootAndCompress();

    double amountPerContainer = amount / root.size;
    if (root.amount + amountPerContainer < 0) {    ❷ Precondition check
        throw new IllegalArgumentException(
            "Not enough water to match the addWater request.");
    }
    root.amount += amountPerContainer;
}
```

Finally, you can run the unit tests we developed in chapter 6 on this version of Con tainer with no changes, and they all succeed.

Summarizing, this final version is strong on time performance and readability, and moderately hardened for reliability. The precondition checks defend against external misuse, whereas the test suite provides some confidence in the internal reliability of the class. If this class was part of a safety-critical system, you could easily increase its sensitivity to internal defects using one or more of the following techniques:

- *Adding precondition checks to the private methods, as `assert` statements*—For exam-ple, `linkTo` could check whether `this` and `otherRoot` are indeed two roots.

- *Adding invariant checks, as explained in section 5.4*—For example, `addWater` and `connectTo` could check that the amount of water held in a container is always non-negative.
- *Adding implementation-specific (that is, whitebox) tests*—The tests we developed in chapter 6 are based on the method contracts only, not on their implementation. That's a perfectly fine blackbox approach. However, the parent-pointer tree implementation used here and in *Speed3* is quite tricky. It may be worth adding tests that specifically target this implementation to ensure that you got the various cases right. For example, you may test the link-by-size policy by connecting containers having varying group sizes.

index

RELATED MANNING TITLES

Modern Java in Action
by Raoul-Gabriel Urma, Mario Fusco, Alan Mycroft

ISBN 9781617293566
592 pages, $54.99
September 2018

Spring in Action, Fifth Edition
by Craig Walls

ISBN 9781617294945
520 pages, $49.99
October 2018

Cloud Native Patterns
by Cornelia Davis

ISBN 9781617294297
400 pages, $49.99
May 2019

For ordering information go to www.manning.com

Object Design Style Guide
by Matthias Noback

ISBN 9781617296857
288 pages, $39.99
December 2019

Practices of the Python Pro
by Dane Hillard

ISBN 9781617296086
248 pages, $49.99
December 2019

C# in Depth, Fourth Edition
by Jon Skeet

ISBN 9781617294532
528 pages, $49.99
March 2019

For ordering information go to www.manning.com

RELATED MANNING TITLES

Functional Programming in Scala
by Paul Chiusano and Runar Bjarnason

ISBN 9781617290657
320 pages, $44.99
September 2014

Functional Programming in Java
by Pierre-Yves Saumont

ISBN 9781617292736
472 pages, $49.99
January 2017

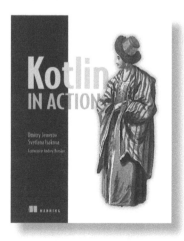

Kotlin in Action
by Dmitry Jemerov and Svetlana Isakova

ISBN 9781617293290
360 pages, $44.99
February 2017

For ordering information go to www.manning.com